Psychoanalysis and Culture

To Kathleen and Sydney

Psychoanalysis and Culture

Contemporary States of Mind

ROSALIND MINSKY

Polity Press

The right of Rosalind Minsky to be identified as author of this work has been asserted in accordance with the Copyright, Designs and Patents Act 1988.

First published in 1998 by Polity Press
in association with Blackwell Publishers Ltd.

Editorial office:
Polity Press
65 Bridge Street
Cambridge CB2 1UR, UK

Marketing and production:
Blackwell Publishers Ltd
108 Cowley Road
Oxford OX4 1JF, UK

ISBN 0-7456-1579-1
ISBN 0-7456-1580-5 (pbk)

A CIP catalogue record for this book is available from the British Library.

Typeset in 10 on 12 pt ITC Garamond
by Best-set Typesetter Ltd, Hong Kong
Printed and bound in Great Britain by MPG Books Ltd, Bodmin, Cornwall

This book is printed on acid-free paper.

The truth did not come to me suddenly,
It came quietly, circumspectly, snuffling and whimpering,
Looking to be let in many times before.

Paul Scott

Insight into the truth is the flash which, in live
conversation upon serious matters, carries one beyond
words.

Iris Murdoch, *Metaphysics as a Guide to Morals*

There's a cool web of language winds us in
Retreat from too much joy and too much fear:

Robert Graves, 'The Cool Web', *Collected Poems*

Contents

Preface

Despite the regular appearance of ill-informed and often hostile articles about psychoanalysis and psychotherapy, in all sections of the press, based on a surprisingly low level of enquiry, there have been two major areas of developing interest in psychoanalytic ideas. One of these is the increasing number of women entering training institutions in analytical psychotherapy, significantly, perhaps, in a cultural climate where ordinary human need and intuitive, empathic forms of knowledge and containment have often been sacrificed to economic expediency. The other is the continuing interest in psychoanalytic ideas in universities. More and more, sociologists, anthropologists, historians and psychologists are becoming interested in how unconscious as well as conscious processes manifest themselves in their areas of study as well as those involved in literary, cultural, film and women's studies. These latter were the first to dip their toes in the glinting waters of psychoanalytic knowledge, particularly in relation to our understanding of the complexities of gender.

In contrast to the clinical world of psychotherapy and psychoanalysis, much of the 'take up' of psychoanalytic theory in arts and humanities departments in universities has centred on the post-modernist work of Lacan. But intriguing and intellectually seductive as this theory is, it represents only a very small part of the richness and subtlety of psychoanalytic approaches as a whole, including those of object-relations theory or what is sometimes called the British School.

In this book I have tried to suggest some of the flavour and cultural relevance of the intellectual, imaginative and intuitive depth and range which are characteristic of psychoanalytic perspectives generally, none of which, given the complexity with which contemporary culture confronts us, I think we can afford to ignore in our attempts to make some kind of sense of what is 'going on'.

In spite of the cultural dominance of science and reason, the end of the millennium sees an increasingly fragmented, disordered world which, particularly in the contexts of globalization, the electronics revolution, the environment and poverty, often appears to be already running out of our control. Perhaps, in this context, a desire to feel in control explains our need, sometimes, to ally ourselves too exclusively with perspectives which offer us the greatest sense of mastery of what we may find painful or disturbing even if they leave out crucial and valuable dimensions of our existence. Psychoanalytic insights cannot offer us any precise solutions but they can enable us to see some problems more clearly because they take account of the irrational as well as rational elements that are inherent in them.

All psychoanalytic theories confront us with uncertainty, unpredictability, contradiction and ambiguity and the need to recognize and accept difference. However, I want to suggest that an eclectic use of these theories can allow us to remain in touch with the notion of wisdom, value or the best ways to live well (in the Greek sense), without falling victim to idealization, demonization or totalizing, rigid versions of 'truth'. An awareness of psychoanalytic knowledge and the emotional resonances and insights it often generates offers the possibility of finding 'artistic' ways of understanding culture rather than exclusively scientific or rational ones which leave out so much of what the experience of living feels like. Such 'artistic' ways of thinking aspects of culture depend on extending our cultural capacity to appreciate forms of knowledge which, like most forms of art, reflect and value some level of emotional as well as intellectual integration and creativity. This seems more realistic, and potentially more productive, than a defensive resort to denial and control of what makes us feel uncomfortable. In the context of postmodernism, this may include a blanket rejection of any notion of value because of its perceived source in the arbitrariness of language. In this view, values which might spring from our earliest sensory and emotional experiences of infancy and the mode of being which emerges out of them are deemed to be theoretically beyond the pale. At an important level, psychoanalytic approaches suggest that culture does not entirely 'live' us. We live ourselves in our different ways partly as a result of what has been available to us as embodied, emotional creatures from the moment we are born.

The tendency for academic fashion to see-saw from one binary position to another, just like fashion in other areas of life, also seems to be a reflection of the emotional need to exclude huge areas of our experience in order to sustain a sense of identity, coherence and security. This book, among other things, emphasizes the possibility of a degree of emotional integration as well as precariousness in our identity. It is this, psychoanalytic theory as a whole suggests, which can enable us to have confidence in some values about how to live and in our ability to make some helpful sense of the complexity and contradictions within ourselves and culture and act on it intuitively and imaginatively as well as rationally.

Acknowledgements

I would like to thank my partner David Pickles for his unstinting support and for his invaluable comments at every stage of this book, Marina Voikhanskaya for her continuing generosity and interest, and Peter Lomas and Gerald Wooster for their encouraging comments on some of my ideas. I would also like to express my gratitude to my students at Anglia Polytechnic University from whose responses to psychoanalytic ideas I have learned so much. I am also grateful to Andrew Winnard, Anthony Giddens, Gill Motley, Julia Harsant and Annabelle Mundy at Polity Press for their help and advice.

The author and publishers gratefully acknowledge permission to use short extracts from the following copyright works as epigraphs:

Sigmund Freud: from *The Standard Edition of the Complete Psychological Works of Sigmund Freud*, Volume 19, translated and edited by James Strachey, reprinted by permission of Sigmund Freud © copyright The Institute of Psycho-Analysis and The Hogarth Press Ltd; and from the US edition, *The Collected Papers*, Volume 5 edited by James Strachey, published by Basic Books, Inc. by arrangement with The Hogarth Press Ltd and The Institute of Psycho-Analysis, London, reprinted by permission of Basic Books, a subsidiary of Perseus Books Group, LLC.

Robert Graves: lines from 'The Cool Web' from *Collected Poems* (1997), reprinted by permission of the publisher, Carcanet Press Ltd.

Nick Hornby: from *Fever Pitch* (1992), reprinted by permission of the publisher, Victor Gollancz Ltd.

Ian McEwan: from *The Child in Time* (Jonathan Cape, 1987), reprinted by permission of Random House UK Ltd.

Iris Murdoch: from *Metaphysics as a Guide to Morals* (Chatto & Windus), reprinted by permission of Random House UK Ltd and of Penguin Books, USA.

Susie Orbach: from 'Revenge Tragedy' first published in the *Guardian*, 16.8.97, copyright © The Guardian 1997, reprinted by permission of Guardian Newspapers Ltd.

Paul Scott: quotation reprinted by permission of David Higham Associates.

Abbreviations

The following abbreviations have been used throughout:

SE *Standard Edition of the Complete Psychological Works of Sigmund Freud*, vols 1–24, 1953–74, London, Hogarth Press and The Institute of Psychoanalysis.

PFL *Pelican Freud Library*, 1973– , Harmondsworth, Penguin.

Introduction

Contemporary culture in the Western world confronts us with social, political, technological and economic changes which are often confusing and contradictory and sometimes disturbing and frightening. This seems likely to be related to the sheer scale of change on so many fronts of our existence. These include changes in the relationships between men and women, family breakdown and the increase in lone-parent families, the ending of the Cold War, the decline of European control and the emergence of Asian economic power, globalization, the electronics revolution, the growing divide between rich and poor in the West and between the northern and southern hemispheres, a growth of a sense of social fragmentation rather than cohesiveness (in spite of the con- notations of a global village) and environmental damage, such as global warming and a hole in the ozone layer, in a context in which nations, so far, seem helpless in putting limits on unbridled economic growth. In many places both science and economic growth seem to be leading to disorder rather than order and to more, rather than less, global poverty, violence and environmental damage. The world, now divided into a natural and an electronic one, seems to be rapidly spinning out of control. Globalization seems to have replaced imperialism and to be operating outside human beings, national boundaries and material reality. Society, it seems, is fast becoming a mere adjunct to the global economy. As Wolfgang Sachs (1992) argues, the language of control seems to have been replaced by the language of management and monitoring. Our sense of having control, the world at our fingertips, as it is in the famous 'Armada portrait' of Queen Elizabeth I and in Michelangelo's painting *The Creation of Adam*, is waning fast. Being able to measure the world, or make computerized predictions about it, or look down on it from space, no longer seems to offer us the sense of omnipotent control that it used to. The world seems to be becoming less predictable and old certainties seem to be breaking down. Sachs (1992) offers us the strange contradiction between Bosnia and Rwanda and computer-based globalization.

Psychoanalytic knowledge suggests that we cannot think about the immense complexity and diversity of culture and cultural change adequately if we use only the language of consciousness and rationality. Like our own identities, culture is underpinned by powerful, hidden unconscious as well as conscious processes. Psychoanalytic approaches suggest that history directs and produces outlets for these unconscious processes which take different forms in different historical epochs. Difference is central to this process in the sense of who, at any particular moment, is defined as the scapegoat 'other' against which we bolster our own sense of identity (for example, woman, Protestant, Catholic, Jew, Muslim or homosexual). The aim of this book is to explore how unconscious processes may be manifested in culture. Psychoanalytic knowledge does not offer us control. Rather it can offer us some insight into the sources of the irrational dimensions of culture which are not so available within other areas of knowledge. This includes insight into language and representation but it is not confined to them. Although at one level our experience of the world is mediated by thought and language, a recent emphasis primarily on these as the home of the unconscious as well as consciousness has often meant that embodied experience and the psychosomatic emotional dimension of our existence have been ruled out of court. Although the internal structure of Jacques Lacan's influential psychoanalytic theory justifies this rejection of the value of experience, there are other powerful and compelling psychoanalytic perspectives which inform clinical practice which do not compel us to believe that we are entirely created by our words and that life consists only of events in language. Nor do they assume that we and the knowledge we produce are anything but precarious and imperfect because of the potential subversion of who we are by our unconscious. But they do suggest that there are degrees of precariousness and that some level of emotional integration and way of being deriving from a sphere which pre-dates language is both possible and desirable for a creative, fulfilling life and the ability to learn from experience, something we perhaps call wisdom. In this book I want to suggest that it is time to take another look at identity and culture using a broader spectrum of psychoanalytic ideas.

For a long time, psychoanalytic knowledge has been largely confined to psychoanalysts, psychotherapists and their patients, even though in the past hundred years such ideas as the unconscious, repression and the name of Freud have become common currency. But in the past twenty years, in relation to knowledge and how we 'think' gendered identity and culture, universities have been mainly interested in Lacan's ideas about language and meaning. If we attempt (always eclectically and suggestively rather than with a psychoanalytic sledge-hammer) to apply a broader range of psychoanalytic ideas to culture we may gain more insight even though the process is inevitably going to be different from that which goes on in the psychotherapeutic one-to-one relationship in what the French analyst Pontalis called 'the private theatre of transference' (Weatherill 1994: 6). In the therapeutic session, through a process of free association or saying whatever comes to mind, one person, re-entering his or her own history, constructs a story or narrative which resonates emotionally in the other. This other person, the therapist, in a state of what Freud called 'evenly suspended' or 'free-floating attention' and Bion called a state of 'reverie' which is neither judgemental nor demanding, may then, through the provision of emotional containment, be able to help the patient begin to digest, 'think' or speak what has previously remained unsymbolized and disruptive. The process of psychotherapy which depends on the therapist's access to both her or his own empathic, intuitive feelings and awareness of a range of psychoanalytic ideas provides a means of understanding the patient's unconscious predicament and often generates a positive qualitative change in the life of the patient. Without resorting to a crude reductionism, in a similar way, if we make eclectic use of psychoanalytic ideas and our own empathic, intuitive responses to identify the unconscious elements which may be present within such cultural phenomena as women's subordination and changing relationships between men and women, the role of fathering, public and personal forms of violence and destructiveness, the consumption of cultural 'goods', the preference for some kinds of knowledge over others, we may gain insights which can suggest new directions for cultural change. A focus only on conscious processes may leave these buried and 'unthought'.

In encountering psychoanalytic ideas, it is important that we pay attention to the emotional resonances that these trigger in ourselves since these are what allow us to gain emotional as well as intellectual insight. They give us some access to our own unconscious processes and help us to be more emotionally open to possibilities. One of the arguments raised against using psychoanalytic ideas outside the clinical sphere is that they can be used defensively for intellectual control rather than emotional insight. Although this is a real danger for a few people, it does not seem to me to justify steering clear of psychoanalytic ideas when they are so rich and potentially illuminating for many of us. All knowledge can be (and a considerable amount is) used defensively to shore up identity and compensate for a sense of powerlessness.

If individual psychotherapy offers the opportunity for the individual to tell another, richer, more authentic story than his or her customary one and subsequently allows him or her to live a more creative, fulfilling, less inhibited, life, then an awareness of and emotional openness to psycho-analytic ideas may enable us to tell new, more authentic cultural stories which may radically affect the way we think about some aspects of culture and what we try to do about them. But since we all live in a social as well as unconscious or psychical world, our use of psychoanalytic ideas needs to include a continual awareness of the power of culture and historical contingency. The question of whether or not these originally stem from unconscious sources must remain an enigma but there is inevitably a complex dialectic in play between them.

Modernist and post-modernist approaches

Much recent interest in psychoanalytic ideas has focused on the post-modernist work of Lacan and his attempt to re-work Freud's ideas specifically in relation to language. However, as I have suggested, psychoanalytic theory represents a rich and varied body of modernist as well as post-modernist ideas. These, when used eclectically, can be immensely valuable in helping us to unravel the complexity of ourselves and contemporary culture. Although in recent years identity and culture have frequently been discussed in terms of modernism and post-modernism, like the old binary categories of 'masculinity' and 'feminin-ity', nature and culture, 'right' and 'left', this oppositional way of thinking about ourselves and the world often seems to need to exclude every-thing that smacks, in any way, of the 'other' (approach). In order to survive as conceptual 'identities', opposing theories and ideas often also exclude, as we ourselves often do, the unpalatable realities of ambiguity, contradiction, unpredictability and uncertainty. This may mean some-times that we dare not think about certain ideas because they lead us into personal or political spaces where we would rather not be 'found'. This can often distort the way in which we think about very complex matters which persistently resist incorporation into any single approach. We need a broad and varied palette of both modernist and post-modernist approaches to allow us insights into important, if not crucial, contempo-rary questions. We need insight into such questions as: How important is male envy of women's capacity to procreate in women's historical subordination and in what is sometimes seen as a contemporary crisis in male identity? What constitutes 'masculinity' apart from power and control or, more recently, the capacity to be a substitute mother? How important is the father, actually or symbolically, in children's emotional development in the context of lone-parent families and absent fathers?

Why is so much of culture so violent and destructive? Why is the 'consumer society' so attractive to so many people and why is it so difficult to put limits to economic growth even in the context of environmental disaster? What does the idea that our identities and bodies are constructed only in language and culture leave out? Is biology any more a cultural, historical construction than post-modernist theory or do both inevitably reflect their own conscious and unconscious interests? And, if some of these questions seem personally or politically 'risky', why do they? What of our selves do we unconsciously invest in ideas and theories, and why? These are large questions and this book attempts only to give the flavour of a psychoanalytic way of thinking about them but they are so important that we need to confront them.

Understandably, since our psychical survival depends on the belief that we have some grasp of what is going on, we are often tempted to over-simplify, even when using difficult and powerful conceptual language. With modernism we often had to endure the unifying rigidities and omnipotence of 'grand narratives' which often imperiously silenced different others, but more recently post-modernism, while celebrating difference, has argued that since identities exist only in language, there can be no grounds for valuing any one view over any other. This then fails to distinguish between outcomes which are destructive and cause suffering and those which do not and denies all notions of coherence, value or moral purpose, even in the Greek sense of knowing how to live. In the context of the potentially overwhelming complexity of contemporary culture, it hardly seems surprising that neither modernist nor post-modernist approach can be adequate on its own. Both these positions, in their 'all or nothing' quality, in different ways, suggest the need to gain some sense of having said the last word about a world which is always unpredictable and uncertain and where there is a vital need for the acceptance and celebration of difference but also for values and boundaries. Neither of these positions on their own represents a tenable position with which to try to address the complexity of the next millennium. All psychoanalytic perspectives suggest that intellectual health depends on a degree of psychical health and the capacity to integrate different, apparently incompatible, elements rather than splitting them off. This means we need to be able to think in the grey area between the structuring binaries of black and white, post-structuralist and humanistic theory, in order to think creatively.

Although Lacan has intriguingly and usefully focused our attention on the fragility of cultural 'masculinity' and the mastery involved in language, his work, in focusing so much on signification, has denied the force and validity of embodied experience, including intuitive, empathic ways of knowing. Object-relations psychoanalytic writers such as Winnicott, Klein and Bion, in particular, who represent the second main strand of psychoanalytic theory (the first being Freudian), would argue that, although we speak our 'selves' in language which pre-exists us, we are not all interchangeable. Part of us is determined from birth by our psychosomatic experience, our experience of ourselves as embodied beings, as well as by the narratives we eventually produce in language. Lacan's theory, while focusing our attention on the precariousness of cultural identity is, paradoxically, a very 'masterful' theory in itself in that it writes off early pre-verbal emotional, intuitive and empathic experience with the mother as delusory and, in entirely substituting language and signification in the place of psychosomatic experience, dramatically perpetuates the old, intellectually and emotionally crippling mind–body split. In this way, Lacan's theory, coherent as much of it is, excludes large areas of what, as Winnicott, with his customary down-to-earthness, put it, 'makes life worth growing up for'.

The problem of grappling with complexity seems to be as much of a problem in the humanities as it is in the sciences where it is now seen as the over-riding task. In science there is a movement from linear prediction to the idea of chaos and unpredictable systems in a world where both the natural and the electronic seem beyond human control. It has been said that, with the aid of computers, satellites and sensors, we now watch the world as if it were an ailing patient.

The unconscious, identity and culture

Psychoanalytic theory is primarily concerned with how early bodily and emotional experience in infancy and early childhood is transformed symbolically into the unconscious ways in which men and women live out their lives as male or female, 'masculine or 'feminine' within culture. This includes, as Freud put it, whether we have the capacity creatively, both 'to love and work' as reasonably independent human beings (where culture does not make this impossible) or whether we feel an underlying sense of anxiety, inhibition or inner impoverishment which cannot be attributed directly to cultural deprivation or frustration. Freud distinguishes between what he called 'neurotic unhappiness' which stems from unconscious conflicts in our inner world and 'ordinary unhappiness' which results from our encounters with the frustrations and deprivations presented by culture or the external world.

Psychoanalytic approaches assume that our first experience of both the social and psychical worlds takes place within the context of the

family. This is at first mainly our mother's (and increasingly both parents') emotional way of being with us. We construct our earliest sense of
who we are, our own personal way of being and relating to others in
relation to the mother's body and what Christopher Bollas calls the
mother's 'personal grammar of being', even though our identity is at first
fused with that of the mother. This initial fusion is likely to be related to
the fact that we have previously existed as a part of her body. So to the
extent that our mother, and later father and siblings, constitute our first
environment, with whom we initially identify, and who occupy a part of
the social world, we are socially inscribed from the very outset. As Freud
suggested, the unconscious can never escape culture. Even the most
delicate moments in our psychical development run their course in a
social situation. He writes 'in the mental life of an individual, the Other
enters quite regularly as ideal, as the object, as helper, as an adversary;
hence individual psychology is from the outset social psychology at the
same time' (PFL 12: 91).

However, psychoanalytic theory suggests that we only begin to experience ourselves consciously as a part of wider culture, able to
participate in the shared meanings in language and wider social relationships once we are able to separate from our merged state with the
mother and cope relatively independently. It is then that, according to
Freud, we internalize culture, the world beyond the mother's body,
through our identification with the symbolic father or a substitute. In
Lacan's theory, our identification with the actual father as the symbolic
representative of culture is replaced by our identification with the
meanings and conventions of language, what he calls the 'place of the
father' rather than the actual father. This re-making of our selves out
of culture through our capacity for identification, that is the projection of
our self into an Other, language, which we then internalize as part of
who we are, helps to fill the empty space left by the need to separate
from our mother. Crucially, it is our separation from the mother which
allows us to enter into our humanity through our entry into the symbolic
realm of language. This process of separation continues in adolescence
but psychoanalytic theory suggests that many of us spend large tracts of
our adult lives unconsciously trying to complete this difficult transition
within our subsequent relationships. Freud and Lacan insist that despite
our efforts to find substitutes, nothing can ever entirely fill the space
left by the loss of our mother from whom we took our first identity.
We are left with an unfillable gap between what we are and what we
want to be, that is perfect and unified in a state of fused bliss with
our mother for ever. It is this psychical domain of loss and lack, of
unfulfilled longing for perfection which Freud designates 'unconscious

desire'. Subsequently, many of us unconsciously seek symbolic substitutes for this unmet phantasy of blissful merger.

Recently, however, psychoanalytic therapists who want to emphasize the role of culture, as well as the unconscious dynamics of our early experience of the family, have emphasized the need for culture, as well as parents, to provide the emotional containment and reinforcement necessary for emotional or psychical growth. They see emotional growth as the development of identities which have the capacity to integrate conflicting emotions and needs sufficiently to allow them to cope creatively with both the conflicts and contradictions and the challenges and opportunities with which life presents us. They suggest that contemporary Western culture, increasingly characterized by fragmentation and uncertainty, provokes a high degree of anxiety, insecurity and an underlying sense of worthlessness and lack of meaning and value in many individuals. In this sense, culture, through an increasing decline in 'containing' institutions which support ordinary human needs and a sense of mutual concern (such as the provision of adequate publicly funded welfare and health services), frequently reinforces many people's inner anxieties and sense of helplessness. Psychoanalytic knowledge suggests that this has enormous potential for destructiveness and self-destructiveness. This means that for a large minority of people, in the developed as well as undeveloped world, culture still seems to be experienced as a form of assault on human needs and aspirations rather than as a container.

A degree of integration

Most psychoanalytic writers, while recognizing the relative precariousness of all identity because of the existence of the hidden dimension of the unconscious and, at one level, the necessarily illusory nature of all the meanings we build in language, see the achievement of a *relatively* integrated identity as possible, desirable and liveable. They argue that the human subject has a genuine capacity for a personal identity or self capable of real emotional depth and creativity. This self is not pre-given or fixed by biology but constructed in a dialectical relationship with the external world of culture 'out of bits and pieces of experience' (Frosh 1991: 31). Identities are 'real' and embodied and not entirely fictitious as post-modernists such as Lacan want to argue. They are not entirely socially constructed because they contain elements which are not identical with cultural meanings. The unconscious continually disrupts and subverts consciousness and cultural 'arrangements' of meaning but, as

Frosh argues, individuals can resist, create, become infused with loving, reparative values in the most inauspicious and demoralizing circumstances (Frosh 1991). Most psychoanalytic theory suggests that, given enough 'containing' early emotional experience with the mother or both parents, or later in psychotherapy, it is possible to 'work through' our loss and lack emotionally rather than denying it. Through this experience of what Winnicott calls emotional 'holding' we become able to gain a clear enough sense of the distinction between unconscious phantasy and external 'reality'. This allows us to embark on spontaneous rather than defensive ways of relating and realistic, creative and imaginative ways of living which do not continually confuse our 'self' with projections of this self onto objects or others in the external world. This represents a capacity for a precarious but viable identity involving a certain kind of emotional resilience which allows us to 'keep on going' without being overwhelmed or evacuating painful experience destructively onto others or self-destructively onto our self. Denial or projection of large parts of ourselves onto other people or 'objects' in the external world who are then idealized or denigrated rather than perceived more realistically as a mixture of good and bad qualities, denudes us of an inner world and makes us feel painfully dependent on these people, objects or ideas because they now contain so much of our self. We normally refer to this predicament as 'paranoia'. At the level of culture this may express itself in racism, sexism, class, religion ethnocentrity, destructive nationalism, tribalism, homophobia which, at their most extreme, may involve domestic and public forms of violence, murder, rape and war. This is no less true of the twentieth century than of earlier periods of human history. This century has witnessed repeated acts of genocide against those who have come to represent the different and therefore denigrated and 'feminized' 'other'.

Psychosomatic experience

Psychoanalytic approaches suggest that, while appreciating the crucial role of culture and history, all meanings, conscious and unconscious, have their origins in early bodily and emotional experience and the phantasies associated with them. Central to this experience is our passionate desire to keep our mother for ourselves for ever and our eventual, inevitable loss of her. This includes the little girl's shock at discovering that the mother desires someone with a different kind of body from her own and the small boy's shock when he discovers he cannot have babies like his mother (which up until that moment he thought he could because of his fused identity with her). These, and the sometimes intense experience of sibling rivalry, may be universal unconscious structuring experiences which run across different cultures and history and ones over which we have little control. Psychoanalytic theory generally suggests that we are a product of our entire personal psychosomatic experience or history (with a small 'h') which is inevitably often more than we can signify even in the most poetic language. Object-relations versions of psychoanalytic theory, in particular, emphasize that our beginnings lie ideally in an emotionally containing, intuitive, empathic relationship with the mother (and, more recently, father) out of which, as Bion (1991) argues, the first primitive forms of organization of meaning and thought emerge. It is these first intuitive, empathic patternings of our early emotions, anxieties, needs, impulses, drives and phantasies which make possible our eventual capacity for symbolization and language.

In contrast to other areas of knowledge, psychoanalytic theory rests fundamentally on how the baby and then small child comes, unconsciously, to discover a way of being rather than existing and to make sense of itself, its parents, siblings and the non-sense of the world in which it tries to place itself. So, to understand psychoanalytic ideas, we need to be willing to enter what may seem to us, as rational adults, a bizarre and sometimes politically incorrect world of bodies, emotions and infant and childhood phantasies, that is, primitive ways of making sense of what is going on which pre-date rationality. This, of course, is the stuff of myths and fairy-tales. However, this world becomes much less strange and mystifying if we can allow ourselves imaginatively to enter this infant or childhood reality and experience what it might be like. This capacity for entering another's world intuitively, of walking around in another person's skin without becoming them, is often described as 'empathy'. This is a source of knowledge based on emotional insight or intuition rather than reason or theoretical insight. If we don't make this imaginative leap, psychoanalytic ideas may seem unworthy of our consideration unless they are scrubbed clean of their bodily and emotional content and colonized entirely by linguistic concepts.

One of the difficulties of writing about unconscious processes in the language of consciousness is that psychoanalytic theory suggests that language may be seen as, among other things, an attempt to master or control unconscious desire and anxiety. (We may speak to fill silence which makes us feel uncomfortable or write lists or letters when we feel emotionally upset.) In language, the unconscious often makes itself felt through a series of resonances and reverberations rather than through rational words and syntax. Recently, in the context of Lacan and

Foucault's work, many of us are increasingly aware of the ideological interests which may lurk behind the surface of language and knowledge, so we may, in one sense, never know the world directly. But object-relations theory suggests that there are also powerful emotionally created means of knowing involving intuitive, empathic capacities which draw directly on the unconscious in an uncomplicated and creative way which cannot be reduced to either consciousness or the unconscious when it is defined exclusively as repressed desire. These forms of awareness (which some would argue constitute our humanity) are created in infancy in what Bion describes as, ideally, the container-contained relationship between the mother and baby, in a context of empathy and openness rather than mastery, and represent what may be seen as an alternative form of consciousness. This kind of understanding, which is often undervalued by culture, frequently gets lost, distorted or squeezed out by the rational categories through which we try to know ourselves and the world.

An eclectic approach

To be able to use psychoanalytic theory creatively, I think we have to work eclectically, using the two main strands of psychoanalytic theory, Freudian and object-relations theory, as do many successful practising analytical psychotherapists and analysts. Freudian theory focuses on sexuality, desire, difference and the father as the source of identity, whereas object-relations theory is primarily concerned with the quality of the relationship with the mother and later both parents and the development of the capacities for emotional containment, insight and creativity. As Freud's theory emphasizes, small children identify with and feel desire for both parents and we normally refer to this potent mixture of emotions as 'love'. This means we need a range of theory which will allow us to reflect on the reality of the two different and complicated zones of psychical experience many of us have had in infancy – one related to the mother and the other to the father. This is what makes possible the variety of male and female identities that exist – the masculinities and femininities which constitute the fluidity of identity. Although these different approaches seem in many ways theoretically incompatible, this should not prevent us from using them eclectically. As we cannot be totally whole, unified, coherent and perfectly integrated ourselves, we cannot expect to find or produce the perfectly integrated all-encompassing theory. Theories as well as we, ourselves, have to learn to live with precariousness and contradiction. As well as needing to think eclectically, it is often necessary to turn concepts upside down or inside out to get to something which may have been left out or underestimated in existing psychoanalytic theory. As I have argued elsewhere, like all forms of writing, psychoanalytic texts contain absences and presences which reflect the psychical state of their creators. They, like all of us, writers and readers, unconsciously protect themselves, sometimes, from knowing too much (Minsky 1996).

Encountering psychoanalytic material

The capacity for psychoanalytic material to disturb us is very real and reading about psychoanalytic ideas for the first time sometimes provokes anxiety. Certain ideas may make us feel confused and dizzy when they resonate with something we don't yet know about ourselves, what Bollas (1991) calls the 'unthought known'. They seem to know more about us than we know ourselves, which we may experience as emotionally undermining. There may be times in our lives when we feel particularly fragile and anxious when it might be best to delay an encounter with psychoanalytic theory. However, under normal circumstances, if a particular passage does suddenly trigger off anxiety, anger or boredom it is probably best to abandon it and move on to other areas that feel more comfortable. Often, at a later date, we can go back to a previously disturbing idea that made our mind empty or come to a standstill and find that, without our conscious awareness, imperceptibly, we have integrated the new idea into what we now know about ourself and it no longer confuses or disturbs us. We've turned it into emotional insight.

Freudian and object-relations theory

Freud's theory confronts us with the mystery of the unconscious, a restless, split-off part of our identity which represents the history of our psychical rather than cultural experience and which is largely unknown to us. Normally, unless we have analytical psychotherapy or, perhaps, a life-threatening experience which suddenly faces us with the question of who we 'really' are, we have very little access to this silent, remote part of our self. But Freud argues that the signs of it are most clearly articulated in the timeless condensations and displacements we see in dreams, and in hesitations, bungled speech, jokes and in symptoms such as anxiety states, depressions, phobias, obsessions, compulsions, psychosomatic ailments and illnesses and acute feelings of emptiness and insubstantiality. Individuals often decide to have therapy when they feel something from within rather than outside themselves is inhibiting their capacity to live a creative, fulfilling existence. They frequently feel that although they are living they are not fully alive, that something is sabotaging their life to a greater or lesser extent. Often, analytical psychotherapy enables the patient to articulate or symbolize unconscious feelings or wishes which were previously expressed in phantasies or physical symptoms rather than words. It also often involves the patient in the experience of a containing relationship with the therapist which he or she may never have experienced before. This means that in the future the patient has the awareness of a creative, fulfilling, intuitive way of relating which can serve as the measure for other relationships. This may mean that the patient stops accepting, or even unconsciously seeking, destructive relationships out of psychical ignorance of what other kinds of more creative ones might feel like.

In Freud's theory, the father's role is central in that he stands as the third term of the triangle symbolizing the world of 'not the mother', 'not me', that is culture. This is irrespective of whether the actual mother is a high court judge or a housewife. The father's symbolic role as culture is about not being the body in which the baby has been carried, suckled and about which the baby phantasizes a perpetual, fused future. For Freud, the father represents the child's first encounter with the cultural reality of the law against incest which insists that small children cannot be allowed to run away with their mother. In this sense, the father sets realistic limits on the small child's and later adult's omnipotent phantasies that anything and everything is possible.

Object-relations theory, in contrast to Freud's theory and Lacan's development of it, makes the mother's rather than the father's role central to the construction of our identity, although nowadays modern object-relations therapists consider the father's role to be also very important. Object-relations theory is developmental rather than structural and assumes the possibility of a relatively coherent and stable identity developed in the context of the child's relationship with the mother, both phantasized and actual. The object-relations writers Klein, Winnicott, Bion and Bollas suggest that identity is only seriously unstable and precarious as a result of maternal deprivation, and in their theories our perception of the mother's power when we were helpless babies is seen ultimately as more important in our construction than political or economic power. The unconscious is conceptualized as a well of deprivation rather than as an 'other scene' or place. Winnicott highlights the very depressed mother as an example of the mother who may be experienced as particularly powerful because she is unable to be 'good enough'.

Instead, she unconsciously compels the child to comply with her needs and responses to the world rather than the child's, leaving it unable to establish a viable identity of its own. Joyce McDougall (1989: 47) describes this kind of psychical predicament in an adult patient.

> Long before the acquisition of language, gestures, movements and the free expression of emotional states may be experienced by the patient as forbidden . . . the growing child understands that it is forbidden to *think* – the only permitted thoughts are the mother's, so that the child must eventually invent its own vision of the world in order to escape the terror of being entrapped in the mother's mind.

Most psychotherapists would now argue that an emotionally unavailable or, more extremely, violent father may also have devastating effects on psychical development. Criminal violence is highly correlated with a history of violent fathering.

Although in many ways Freudian and object-relations theory appear incompatible, they often seem to be referring to the same unconscious phenomena but within different conceptual frameworks. Both approaches emphasize the vital need for separation from the mother as part of the transition from phantasy to reality. The period in which the small child or baby makes this transition from merger with the mother to separation, from phantasy to culture or 'reality', is conceptualized in different ways in the different theories. Freud describes the three- or four-year-old child's repression of its early love for the mother and the internalization of culture as a substitute for her through an identification with the father, as the Oedipal crisis. His follower Melanie Klein thinks that the phase of transition occurs much earlier in the baby of between three months and a year when it painfully negotiates its way through what she calls the depressive position where it gradually learns to abandon its idealizing and denigrating phantasies of the mother's breast (and itself) and see her (and itself) more as a whole person capable of being a mixture of good and bad qualities. Winnicott, building on Klein's theory, refers to it as the 'transitional space', a psychical place in which the small child plays its way from phantasy to reality through the make-believe intrinsic to play. Lacan, from a post-modernist perspective, focuses on our transition from our infant identity based on our reflected image of ourselves (usually first from our mother) to one formed out of our identification with the pre-existing meanings of language which waits to be inhabited fully by us.

All psychoanalytic theory takes for granted the existence of an unconscious which is seen as what is repressed, split off or disassociated. Specifically, in Freud's and Lacan's theory it consists of desire, loss, lack, a 'want-to-be' or, in object-relations theory, as defence mechanisms (Klein) or a well of deprivation (Winnicott). Psychoanalytic approaches see language or consciousness as the main means by which we creatively finally bring our 'selves' into cultural existence. Most psychoanalytic theory suggests, explicitly or implicitly, that the construction of identity is an infinitely complex process which involves both the child's identification with and desire for the mother and the emotional quality of the mother–baby relationship and, ideally, the presence of the father or a substitute as an alternative psychical space. They also suggest that identity is always likely to be precarious because all babies experience some degree of deprivation, loss or 'castration' at different stages of their development and ultimately have to separate from the mother, which means that something always has to be repressed or dissociated. But they suggest that some identities are more than usually precarious because some people have experienced greater difficulties in early childhood. There is also the added dimension of precariousness brought about by social change and social deprivation and injury. So in spite of the importance of the notion of fluidity of identity, and the need to live with a degree of precariousness, most psychoanalytic perspectives suggest that we still have to make some distinctions on the basis of whether an individual is able to cope relatively autonomously and self-reflectively with life. Winnicott took the optimistic view that it is possible for any baby to grow up with a healthy, integrated identity capable of spontaneity and emotional and intellectual creativity if it has had a mother, or parent, who was herself these things and was capable, through the provision of enough loving attentiveness to be 'good enough'. But Winnicott recognized the defensive need for varying degrees of a 'false self' in some emotionally deprived individuals and also the potentially damaging effects of such alienation from the self.

In areas such as literary, cultural, film and women's studies, object-relations theory, compared with Freudian and, particularly, Lacan's psychoanalytic theory, has been somewhat neglected in universities, even though it forms the basis of so much contemporary eclectic psychoanalytic practice. Part of the reason for this may be because it makes the assumption that at least some of our gender is biologically determined, although this can be dramatically modified by our experience within culture. The idea of any biological essence has been very controversial in recent years when a culturalist approach to difference has tended to prevail. While Lacan's version of Freudian theory is associated with culturalist accounts of the world, much of Freud's work and object-relations theory rests on more humanistic foundations which do not rule out the role of some biological factors in the formation of our identity.

Theory and control

Let us consider for a moment just what may be unconsciously as well as consciously at stake when we feel the need to ally ourselves with one view of the world to the exclusion of all others. Psychoanalytic theory as a whole suggests that the recent popularity of culturalist theories which argue that identity is an exclusively social or cultural construction, may be a reflection of a widespread unconscious need to feel we are in control in a world which we sense may be running out of our control. The domination of science and technology, rather than being able to save us, increasingly appears to be the source of much of the impetus towards disorder and to represent an alarming retreat from, rather than secure guiding light towards, progress. This need for control may involve a reluctance to face up to the implications of unconscious or biological factors *as well as* cultural and historical ones because this provokes feelings of increased anxiety and powerlessness. We may feel, with justification, that we cannot control biological or unconscious processes as easily as social or cultural ones. A perpetuation of the mind–body split makes us feel safe. The problem is that our own psychical absences, what we unconsciously know but which remains 'unthought' or unsymbolized, may lead us to mirror these absences in the knowledge we produce and undermine its potential integrity in terms of emotional honesty. Just as we may unconsciously project what we cannot accept about ourselves onto despised others, some theories may project what they cannot cope with emotionally onto theoretical 'others' which are then denigrated and rejected. This returns us to the idea that, since neither we nor our theories can be perfect, for the production of emotionally as well as theoretically 'healthy' knowledge, we need to avoid extreme black-and-white positions if they leave out large areas of what life is about and opt for a more eclectic, nuanced approach. It seems unwise to throw away anything that can be of use to us in addressing the complexity that confronts us. We need to be able to allow ourselves access to a range of psychoanalytic insights, those which are body-oriented and potentially 'smelly' as well as those which, it could be argued, have been made conceptually fragrant through the mediation of the sweet (intellectualized) scent of signifiers, making them less threatening and more 'thinkable'. Psychoanalytic knowledge suggests that we need feelings as well as intellect.

Winnicott's concept of the transitional space as the psychical space which enables us to participate in cultural experience creatively and imaginatively suggests the kind of artistic rather than scientific spirit with which I think we need apply psychoanalytic insights to an analysis of culture. Winnicott describes the delicate psychical place between the mother and baby as the 'transitional space', a space in the mind in which the child plays out the gradual transition from emotional holding and phantasy to relative independence and reality, the relationship between inner and outer, 'me' and 'not me', subjectivity and objectivity. Winnicott compares this psychical space, in which the child plays with the 'as if' of make-believe, with that which the creative artist inhabits. He sees the experience of the artist as the same as the child's attempt to integrate its inner and outer, psychical and material, worlds through playful creativity. Winnicott stresses the vital characteristics of the transitional space as those of provisionality and inconclusiveness. Artistic creativity or forms of 'truth' ideally seem to stem from a way of being which engages creatively with the possibilities offered by inner experience and the external possibilities and constraints which characterize the chosen medium (paint, canvas, musical instruments). He or she draws on the resources of both inner and outer 'reality' at the same time and on experience of loss and negation as well as fullness and pleasure. Marion Milner's ideas about artistic creativity illuminatingly develop and elaborate Winnicott's views (Milner 1971). In using psychoanalytic ideas to shed light on aspects of culture, Winnicott's idea of the transitional space suggests that, like artists, we need to allow the emotional resonances in ourselves to inform the way we 'imagine', make sense of, symbolize or 'think' the external world of culture. In attempting to analyse culture, in some sense, as if it were a patient, we need, if we can, to combine the emotional reverberations culture provokes in us together with psychoanalytic ideas in which we have confidence because of their capacity to elicit emotional resonances in us. These resonances are the only evidence we can have for the emotional 'truth' of these theoretical ideas. In some way, we have to be able to 'feel' aspects of culture before we can try to make some kind of provisional interpretation using our own emotional rapport with the unconscious dimensions of particular theoretical ideas.

Part I of this book introduces the two main strands of psychoanalytic theory, Freudian and object-relations. It provides a brief, accessible outline of the ideas of four major psychoanalytic writers, Freud, Klein,

Winnicott, Lacan, to provide readers unfamiliar with psychoanalytic ideas with the broad background necessary to understand the psychoanalytic ideas which they will encounter in part II. (For a fuller, more detailed but still accessible account of the work of these writers, see Minsky 1996.)

The chapters in part II elaborate on these overviews and introduce the work of other writers, within the context of particular contemporary cultural themes: difference and the fluidity of gender, women's reproductive creativity, male envy and changes in relationships between men and women, the meaning of fathers, the prevalence of private and public violence and destructiveness, consumption and creativity and the production of knowledge. In each of the chapters, I shall take an eclectic approach on the assumption that since no single psychoanalytic or other theory represents any over-arching or absolute truth, the most productive approach is to use whatever theory helps us to illuminate different dimensions of culture, even though these theories may be incompatible when considered as complete and coherent in themselves. Our desire for tight, theoretical cohesiveness may always compel us to leave out too much that is important.

Part I
Psychoanalytic Perspectives

1

Freud: sexuality and the unconscious

The unconscious

Freud invented the theory and practice of psychoanalysis. In his work, which spans nearly fifty years, he suggests that we are never in a position to know the whole 'truth' about ourselves or the world of culture we produce. He argues that this is because of the existence of a largely unknowable unconscious dimension in us all, which creates a radical split in who we are. This is a rift between a consciousness which is knowable through language and a hidden, wordless unconscious. In *Civilisation and its Discontents*, written late in his career in 1930, he takes the view that culture is inevitably the reflection of the unconscious conflicts which inhabit individuals.

Freud argues that the concealed unconscious dimension of our identity is created as the result of repression. This is a blocking mechanism through which consciousness shuts off potentially painful aspects of our early experience and produces an entirely separate place in our psyche which Freud refers to as 'another scene' of our existence. However, although these unpleasurable, unacceptable parts of who we are cannot be articulated consciously in language, they remain in a dynamic state in the unconscious. They constantly threaten to sabotage the apparent coherence and stability of who we take ourselves to be with sudden eruptions of unconscious loss and desire. Rather than expressing themselves in the symbols of ordinary language these feelings often emerge as physical or psychological 'symptoms' but most strikingly, in the symbolic language of dreams which Freud regarded as the 'royal road' to the unconscious. He thought that dreams, but also jokes and bungled speech and action all share the same kind of symbolic structure as neurotic symptoms such as anxiety, depressions, obsessions, phobias and psychosomatic illnesses. Frozen or 'paralysed' meanings which derive from memories of very early childhood emerge in two complimentary symbolic forms, condensation and displacement, which, Freud suggests in *The Interpretation of Dreams* (1905), represent the invisible structuring rules or patterns of unconscious meanings. Condensation occurs when one idea with several associations is symbolized by a single symbol or metaphor. For example, in a dream, a derelict house might symbolize the body, feelings of insecurity and fragility or an unreliable project. Displacement occurs when one idea is displaced onto other ideas which originally had less intensity but which are related to the first idea through a chain of associations. Freud thought, for example, that ladders and staircases represented sexuality (see Minsky 1996: 28–9). Later, Lacan was to relate the crucial structuring role of condensation and displacement in the creation of unconscious meaning to the two principles of metaphor and metonymy which provide the underlying pattern for the conscious meanings of language.

In his paper 'The Unconscious' (1915), Freud elaborated further on his ideas about the relationship between consciousness and the unconscious and distinguished carefully between two kinds of memories characteristic of these different domains. The unconscious stores memories as 'thing-presentations' whereas memories can enter language or consciousness only as 'word-presentations'. Repression prevents the painful 'thing-presentations' in the unconscious from being translated into words so that they remain attached to the unpleasurable idea in the unconscious. But Freud suggests that these unconscious representations of memories can suddenly be mobilized by some wish or desire. Only when we convert the silent 'thing-presentations' into 'word-presentations', that is into the conscious words of language, can they lose their potential for the subversion and disruption of who we are. The process of speaking what previously remained 'unthought' in the unconscious forms a significant part of what happens in the psychotherapeutic session.

Freud suggests that we can have access to the 'truths' of the unconscious through the medium of what he calls 'free association' in the course of the experience of psychoanalysis or, more usually nowadays, psychoanalytic therapy. This means that the patient is invited to begin wherever she or he chooses and to say whatever comes into his or her head. In the production of this narrative, which in some ways is very like the artist creating or telling a story, the patient creates a self out of the unconscious disruptions and repetitions which emerge in this narrative within the emotional context of the therapeutic relationship.

Freud constantly re-worked, elaborated and changed his ideas and these have been used subsequently in different ways by others to produce new theories. But Freud's theory, in both its modern and postmodern dimensions, has given us infinitely rich, complex and subtle ways of thinking and speaking about identity, difference, sexuality, the body, knowledge, language and culture. These underlie many of the theoretical developments which came after him despite their different ways of conceptualizing the construction of identity and their changes in focus and emphasis. Despite its imperfections, limitations and omissions, even in the light of powerful later developments, Freud's theory has opened up crucial and momentous insights about how we come both to be and not be ourselves and, jointly with others, create and be created by the meanings of language and culture. In particular, Freud's theory, taken as a whole, suggests not simply that from our earliest childhood we are driven by a variety of biological drives as some have suggested but, in a much more complicated way, how we construct ourselves and culture out of what we unconsciously 'make' of our earliest bodily experiences and, crucially, the passionate emotional entanglements which arise out of these experiences within our particular historically and culturally situated families. Freud's theory allows us to begin to imagine how we create and live out our gendered identities as 'masculine' and 'feminine' men and women in culture, to a greater or lesser extent divided within ourselves, as a result of these experiences. The unthought and unconscious part of who we are (sometimes referred to as the id) together with the part of us which can be expressed within language or consciousness (the ego) are always embedded together within the con-tingencies of history and place. This does not exclude the possibility that some elements of the unconscious dimension of who we are may well be universal human phenomena because almost all of us had our earliest experience of intimacy, love and separation with our mother or substi-tute mother who was female. However, it is probably wiser to argue that since Freud's theory grew out of European culture his theory as a whole is likely to apply particularly to individuals brought up in that culture. Analytical psychotherapists working with patients from Indian and African cultures frequently comment on their difficulties in thinking about these patients from within a Freudian framework; there is always a sense, they suggest, that 'something else is going on'.

The difficulty with Freud's concept of the unconscious (which, as he himself observed, existed in a less rigorously defined form before him in the work of many writers and poets) is that we cannot have direct access to it because, by definition, the nature of the unconscious is to protect us from what is too painful for us to live with consciously. Sometimes, when we catch a glimpse of the unconscious in ourselves, it feels as if we both know and don't know the content of it at the same time. We may suddenly recognize it when we hear the cry of loss and longing in a popular love-song (which may be as much about separation from and loss of the mother as it is about a later lover), in a haunting visual image, or a line in a poem, play or novel which makes us catch our breath and throws us momentarily off balance because it hooks up with something in us that we didn't know we knew.

Sexuality and infantile sexuality

Freud's focus was primarily on what we 'make' imaginatively of bodily drives and sensations rather than on relationships. (The latter forms the basis of the object-relations-based psychoanalytic theory which came after him.) Freud argued that the unconscious, sexuality, and the body are intrinsically interwoven. He thought the central moment which achieved the vital conjunction of these different dimensions of our identity is the *Oedipal crisis*, which occurs when the child is between three and five years old. This is the moment when we emerge from our phantasies around the body of the mother into fully fledged human beings. Before this time, we shared a fused identity with the mother which is initially supported by primitive sensations of pleasure associated with what Freud called 'component instincts' or drives connected with particular areas of our bodies – mouth, anus and penis or clitoris. At first, Freud, for whom sexuality means something much broader than what most of us mean by this term, very controversially described these drives and their potential for pleasure as *infantile forms of sexuality* because they are associated with both pleasure and our earliest sense of having an existence or identity (Minsky 1996: 31–3). In *The Three Essays on the Theory of Sexuality*, Freud systematically describes these overlapping drives (Freud 1905). Oral pleasure is associated first with the baby's sucking or 'incorporation' of both milk and the comforting idea of the breast (and later fingers and other more controllable objects). Anal pleasure is derived from the satisfaction the baby derives from 'holding on' or 'letting go' of faeces, what Freud sees as the baby's 'gift' of its internal contents to the mother. Phallic pleasure is associated particularly with masturbation in the context of phantasies of having total control and dominion of the mother whose care is associated with so much pleasure that it imagines the power of its love can captivate her for ever. During this phase, Freud tells us children of both sexes assume the mother has a penis because, as the centre of their world, she seems so powerful. Only later, at the end of the Oedipal crisis, do they discover their mistake. As he pointed out to his critics, the adult sexual practice of fetishism seems to bear this out. This is pursued by men who have, in phantasy, partly disavowed the meaning of sexual difference, that is that their mother does not have a penis. Something, such as a shoe or item of clothing, comes to stand in for the penis on the body of their female lover whose lack of a phallus is experienced as terrifying even though, contradictorily, this absence is partly consciously recognized. It is as if the unconscious negotiation of the reality of sexual difference is still going on and cannot be fully accepted so for love-making to be possible, a substitute for the phallus must be present on the body of the woman.

In thinking about Freud's theory of infantile sexuality, it is very important to remember that the different oral, anal and phallic forms of bodily pleasure, like adult sexuality, yield not only pleasure but also a crucial sense of having an existence, of feeling alive, that is of having an identity capable of spontaneity and creativity. So, in the adult, orality (for example, drinking, smoking, comfort eating, mindless watching of television and video), anality (a pre-occupation with control through meanness with money, food or heat, dieting, over-exercising, excessive tidiness, being a workaholic) and being phallic (omnipotent, dominating 'macho' behaviour which involves showing off, being exhibitionist, pushy and 'ostentatious') are defences learned in earliest childhood and are concerned, crucially, with not just pleasure but the business of 'self' preservation or the survival of a sense of having a viable self. If the baby experiences a level of trauma which interferes with the oral, anal or phallic pleasures of infancy, the baby and later adult may be left with a destructive residue of feelings of emptiness, worthlessness, humiliation, inferiority or shame, rather than with the capacity to 'take in' good experiences freely, 'let go' spontaneously and creatively and enjoy sexual experience without guilt or inhibition.

Narcissism

In 1915, long after the publication of *The Three Essays* in 1905, Freud developed his theory of identity to include the concept of *narcissism* which became central to his theory and those of his followers. He suggested that what he called 'narcissism' represents a form of identity which exists between one based on pleasure from the baby's own body (auto-eroticism) while it is still merged with the mother and one which is separated from the mother in a successful outcome of the Oedipal crisis. He argued that the child's narcissistic identity is based on a middle position in which the child projects its self onto the mother. Then, because it is already in a state of fusion with her, the baby takes an identity from the mother which already contains a substantial part of its self. In this way the child achieves a sense of identity but one which is very dependent on a reflection from outside itself in the external world which, paradoxically, is already suffused with its self. If, as adults, we still rely, for our sense of identity and coherence, primarily on the approval of other people or things onto whom or which we have already projected ourselves, we cannot avoid constructing ourselves out of reflections or shadows of ourself which lie outside us. This means that disapproval, rejection or disappointment always threaten us with a potential collapse of identity because our inner world is so dependent on the world outside. It has no filling or inner resources of its own. Most of us carry round vestiges of narcissism, although Christopher Lasch (1980) suggests that we have constructed a culture which actively encourages narcissistic identities in the form of 'quick fix' instant cultural gratifications which we mistake for ourselves. This leaves us in a blind alley of projections without the capacity to make authentic relationships with people who we can see as distinct and separate from ourselves.

Since the Oedipal crisis is so often incompletely resolved, Freud recognized the widespread potential for narcissism. He thought it could be seen in our relationships with children or partners who may become extensions of ourselves, with much younger lovers who may represent what we once were or would have liked to have been, and in the mechanisms involved in bereavement and loss. In the latter case of loss, we have to free ourselves of the inner object (the part of the loved and lost person who has become part of our self) before we can let go of the person in the external world who has been lost (see Minsky 1996: 39). The concept of narcissism is elaborated in chapter 9 on consumerism where it forms a central part of the discussion.

For Freud, what he calls the ego or largely conscious self (except for that part of the ego, the super-ego, which is unconscious) forms the basic building block for identity and represents the means by which we become a human subject. The ego or self is constructed out of the child's earliest emotional ties or what Freud calls 'identifications', together with the symbolic remains of abandoned attachments to other people and things, what Freud calls 'objects' which subsequently form part of the internal world. Identification with another person or someone we would like to be becomes the means by which we come into being through the successive internalizations of the qualities and attributes of these objects. The ego therefore is part of both the past and the present and must be anchored in 'word presentations', those memories which are grounded in language which provide it with a degree of mastery against the symbolic 'thing presentations' which characterize memories which remain unconscious (see Minsky 1996: 28–9). However, he thought that this makes the ego permanently precarious because the unconscious always contrives to be heard in the stumblings and hesitations of language. This emphasis on the construction of the ego through identification with other people, ideas and things, and the role of language in this process, are crucial to Lacan's re-working of Freud's ideas.

But it is the Oedipal crisis that, Freud argues, allows us to make the transition from our merged, narcissistic identity with the mother, and our passionate phantasies about keeping her to ourselves for ever, into human beings capable of being able to lead a relatively creative, self-reflective, autonomous existence.

The Oedipal crisis

Freud argues that we are precipitated into the Oedipal crisis by falling in love with the mother who has cast a spell over us through her care and love and all the touching, wiping, stroking and hugging this entails. But this new stance in relation to the mother, now phantasized as a potential lover we can steal from our father, and, if possible, siblings and anyone else, coincides with another tumultuous discovery in the child's so far body-preoccupied experience – the discovery of sexual difference. For Freud, largely on the basis of what his many female patients told him, the child's first awareness of sexual difference is based on the visual perception of the presence or absence of the penis on the bodies of those around it among whom it must eventually find its place. However, it is at the moment of discovery of bodily difference based on the presence or absence of the penis that Freud introduces the most dynamic concept in his theory of the construction of gendered identity, the *castration complex* and the role of the *symbolic father*. At this point let us look at the experience of the boy and girl separately.

In the context of both his guilt in relation to his father, who is perceived as a rival for his mother, and his perception of the mother's or girl's lack of a penis, the boy falls prey to the terrifying idea that girls have been castrated and that therefore he may fall victim to the same fate. This, he phantasizes, is likely to be at the hands of his father as a result of his sexual ambitions to steal away his mother. It is important to understand that, for Freud, the small boy's fear of castration is experienced symbolically and not only as the threat of being physically mutilated. At the symbolic level, castration anxiety is the threat of the extinction of his fragile and emergent sense of identity which at that time centres around the pleasure derived from his penis. Castration anxiety threatens the small boy with a potentially overwhelming catastrophe, that of psychical annihilation. It also threatens those adults who remain in a state of residual, unresolved castration anxiety as some, perhaps many, men do. As Freud recognized, large numbers of us emerge from the Oedipal crisis with infantile conflicts which, for a variety of complicated emotional reasons, have not been fully resolved.

Desperate to avoid potential annihilation, Freud argues that the small boy is finally persuaded by his castration anxiety to give up his mother and reconcile himself to the deferment of his phantasies about her until he is an adult and can find a woman of his own as a substitute. From this moment on, if all goes smoothly, the small boy gives up both his earliest identification with his mother and his desire for her and at the same time makes an alternative identification with his father. This is someone of the same sex, that is someone with a body like his own who may be able to fill the void left by the loss of his mother. Although Freud does not elaborate on this aspect of the boy's experience, if his Oedipal crisis is resolved successfully, in order to achieve his cultural 'masculinity', and the power this confers, the boy has to lose his mother in two ways – both as his first source of identity and as his first love-object (phantasized lover). In her place, he identifies with his father, although highly ambivalently, because he has to internalize someone who is both loved and feared at one and the same time. The internalized father continues to inspire murderous feelings and guilt but now the boy is under surveillance from within rather than from outside. In this sense the small boy's new identity is composed of a potentially divisive mixture: both himself as potential victim and his father as potential executioner. Henceforth, the father exists in the psyche of the boy as what Freud describes as the *super-ego*, as an internal representative of the external laws of culture and moral authority, not least the law forbidding incest and the law of who belongs to whom within families. It is through the child's crucial identification with the symbolic father, someone beyond the enticements of the mother's body and being (or what Lacan calls the place of the father, that is, language and cultural representation), that culture makes its unconscious impact on the child's identity through its entry into the symbolic world of language. For Freud, this entry into the laws and values of culture represents the child's entry into its humanity, its vital transition from phantasy to reality and the setting of boundaries on its desire. But, crucially, it eventually also offers us the only opportunity, emotionally, of 'growing up' through gaining access to the creative possibilities of language and symbolization (see Minsky 1996: 42–5).

It is at this crucial and emotionally fraught time, Freud argues, that the unconscious is formed out of the *repression* of the boy's love for and loss of the mother. The formation of the unconscious allows the pain of this loss to be concealed from consciousness but results in a divided subject.

This means that consciousness, what we think we know about ourselves and the world, is always vulnerable to sabotage from the sudden eruption of hidden desires and loss. If the boy is unable to identify sufficiently with the father for him to feel able to separate from the mother, Freud argues that he will continue to be dominated by phantasy involving possession of the mother and castration anxiety which will inhibit his ability to cope with the demands of reality and relationships. What Freud does not emphasize is that early separation from the emotional, bodily world of the mother entails the boy being permanently cut off also from this vital dimension of himself. The small boy has to survive the double loss of both his identification with his mother and his mother as his first love-object. The power of the phallus as the apparent lynchpin of cultural 'masculinity', and the pleasure and sense of identity it offers, seem to provide the only hope of compensation. This is in dramatic contrast to the girl's predicament if she manages to emerge successfully from her Oedipal crisis. Freud suggests that for many boys, in the context of their lingering castration phantasy, 'femininity' is inevitably viewed as a position of loss and castration and therefore one of inferiority even though in their earliest identification with the mother they were a part of this 'femininity'. This rejection of 'femininity' may go a long way in explaining some men's fear of women and their need to dominate and control them.

In his lecture 'Femininity' (1933), Freud describes how at the beginning of her Oedipal crisis, the girl, also passionately in love with the mother, discovers sexual difference and, according to Freud, perceives herself as lacking in relation to the boy's penis (and, retrospectively, understands the cultural inferiority this implies). In spite of the pleasure involved in her own version of masturbation in relation to the mother based on her clitoris, she angrily rejects her mother for not giving her a penis and for wanting someone else. Recognizing difference and the power of the penis/phallus over her mother's desire, she subsequently gives up her clitoris as second best. This means she gives up the *active* dimension of her sexuality in favour of the passive form associated with the vagina which Freud believes she discovers only later in puberty. It is important to emphasize here that her anger with her mother seems to be primarily provoked by her mother's apparent wish (in the child's phantasy) to remain with her father or a substitute rather than the little girl herself. This is at the root of what Freud, controversially, describes as *penis-envy*, the female version of castration anxiety – wanting to have, be, what the mother *desires* rather than what she *is*. Apparently the mother is not interested in bodies like that of her daughter but only, it seems to the little girl, in those of the opposite sex. In the girl's jaundiced

and disappointed eyes, it is not difficult to imagine why she should come
to the conclusion that female bodies are inferior to those of men and in
this sense she, like the little boy, rejects 'femininity' as a desirable state
to be in. So it is the fact that the mother is always female and that her
usual heterosexual desire is for a body which is different from rather than
like her own, together with the assault on the little girl's narcissism,
which provokes the rejection of 'femininity' in the unconscious of the
little girl as well as the boy. But, according to Freud, the girl never
completely gives up some vestiges of her penis-envy, that is her early
homosexual love for the mother, and he thought that most women,
although most of them are heterosexual and eventually have children,
never completely give up their yearning to be what their mother wanted,
that is a man. This is why Freud thought that, importantly, although both
men and women are bisexual (small Oedipal boys fall in love with their
fathers as well as their mothers), because of the prevalence of penis-
envy, women were particularly so.

For Freud, it is penis-envy which achieves what he thought was
impossible to accomplish without it – the girl's crossing over from her
homosexual love for her mother as the primary object of her affections
to her heterosexual desire for her father, and eventually other men.
Freud rejects biological explanations for this change of heart, suggesting
that there is very little reason why the girl, now sexually self-sufficient
with her clitoris, should ever be drawn towards her father except,
initially, as the one evidently favoured by her mother and therefore
perhaps the most promising source of access to a penis through an
identification with him. Eventually, when this unrealistic project fails,
Freud argues that the girl abandons this temporary identification with her
father and falls in love with him. Now she phantasizes having a baby
with him instead of her mother, while at the same time making a
secondary identification with her mother. This, for Freud, achieves a
successful outcome for the girl's Oedipal crisis, not least because it
entails abandoning phantasy for reality.

At this point in his theory, Freud introduces another controversial
concept, the idea of the ancient symbolic *penis–baby equivalence* which,
he argued from his knowledge of anthropology, is culturally widespread.
Like penis-envy, this concept has often been misunderstood. In the
context of trying to understand how the phantasy-ridden little girl comes
to terms with the realistic possibilities of her own body rather than
wishing she was someone else (at first, her father), Freud concludes that
most girls never completely give up their residual penis-envy which
always makes them unconsciously feel at a cultural disadvantage because cultural denigration meshes with their own unconscious view of

themselves. However, Freud thought that there are some women who manage to resolve their initial penis-envy because they have no trouble in perceiving their capacity to have babies as conferring equal status and power in their own, if not culture's, eyes. These women are not unconsciously undermined by penis-envy and an underlying sense of inferiority and therefore do not look nostalgically backwards towards the mother. More realistically, they abandon the phantasy of being what the mother *wanted* for being *like* her. This means that, as adult women, they will be unlikely to be undermined by neurotic symptoms caused by an unconscious sense of lack coming from within rather than from external, male-dominated culture.

Freud's argument does not, as some have suggested, seem to be that women should stay at home to have babies even though this is what most women were expected to do throughout most of the period of his career. Such a view would be in dramatic contrast to what is known of his life. In his psychoanalytic practice, Freud dramatically altered the prevalent view that women suffering from hysterical conversion symptoms were degenerate, emphasizing instead the intellectual gifts of many of these women whose symptoms, he argued, resulted from repressed sexuality and social exclusion. Among his professional colleagues he was surrounded by highly intelligent and gifted women, many of whom had families, and with whom he reputedly had entirely egalitarian relationships (Appignanesi and Forrester 1992). Freud's undoubted ambivalence towards women and his over-valuation of the penis/phallus seems likely to have been a defensive way of protecting himself from anxieties (frequently shared by other men) about the authenticity of his own 'masculinity' (see Minsky 1996: 72–4). If we understand the symbolic rather than physical meanings associated with the penis and difference, the controversial idea of penis-envy or the penis–baby equivalent seems to be most significantly about the little girl's unconscious desire for exclusive possession of her mother's heart and some women's successful resolution of this painful unconscious phantasy.

There are tensions and contradictions in Freud's work which reflect the tensions and lack of coherence in us all. However, his theory is so rich, suggestive and wide-ranging in scope that, in my view, its implications sometimes extend beyond Freud's conscious perceptions at any particular time. At the heart of Freud's theory is the idea that the price of a viable cultural identity and the necessary separation from the mother is a divided self. At the core of our being we are unavoidably split into consciousness and the unconscious. This means that our gendered identities are not fixed comfortably in the traditional cultural categories of 'masculinity' and 'femininity' but occupy many positions within a continuum in between. Freud's theory insists that gender exists across the boundaries of the body.

Freud believed that if we manage to resolve the Oedipal crisis successfully, and he argued that many of us for a variety of complex reasons do not, we have the potential, all other things being equal, to live a relatively independent human existence, but to do this we have to *repress* the desire and loss of the mother into our unconscious. Without this repression, Freud suggests, with so much emotional loss to bear, we would never be able to pick ourselves up, dust ourselves down and get on with the business of living. The problem is that desire and loss don't just disappear. They continually threaten to make an appearance within the gaps in consciousness and, most frequently, in the displacements and condensations which underlie the symbolic language of dreams.

It is difficult in this brief summary to give a sense of the sheer scale, richness, imaginative grasp and inventiveness of Freud's work, which has often been misunderstood and criticized because ideas have been taken out of context and there has been an insistence that Freud's weaknesses (for example, his emphasis on sexuality, patriarchal cultural assumptions and phallocentrism) obliterate the enormous imaginative sweep of the theory as a whole. Virtually all those developments which came after him grew out of ideas embedded in the rich and suggestive weave of Freud's complex work, which for a variety of practical, cultural and psychological reasons he left for those who came later. (For a fuller account of Freud's ideas and a commentary on his paper 'Femininity', see Minsky 1996: 25–77.)

2

Klein: phantasy and reparation

Although Klein is often referred to as a second-generation Freudian, many regard her as the founder of the second major strand of psycho-analysis known as object-relations theory (the second stream of object-relations theory is associated particularly with the work of Winnicott). However, although Klein drew heavily on many of Freud's ideas, her theory eventually became so distinctively different from his that it became an independent school in its own right. In contrast to Freud, Klein was interested in the baby's very early, pre-Oedipal relationship with the mother long before the small child's entry into Freud's Oedipal crisis and culture. Klein's theory, unlike Freud's, is centred around infancy and, as she sees it, the emotionally fraught experience of the very young baby dominated by conflicting phantasies. However, although culture is not central to Klein's theory, it and developments of it by post-Kleinians, and particularly Bion, have been widely used to shed light on the unconscious dimensions of cultural issues.

With Melanie Klein we move from Freud's view of an unconscious dominated by desire to one permeated with anxiety and the experience of the very young, helpless baby. In her clinical work with small children, Klein was able to look behind the Oedipal territory with which Freud was preoccupied to the conflict-ridden world of the infant which she thought underlies the reality of all of us. Klein argues that it is the baby's anxiety arising out of its instinctive emotional ambivalence towards the mother rather than sexuality or desire that is the major problem with which the small baby, and later the adult, have to contend. From the moment of birth, she argues, the baby is plunged into a desperate conflict between alternating emotions of love and hate which cause acute anxiety. Phantasy provides the means by which these instinctual emotions may be directed towards both the mother and the self.

Klein's approach to the construction of identity is usually described as 'developmental', that is, something which happens step by step in the baby's or individual's life, but she writes about 'positions' rather than 'phases' of development to emphasize that both infant and adult can move from one unconscious structure to another throughout life.

Klein was primarily interested in what she perceived as the baby's struggle to relate to other people, or what Klein calls 'objects' (at first the mother) by taking them into its inner world as phantasy objects and then building an identity out of them. It is the primitive, pre-verbal and extra-verbal language of these internalized objects – what Klein called 'phantasies' – which is the major focus of her work. By 'phantasy' Klein means a kind of primitive thinking consisting, in the first place, of what the baby constructs out of its experiences, both inside and outside itself and by which it communicates with itself. Klein thought the perceptions of the external world by young babies, but also children and even adults, were dramatically coloured by their emotional state. Klein found that her four- or five-year-old son, Eric, saw her as a wicked witch threatening to poison him when he felt sad and unhappy. But when he was feeling happy and secure, he saw her as a princess he wanted to marry. For Klein, such phantasies of loving and hating form the basis of a rudimentary sense of identity consisting of impulses, defences and relationships. She saw the creation of phantasies emerging out of primitive defence mechanisms as crucial to establishing future relationships and rational ways of thinking. Such thinking evolves from phantasy as the baby gradually gains a more realistic view of the mother and the rest of the world and needs to defend itself less by dividing the world and itself into black and white. But Klein became convinced that an identity constructed only out of phantasy objects was a feature of both the mental life of the very young baby and the psychotic child or adult and that phantasy is a precursor of any engagement we can have with reality.

Klein took the view that the baby's primitive phantasies of love and hate are based on early biological instincts and this partial reliance on biology is reflected in her assumption that 'masculinity' and 'femininity' are also biologically determined but reinforced during early childhood. This returns to the idea that there is some underlying biological component in gender formation which, for Klein and her contemporaries, seems to have been inspired by a wish to detach 'femininity' from the dependence on the perception of the penis proposed by Freud. For Klein, the first sign of difference is not the penis or lack of it but largeness or smallness, breast or no breast. As we shall see, her concept of envy of the mother in her book *Envy and Gratitude* is based on the impact on the infantile mind of these experiences (Klein 1957).

As Maguire (1995) emphasizes, Klein, redefining the Oedipus complex, focuses much more on emotional and intellectual development than on sexual desire. The child's envy and fear is related to the mother's body rather than the fear of castration, and the achievement of psychical health, including the capacity for self-reflection and symbolic thought, depends on it being able to recognize that the mother has a life of her own including a sexual relationship with the father (Maguire 1995: 35).

Loving and hating phantasies

Klein took Freud's idea of a life and death drive (described in chapter 8: 155–7) and converted it into instincts of love and hate through which the baby first constructs a sense of the mother and itself. For Klein, the baby's first fragile identity is carved out of its defences against anxiety in relation to these instincts resulting from its extreme helplessness and dependence on the mother at the beginning of its life. Although the struggle between these powerful opposing emotions produces huge anxiety, Klein sees this as the necessary and eventually humanizing trigger for the child's potential to develop a separate identity of its own. Loving and hating phantasies of the breast are the baby's first experience of relating to the mother and (since the baby's identity is fused with the breast because it does not yet have an identity of its own) of filling itself up with a good or bad phantasy of the breast thus creating a primitive sense of having a self. It is the mother's presence or absence which determines whether the baby can incorporate or 'introject' a good or bad phantasy of the breast and later whole mother. For Klein, the young baby must manage to allow its love for the mother to overcome its hate so that it can incorporate her and everything she represents (the breast but also other internal objects such as the father's penis, another symbolic part-object that has a claim on the mother) as good objects and therefore experience itself as substantially good rather than bad. This idea develops Freud's idea of the mother as the baby's first distinct, psychological object which it internalizes or introjects when she is perceived to be missing. He had linked this to the baby's sensations of anxiety and helplessness whenever the mother's breast is removed for too long. At such times the baby recreates the external mother, the object, for itself in phantasy inside its inner world. By hallucinating a good feed within its imagination, it creates a phantasy of the breast/mother which then becomes a part of the baby's own fragile, residual self over which it has some control, unlike the external breast (SE 1: 319). This capacity to internalize phantasies, at first of part-objects, such as the breast or penis (also contained in the baby's phantasy of the mother), but later, as a sense of external reality sets in, whole objects or people out of which the baby then creates its self, lies at the core of object-relations theory.

For Klein, in contrast to Freud, it is the baby's relatedness to the mother through phantasy, and not the object of desire, which is incorporated as a self. In Klein's theory, when the baby feels full, in a state of contentment and therefore 'good', it takes into itself or introjects the idea of a 'good breast' out of which it then constitutes a positive, satisfying identity. When the baby feels hungry, insecure and empty, it introjects the idea of a 'bad breast' and, since it still shares its self with the mother, it experiences both her and its self as 'bad' and frightening. In the first months of life the baby needs to hold on to an inner 'good' breast with which it can build a self which will be able to keep it safe from the 'bad' breast or 'bad' object which in phantasy, both externally and internally, threatens to annihilate it. The baby's aggression or hostility towards its bad internalized objects transformed into parts of the self is experienced as so dangerous that it has to be projected out of the baby's self onto other people. This then means that these other people are experienced as potentially damaging because they contain hostile, split-off parts of the baby's own identity. The baby and later child or psychotic adult, as a result of the projection of early oral phantasies, may fear that it will be devoured or torn to bits by women. This, of course, is the mechanism of paranoia – part of the outside world gets muddled up with a hostile part of the self. Such oral phantasies may well underlie some men's attacks on women (the 'bad' mother) inspired by fear of them as devouring monsters, witches or hags. Such phantasies appear in myth, literature, the cinema and in fairy-tales such as the old woman in 'Hansel and Gretel' who eats children, the wolf in 'Red Riding Hood' and in the male phantasy of woman as the *vagina dentata* (the devouring, castrating vagina).

Although Klein built on Freud's idea of the life and death instincts and the idea that potentially wounding aggression could be deflected outwards, she was much more interested in acquiring a detailed understanding of the unconscious mechanisms by which the ego or self protects itself from being overwhelmed and annihilated by its own internalized aggression in the form of bad phantasy objects.

So, in Klein's theory, phantasy is related to both the external and internal world where it is actively used in the construction of the baby's first phantasy-based identity. The first pole of her theory of identity is the self or ego's relationship, through phantasy, to the *external* world of objects at first seen as the mother's breast which includes other part-objects, and later as the mother seen both as a whole and as a combined object (containing the idea of a whole father, rather than the part-object penis) and siblings who also compete for the mother's attention. These objects are either idealized or denigrated through the mediation of love or hate. The second pole is the self's relationship, through phantasy, with its *inner* world containing instincts, impulses, bodily sensations and, most importantly, the baby's anxiety. This fundamental anxiety is the fear of being psychically annihilated by its own internalized aggression and not Freud's much later Oedipal fear of castration by the father seen as a rival in love. Taken as a whole, Klein's work is concerned primarily with how the child copes with what it assumes to be the loss of the mother when she is absent, by splitting her and the external world by means of good and bad phantasy. Significantly, the breast replaces Freud's phallus as the most important feature in the formation of the child's identity.

Unconscious mechanisms

In her clinical practice with disturbed young children, instead of using Freud's method of free association, Klein used her own invention of a 'play technique' which she used to construct a previously non-existing picture of the child's internal world. Klein describes the technique in her 1955 paper 'The Psychoanalytic Play Technique' (Mitchell 1986). It involved the children playing with specially made toys which they used as a way of representing their phantasy life, as a form of language about their inner world. Using this technique, Klein perceived a special system of organization of feelings and impulses through which the baby (and later 'normal' adults and, in extreme forms, psychotics) tries to protect its inner world from annihilation. This includes four central unconscious mechanisms based on phantasy: *splitting, projection, introjection* and *projective identification*, which are mechanisms or defences against acute feelings of fragmentation of identity and emptiness which represent a kind of unconscious, non-verbal language. However, they are not part of another separate, psychical domain as the unconscious is for Freud.

Splitting involves the baby in unconsciously separating the 'good' phantasy object from the 'bad' one in its external and internal worlds. It does this by splitting both the mother and itself into two after, for example, the depriving experience of crying too long. The 'bad' mother is rejected and the bad part of the self is disowned and projected onto the mother's breast which consequently becomes 'bad'. This may then contaminate the part previously perceived as satisfying and good, because it now carries part of the baby's 'bad', anxiety-ridden identity. Sometimes a baby who has waited for the mother too long will turn away from the mother when she finally arrives as if it fears attack from her.

Projection, as Freud had discovered, is the baby's unconscious device for pushing both good and bad feelings within its inner world out onto something or someone in the external world (FPL 11: 187–8). As we have seen, initially this included pushing the split-off part of itself which it experiences as 'bad' (its inner bad objects) onto the external object, the mother, in order to preserve its own feelings of goodness and security. (In a child or adult we call this kind of behaviour 'scapegoating' or looking for someone else to blame for our own feelings of aggression and vulnerability.) As a result, the baby feels hated and persecuted by its split-off feelings now contained in the mother who is now contaminated and experienced as 'bad' and hostile whatever she is actually like. This then produces more bad feelings of anxiety which also need to be split off and projected and so on, so that the baby or psychotic adult is riven by multiple splits. However, since in this nightmare cycle so much of the self becomes split off, this leads inevitably to feelings of fragmentation, emptiness and impoverishment. Sometimes, if the mother conveys to the baby that she can only tolerate its love and idealization, but not its aggression (or is so emotionally needy herself that she envies the baby), the baby may project only its good feelings onto the mother retaining only its bad feelings within itself. This is a feature of depression in adult life where an individual feels all 'goodness' exists outside his or her self, leaving him or her 'inside' feeling worthless and bad. In such a predicament, the individual is being attacked by a part of his or her own self, constituted by the bad, destructive objects inside him or her without any possibility of rescue from the good ones. This may, as Klein suggested, form the basis for psychosomatic illness where the bad objects attack the body which may be experienced as part of the external world. The projection of our 'good' feelings onto an idea of God, an ideal parent, may explain the Christian preoccupation with man's unworthiness as a 'miserable sinner' in need of redemption. (As we shall see, Klein's concept of reparation in what she calls the 'depressive position' fits this analysis.) Projection is also likely to be an unconscious factor in certain forms of racial and ethnic hatred, homophobia and some men's hatred of women. Importantly, the people onto whom these projections have been made have to be severely controlled because, like human psychical dustbins, they contain rejected parts of the self. This may even apply to clothes when we say, very extravagantly, 'I wouldn't be seen dead in it.' Sometimes we may make objects as well as people into despised 'others' on the basis of stark, black-and-white distinctions.

Introjection is the means by which the baby takes in, or internalizes, everything it perceives or experiences in relation to the object (breast or whole mother), both its 'goodness' and its 'badness'. Like Freud's idea of identification, it is the basic building-block of the baby's self and, for Klein, the introjection of sufficient 'good', loved objects is the essential requirement for an autonomous self capable of both giving and taking in love.

Projective identification is Klein's version of what Freud calls narcissistic object-relationships where an identity is taken via projection from a part of the external world with which the individual has already identified. This means that the individual becomes very heavily dependent on the love-object. Klein distinguishes between narcissistic states where the self is taken as the love-object (what Freud termed 'auto-eroticism') and those states and the relationships based on them where the self is projected onto the other and then re-introjected. This is what Klein called 'projective identification'. Initially, with the mother, this involves the baby's projection of good as well as bad parts of the self onto her, having already imaginatively filled itself up or identified with her as part of its fused self. In some adult relationships, based predominantly on a defensive form of projective identification, both partners may tend to lose sight of who each of them is because there is only one fused identity based on mutual identification with each partner then re-introjecting or taking back into the self the other who already contains part of that self. Usually both partners are unaware of how dependent they are on each other. In some cases, unconscious feelings of being potentially enslaved by a partner may mean such people try to avoid close relationships because they inevitably find them too suffocating and psychically exhausting. The problem with relationships based on love-objects who carry too many projected parts of the self is that there is a constant need to control the object and, conversely, a persistent fear of being controlled by it. When bad parts of the self are projected, the partner may become a feared persecutor, and when good parts are projected, causing idealization, there may be a huge sense of dependence. The partner, therefore, has to be controlled at all times because he or she contains a substantial part of the self which has been split off and therefore always threatens to get out of control, while at the same time there is a fear of being controlled by this same controlling part of the self which has been externalized. However, more positively, Kleinians would argue that, in therapy, projective identification may be a form of communication of what is unconscious or split off. The patient unknowingly makes the therapist feel the emotions which they have denied by, for example, making him or her feel worthless and stupid. In other circumstances, projective identification may not be defensive. If we project the good parts of ourself onto the object it can enable us to put ourselves into another's shoes and feel empathy.

Unconscious positions

Klein suggests two primary ways in which our psyche may be organized. She refers to these as 'positions' rather than stages because anyone, as an adult, can find themselves operating within one or other position at any time. They each represent an unconscious system of thinking based on phantasy. The first is what she calls the *paranoid-schizoid position*, which is primarily based on persecutory anxiety (fear of attack) and the defences of splitting and projection characteristic of the baby's first three months. The baby, in a state of total vulnerability and dependence on the mother, fears her retaliation (being devoured, poisoned, having its internal organs damaged) because of its own oral and anal destructive phantasies which have been projected outwards onto her. In the case of a severely paranoid adult, splitting and projection create a terrifying persecutory, external world which in a psychotic state might take the form of hearing hostile, mocking voices, for example, which lead to further persecution from an equally fragmented inner world. Sometimes, as 'normal' adults, we talk of feeling that we are 'going to pieces' and of 'getting ourselves together'. This seems to reflect the unconscious experience of potential fragmentation characteristic of the paranoid-schizoid position.

Klein sees the paranoid-schizoid position as, ideally, a first developmental step in the evolution of identity during which the baby relates to part rather than whole objects. The baby can gradually overcome its fear of disintegration through its first identification with an idealized breast. Gradually, as the baby develops in the second quarter of the first year, it is able to perceive and take in a whole person, normally its mother. This is the beginning of a more realistic view of the world. It learns that both loving and hating experiences can be integrated and co-exist in the same person, in both its mother and itself. Although the baby may continue to feel empty and hostile about the frustration caused by the mother's independent existence (the demands, for example, of its father and other children), its fear of retaliation from the mother is gradually replaced by feelings of guilt and anxiety about its phantasies of destroying her. These are very painful. For Freud, guilt is associated with the much later Oedipal period, and with desire and phantasized murderous attacks on the *father*. In Klein's theory, painful feelings of guilt and anxiety result from the baby's phantasized, murderous attacks on the *mother*. They occur much earlier, at between three and six months, but they represent a major turning point for the baby as it enters what for Klein is the all important *depressive position*. This, not Freud's Oedipal crisis, represents the crux of her theory and the child's entry into its humanity. If the baby can repair the damage to its external world (the mother) and its internalized bad objects through loving, reparative feelings, its inner world can be transformed by re-populating it with good objects – a restored and repaired mother whose loss can be endured. In other words, if, through positive, loving experiences with the mother, the baby can come to trust and internalize an external world of goodness and the possibility of reparation and integration rather than persecution and annihilation, it will have negotiated the depressive position successfully. It will also have achieved the necessary separation from the mother. On the basis of this experience it will be able to form an identity which creatively constructs and repairs rather than destroys, denies or omnipotently seeks to control parts of the self projected onto objects in the external world. In other words, *blaming* the (m)other as a way of defending against feelings of helplessness and dependence, and the accompanying anxiety, is replaced by an ability to own these 'bad' feelings so that they can be integrated within the self instead of disowned and projected onto the outside world. By learning to integrate good and bad qualities in the same person, in its own developing self and in its perception of the mother, the baby is able to make the vital transition from its crude binary, black-and-white phantasies of love and hate in relation to part-objects to the recognition of a more complex reality involving whole people. In Freud's theory, the child makes this transition from phantasy to reality much later in the Oedipal stage through its successful separation from the mother by means of the intervention of the father.

Defences in the depressive position

The two defences characteristic of Klein's depressive position are *denial* and *omnipotence*. These are less violent than those of the paranoid-schizoid position. *Denial* is primarily a denial of dependency (feelings of helplessness) and ambivalent feelings towards the mother. When, as adults, we get involved in denial we may say we don't care about someone or mind about something happening when we do. We may brush things under the carpet and insist that the contrary is true. Associated with this is *omnipotence*, which may express itself in feelings of triumph and contempt which conceal the pain associated with the inevitable loss of the mother as well as the phantasy of total control over her. Freud's concept of repression begins much later in the Oedipal crisis. But, like repression, denial of reality and the phantasy of having omnipotent control over the mother (the excessive feeling of being in control sometimes described as mania) are the ways in which the baby excludes its painful feelings of loss from consciousness. In the depressive position the still helpless baby's anxiety causes depression rather than fear of attack (persecution). This emotional pain is induced by *guilt* caused by anger turned against the self rather than, as before, against someone in the external world. The pain of guilt has replaced the absence of guilt involved in hate or blame. In the depressive position the baby's identity, which has been based only on phantasy, is gradually transformed, through the emotional suffering (depression) involved in owning all its feelings, including painful ones of vulnerability and anxiety, into one based on reality and the possibility of creative reparation and change. (This psychical process seems to be reflected in religious ideas of redemption through suffering.) Klein took the view that most of us never entirely resolve the depressive position throughout our lives because the guilt, the eventual loss of the mother and the process of owning and integrating our own bad feelings are so painful. Crucially, Klein's depressive position highlights the need for human beings to be able to perceive and cope with complexity both in the internal and external world. It is this relinquishing of the seductive simplicity of a world and a self seen only in terms of black and white, in which elements can only be demonized or idealized, which constitutes the rewards of the depressive position – the capacity to see the world more realistically, less precariously and less terrifyingly. For Klein, the possibility of achieving a relative sense of wholeness or integration always exists as it does in the more modernist dimension of Freud's theory where the unconscious can be integrated into consciousness and a more substantial ego or self achieved.

Most people, at certain times, employ some of the defences identified in Klein's two kinds of psychical organization; they are part of what we call 'normal' behaviour. For Klein, the psychoses are psychical predicaments which occur because the depressive position has been so unsuccessfully negotiated that one or other of the defences takes over and dominates other forms of communication. The individual's perception of what we call reality may become so distorted by phantasies – projections and introjections, denials and ideas of omnipotence – that internal and external reality can no longer be differentiated and negotiated. No common ground exists to enable normal communication. Freud describes this closed system of reflections detached from reality as an extreme form of narcissism. In a less severe form it may express itself in adults as a psychical inability to tolerate or take responsibility for feelings of vulnerability or being out of control so that others are blamed for the feelings of anxiety which result. Often, to avoid such feelings, there is an obsessive need for power and control of others to avoid conscious contact with these split-off parts of the self.

Klein's version of the unconscious seems to be modelled as a container of biological predispositions to feelings, impulses and defences rather than a dynamic, potentially subversive system of thought with its own symbolic language, as the unconscious is in Freud's theory. As Juliet Mitchell suggests, Klein, unlike Freud, argues that, from a very early age, people and even part-objects are perceived to have personalities rather than just bodies and that these are the psychical objects with which the baby peoples its world and, at the same time, constitutes itself (Mitchell 1986: 25–30). Through the internalization of good objects, a stable, authentic identity *is* possible in Klein's theory but only if the child manages to negotiate the pain of the depressive position. It has to acknowledge the potentially overwhelming discovery that it cannot be omnipotent and have complete control over the mother, and it must painfully come to terms with her loss. In Klein's theory, if a unified identity is achieved in this way, there is no separate, unconscious place from which this identity can be sabotaged.

The father in Klein's theory

In Klein's work the father is included in the baby's early phantasies of the mother. Whereas in Freud's theory the child takes in the father as a crucial parental figure in the shape of the super-ego during the Oedipal crisis, Klein expands and backdates this idea so that the baby incorporates the father as part of its phantasies about the mother. Like the early phantasy of the mother's breast, the phantasy of the father's penis, contained in the idea of the mother, is also exposed to splitting and projection but it, too, is capable of being integrated more realistically as the child becomes aware of external reality within the depressive position.

In Klein's later work, the baby's working through of the depressive position virtually replaces Freud's much later resolution of the Oedipus complex. Klein transforms the child's guilt and fear of castration by the father in Freud's theory into the child's guilt about and fear of losing both parents in the depressive position as a result of its persecutory phantasies. Here fear of loss is primarily about generalized loss of good internal objects in the form of the mother and father, what Klein describes as the 'combined object'. However, Klein makes the mother of primary importance. The cost, in theoretical terms, of this return of the mother to what many women might consider her proper place is that we lose touch with desire and the intervention of the father which, in Freud, is the catalyst for castration anxiety and the creation of an unconscious which potentially destabilizes all our identities. There is an elaborated account of Klein's view of the father in chapter 7.

Envy and gratitude

Late in her career, in a paper called 'Envy and Gratitude' (Klein in Mitchell 1986), Klein introduced two major new concepts into her theory of the development of identity which have powerful implications for the analysis of cultural issues, particularly in relation to gender construction and the need to spoil and destroy. In this paper she introduces envy into the range of the child's aggressive feelings towards the mother as the baby envies the limitless riches the mother is perceived to possess compared with its own poverty and helplessness. At the same time Klein extends her idea of reparation to include gratitude. She also raises an issue fundamental to the study of gender and the relationship between the sexes – womb-envy.

Klein reasserts the view she held for most of her life that the mother–baby relationship, from its first moments, contains all the fundamental elements of future relationships, and this is based on an innate instinct in the baby which sees the mother not only as the source of nourishment but also of life itself. This is the basis of the life instinct. Pleasure is a source of psychical as well as physical well-being because the baby takes in or 'introjects' the breast as the representation of total love, wisdom, understanding and creativity capable of turning all distress into complete contentment and bliss. The problem is that envy of the mother is provoked by all these riches which lie frustratingly beyond the baby itself. In other words, although there is a biological factor in the baby's capacity to love, this is modified by the baby's experience with the mother.

Klein makes an important distinction between envy, jealousy and greed. Envy is the most primitive and purely destructive emotion. Jealousy involves a relationship with at least two other people and is concerned with the fear of being deprived of someone we love by another. Greed seems to lack the component of malice implied in envy where the desire to spoil the good object is achieved by splitting off and projecting feelings of being bad onto the object. Greed, however, uses introjection; envy uses destructive projective identification. Greed may conceal envy – if we have everything we don't need to envy anyone.

Klein sees envy as the single most dangerous ingredient in the baby's capacity to work through the depressive phase and internalize a good, uninjured and unspoilt breast. She sees the mother's breast, uncontaminated by the baby's phantasized envious attacks, as the core of the baby's healthy sense of identity. It is the foundation for an internal world in which the baby's love outweighs its hate so that in its future life it can establish other good object-relationships with which to identify and stock its inner world. A good experience of the breast (for example, one which does not involve a very depressed or envying mother), Klein argues, forms the basis for the second subject of Klein's paper, gratitude. For Klein, gratitude rests on the belief and trust in good objects, the capacity to love without the interference of the baby's envy, and the wish to reciprocate pleasure. Gratitude is bound up for Klein with generosity – a capacity for gratitude allows the baby in later life to share its gifts freely, to take in other people's goodness and share its own around.

Klein sees idealization in the paranoid-schizoid position as the universal problem. Some people still operate unconsciously within the confinement of a world where they are able to relate to other people only through idealizing or denigrating them. The idealization of someone else, as with the mother, inevitably involves a parallel idealization of the self; it enables those who idealize to fill themselves up with a good reflection of the self. (This is close to what Freud describes as narcissism – falling in love with one's own reflection in the 'other'.) The problem is that, under the weight of reality, this idealization must collapse and both the lover and the self are then perceived without the rosy tint of the 'good' phantasy. The previously idealized person, perhaps perceived as the 'perfect partner', is now likely to be experienced as totally bad. An internal bad object is substituted for the internal good object and the identity of the one who idealizes suddenly feels terrifyingly precarious. This could explain those people who, unable to sustain a relationship after the phase of idealization has broken down, compulsively move from one relationship to another in search of their identity. Sometimes the previously idealized person is subsequently experienced as a hated persecutor, which indicates the origin of persecution in idealization. The subject now projects all his or her envy and hostility onto someone who was formerly his or her ideal self, the apple (breast) of his or her eye. For such people, love and hate have never been sufficiently integrated unconsciously in the depressive position to allow for the acceptance of the reality that good and bad qualities exist together in the same person. Others cannot be experienced with love and generosity for what they are because primitive phantasies of good and evil make idealization and denigration the only possible emotional stances.

There are many cultural examples of this mechanism of idealization, the most striking of which probably forms the unconscious basis for much hostility towards women based on phantasy. The cultural representation of women by patriarchal men as either 'Madonna' and 'goddess'or 'witch' and 'whore' suggests the presence of idealization and denigration and an ambivalent relationship between patriarchal men and women which is saturated with male dependency projected onto women. If integration in the depressive position has not occurred, a more realistic perception of women is unavailable. Similarly, the apparently blind adulation of deities, political leaders or national heroes is also a form of idealization. If the object becomes excessively elevated because all the good parts of the one who idealizes have been projected onto it, the discrepancy between them and those who idealize them may become so great that comparison becomes impossible and envy is alleviated. Worship becomes the only option. This looks very much like the Christian version of the relationship between God and man – the omnipotent perfection of God is split off from man who is so immersed in sin, guilt and unworthiness that envy cannot become an issue.

Klein's distinctive version of the Oedipus complex emerges clearly from her discussion of the difference between envy and jealousy. Jealousy, Klein argues, is based on rivalry with the father who is seen as having frequently distracted the mother and her breast thus depriving the baby of exclusive possession. However, in dramatic contrast to Freud, Klein sees the Oedipus complex emerging very early at the age of between three and six months at the time of the onset of the depressive position. This is the period of development when, earlier in her career, on the basis of phantasies described to her in her analyses of children, she had formulated the idea of the combined parent figure. At this time this idea replaces the mother as the object of the child's phantasies, its projections and introjections. The mother's breast is now seen as also containing the idea of the father's penis and all it represents as a rival focus of interest for the mother. This view of the Oedipus complex (which initiates the Oedipal crisis) and the role of the father represents a major theoretical difference between Klein and Freud. The father, culture, the law against incest, all so central to Freud, are subsumed in Klein's work in the all-powerful figure of the mother and the central role of the depressive position associated with her. The moment when the child becomes a full-blown human being is no longer the successful resolution of the Oedipal crisis but the successful emergence from the depressive position in which the father does not play the decisive role.

Klein suggests that many of us spend our life unconsciously trying to work through the depressive position. At certain moments, particularly of loss, most of us are vulnerable to depressive guilt and the pain of trying to make reparation for the destructive phantasies we have harboured about the one we have lost. The state of bereavement is the commonest form of this kind of experience where the lost object at some level represents a parent or sibling figure and thus reactivates the conflicts of the depressive position. As we have seen in the discussion of narcissism in chapter 1, when we lose someone, and feel angry towards them for having left us, we have to face both their loss in external reality, but also the loss of the good object in our internal world. We are exposed again to feelings of emptiness and, Klein argues, to our primitive, underlying paranoid and depressive fears. If we have not managed to rid ourselves of early phantasies of omnipotence and denial, the death in external reality may be experienced as a death of the actual 'self'. Bereavement may then turn into more prolonged depression or even psychosomatic illness. It is striking that, in old age, partners frequently die within a very short time of each other.

Klein's focus on envy is inevitably concerned with the idea of both penis-envy and womb-envy. As we have seen, Freud saw the girl's envy of the penis as being of far more significance than male envy of the womb. Even in her early work, Klein, like Karen Horney and Helene Deutsch and other women analysts, disagreed with Freud and saw penis-envy in girls as a secondary and not primary reaction. Like Freud, Klein saw it as eventually constituting a girl's bisexuality (her gender-precariousness) but, for her, this is the result of envy of the mother, not the father. The girl first envies her mother's body because this is felt to contain everything – father, future babies, the world. This envy, according to Klein, is then at a later stage projected onto the father's penis when the girl's phantasy of being her father's lover is also frustrated.

Unlike Freud, Klein sees the girl's penis-envy and the boy's similar envy of the riches and creativity of his mother's body as of equal importance. In both sexes, Klein sees envy as primarily envy of the *mother's breast* and body during the paranoid-schizoid position. For her, penis-envy pales into insignificance compared with the envy of the mother as the all-creating, life-giving force. She outlines the repercussions of this phase in adult relationships if it is not adequately resolved in the depressive process of reparation and gratitude. If the girl who has turned to her father still feels dominated by envy of her mother, and her mother's relationship with the father, her desire to spoil the father as a valuable object for her mother will undermine her relationship with him and all other men and, in Klein's view, this may lead to frigidity. (Freud thought that it was women's excessive penis-envy directly in relation to the father which led to frigidity.) This is Klein's version of Freud's phallic, castrating woman who, like the misogynist, constantly feels the need to ridicule and symbolically castrate the opposite sex. The reason, Klein stresses, is that the girl's powerful envy of her mother, and her mother's relationship with her father, compels her in phantasy to spoil and denigrate her father and all men *for* her mother, her rival, and therefore inevitably, for herself also. Female envy for Klein is not primarily envy of the penis, of what the mother is thought to *want*, but rather primitive unresolved envy of what the mother *has*. She argues that it is this envy that may destroy some women's potential for fulfilling relationships with men.

In the context of the boy's relationship with the mother, significantly left undeveloped by Freud, Klein thought that if envy prevails in the boy's relationship with his mother and of course with himself (because envy spoils the inner world as well as the outer), the boy may feel unable to experience successful relationships with women. As in the case of the girl, envy and anxiety will interfere with feelings of intimacy. A boy's excessive envy of his mother, emanating originally from the very early paranoid-schizoid position, will leave him in an essentially 'feminine' identification with her. His unconscious envy will, Klein warns, extend to all feminine characteristics and, in particular, women's capacity to bear children. This envy of the womb, of course, may be omnipotently denied and projected onto women so that only women's penis-envy is acknowledged as a possibility. In this way, womb-envy disappears from patriarchal view. The cultural significance of womb-envy is the main focus of chapter 6.

Envy of the breast, Klein argues, amounts to envy of creativity, of fullness and richness in life generally because the breast, and the milk it gives, is experienced as the source of life. This, frustratingly for babies of both sexes, means that life's source lies outside the self. In both sexes, Klein argues, envy of the breast, and an unsatisfactory object-relationship with it, leads to a wish in both sexes to spoil, take away and denigrate the attributes of the other sex. As we shall see in chapter 6, women's envy of the mother is more likely to be resolved in the realization that they will eventually have the same capacity for creativity, whereas boys cannot take comfort in this knowledge. The wish to spoil the good object, the mother and later all women, may explain some men's violence against women in phantasy in the form of pornography and the violent 'acting out' of spoiling phantasies in rape and other forms of violence against women. Of course, we need to remember that envy does not only exist *between* the sexes. Any kind of success or perceived 'richness' in an individual tends to provoke envy from other people – our family, friends, colleagues at work – whether they are the same or the opposite sex.

As Juliet Mitchell emphasizes, Klein describes integration horizontally in the present rather than on a vertical of past and present more characteristic of Freud's perspective (Mitchell 1986: 26). In therapy, destructive, envious, split-off parts of the self can be accepted and drawn back into the self which has been emptied and impoverished by splitting off so much of itself. Like Klein's view of the young baby, the patient comes to see that both the world and she or he, themselves, are not simply one thing or another but a complex mixture of 'good' and 'bad', loving and hating aspects which have to be acknowledged and integrated as part of the same complex whole. This idea is not the same as an acceptance of or adjustment to the status quo or the dominant ideology as is sometimes claimed. It is concerned with the development of the capacity to appreciate the complexity of reality, not to adapt to it, to convert destructive projection into the capacity for creative thought. This usually implies action and change rather than adaptation.

Many psychotherapists, especially those sympathetic to Winnicott's ideas, dispute the view that ordinary babies are locked in a violent struggle between love and hate. They argue that Klein's theory describes the predicament of the baby who has suffered substantial maternal deprivation, perhaps with a depressed or narcissistic mother. However, the evidence of splitting, projection, projective identification, denial and omnipotence in substantial numbers of individuals, frequently in positions of power and influence, makes Klein's ideas very useful for the analysis of particular aspects of culture.

3

Winnicott: the mother and creativity

Winnicott's work represents the second strand of object-relations theory. It developed directly out of Klein's work as a distinctive object-relations approach of its own. However, although Winnicott's theory shares Klein's emphasis on the role of the mother, for him it is the actual rather than the phantasized mother that is all-important for the baby's development of an identity. And where, in Klein's theory, the baby becomes humanized into culture through the development of its capacity for guilt and reparation, and in Freud's through the repression of loss and desire and the acceptance of a symbolic castration, in Winnicott's theory this transition from phantasy to reality comes about through the make-believe of creative play. This occurs painlessly within the relatedness between the baby and its mother or a substitute. (In fact, Winnicott never draws a clear distinction between phantasy and reality because he believed adults moved in and out of each at will when they became absorbed in day-dreaming or creative activity.) For Winnicott, the baby literally creates itself as a separate, integrated human being given appropriate time and the kind of nurturing and creative maternal environment or quality of relatedness of which Winnicott thought most mothers were capable. Winnicott's theory is often articulated in a cosy, down-to-earth language of 'holding', 'going on being', 'playing', 'bodily aliveness', 'feeling real'. However, this simple and homely style stems from his deep suspicions of the potential rigidity of academic or theoretical language which he thought, separated from feeling and intuition, was prone to slipping into orthodoxy and dogma. He believed that it closes off thought and the emotional as well as the theoretical insight that emerges from being able to relate empathically and intuitively to another person.

For Winnicott, the coming into being of identity involves the gradual development from the baby's initial dependency to what he calls a 'personal way of being'. He sees this as having a sense of 'bodily aliveness', of feeling real in the baby's own body, of 'life being worth living' and of being in touch with its own potential creativity and spontaneity. But Winnicott thought that this sensation of personal 'real-ness' could only be achieved through a special kind of reliable, creative, non-compliant relationship with the mother in early childhood. He frequently uses words like 'holding' and 'handling' to communicate the importance he attached to issues of reliability. He insists that an individual's potential for the development of a creative sense of what he called 'aliveness', of the world being a rewarding place to be in, could be damaged if, as a baby, his or her sense of continuous 'going on being' was interfered with by the trauma of 'waiting too long' or if the baby was emotionally compelled into a pattern of compliance with the needs of an inattentive or depressed mother. Winnicott's highly individual, and inno-vative re-writing of Freud's and Klein's ideas produced a powerful, alternative view of psychical reality which currently provides the basis for much eclectic psychoanalytic practice. Although Winnicott believed that the natural developmental process allowed anyone to make contact with his or her own personal potential for creative living, if he or she had the right kind of maternal environment, he also took the view that this creative self was always ultimately elusive, unknowable and incommun-icable. He distinguished between the ego, which is the perceiving window on the world which replaces the containing mother, and the self, which always remains in hiding. He wrote of the self, 'A word like "self" naturally knows more than we do; it uses us and can command us' (Winnicott 1965b: 158). This idea conflicts with Freud's and Lacan's belief in the central role of language within psychoanalytic practice in which the subject 'speaks' a hidden part of the self.

Winnicott sees the mind and body as an essential psychosomatic partnership and takes the view that the developmental process must include the negotiation of this relationship. In contrast to Klein, for Winnicott the baby's primary task is to get to the stage when it feels it inhabits its own body rather than when it has overcome its hate and aggression. This is in the context of what he calls the 'good enough' mother who is able to act as a kind of ultra-sensitive coordinator of the baby's chaotic emotions. He sees the baby's earliest predicament as being made up of a bundle of conflicting emotions or what he calls being in a condition of 'primary unintegration'. This includes the wish to greedily love the mother, but, later, the wish also to hold her at bay and put her resilience to the test. However, he argues that the baby has a natural developmental tendency to integrate the disparate parts of its self which is only made possible by the mother's special kind of care. The baby, Winnicott insists, is a creature who from its moment of birth enthusiastically wishes to participate in its own development. Winnicott distinguishes between ordinary care and instinctual, intuitive relating which is repeated over and over again. This involves the mother in continually gathering together the variegated fragments of the baby's self into a potentially whole person, while crucially allowing the baby to feel *it* has been responsible for this creative experience. If the mother, who represents the 'holding environment' cannot enable the baby to integrate its self completely, Winnicott thought that the unintegrated part would be split off or 'disassociated', resulting in a blank or blind spot in the baby's sense of being alive. In the early, fused mother–baby relationship, whenever the mother moves away she takes with her the baby's identity as well as her own. It is at this stage of what Winnicott calls 'absolute dependence', before we have developed a psychical 'skin', that we learn to equate loss with our own annihilation. For Winnicott, the unconscious is a well of deprivation which is not a significant part of the identity of the baby who has grown up without too much deprivation. We all suffer the deprivations of weaning, toilet training, loss of our illusions of perpetual oneness with the mother. Maturity, for Winnicott, within a developmental framework, is a condition in which the individual can sometimes return to a state of what he called 'unintegration'. One example of this is day-dreaming, or being preoccupied or 'lost' in some absorbing activity, but in this state, Winnicott stresses, there is always the freedom for such an individual to move back into a state of integration again.

Sexuality and gender difference are not major concerns in Winnicott's work. Like Klein, he took the view that at some level gender difference exists from birth but is reinforced during early childhood. Nevertheless, his perspective offers us important insights into the widespread subordi- nation of women because of the power the mother necessarily wields over us all in early childhood. Winnicott suggests that the mother and, hence, all women are unconsciously associated with the early terror of psychical annihilation by babies of both sexes. For Winnicott, everything depends on the mother's capacity to relate to her baby intuitively which, for him, means the ability to allow the baby to create reality for itself rather than having it imposed on it. This she does through her empathic ability to enter the reality of the baby, that is, to walk around, imagina- tively, in its skin, but also, to move out again into her separate self. As the baby's first contact in life, the mother is the primary agent for the flowering of its potential, unique identity. In contrast to Freud and Klein, Winnicott always emphasizes the qualities of the *actual* mother rather than the *phantasized* mother and the baby's initial dependence on her. In the context of the mother's power, Winnicott believes that one of the mother's most important tasks is to transfer her power to the developing baby through her ability to empathize with its evolving self.

Winnicott transforms Freud's and Klein's concepts of life and death instincts into a single, uncontaminated life-force containing love. He insists that if our love is accepted we feel creative, alive and strong, but when it is rejected we feel as if someone has psychically annihilated us. Winnicott thought that Freud's conception of the drive towards inertia (the death instinct), as an innate destructive drive drawing us (by means of our sadism or masochism) towards dissolution and disintegration, was based on Freud's confusion between the inertia associated with death and that of the creative, unbounded state we are all in at the beginning of life. This is when the baby feels it is part of an unending whole with the mother and the rest of the holding environment including nature. Winnicott takes the view that all our lives we are imbued with a longing for this first unintegrated state of unity with the mother – the original bliss of total acceptance, recognition and plenitude. He insists that only in a situation where there is a lack of love, where the mother is emotionally depriving, do we find that the creative assertiveness contained within the life-force is pathologically transformed into a sadistic projection against others or turned against the self in the form of masochism.

The 'good enough' mother

Unlike Freud's theory of desire and Klein's theory of phantasy, Winnicott's theory of identity is based on the idea of emotional nurture. He was convinced that all babies have the potential from birth for enrichment, creativity, integration and, eventually, a successful separation from the mother provided she can be what Winnicott called 'good enough'. By the *good enough mother*, Winnicott means a mother who actively adapts to the needs of the infant rather than the other way round. Her relationship with her baby is one of reciprocity, mutuality, recognition, responsiveness and acknowledgement of whatever the baby takes itself to be at any time. Through what Winnicott calls an 'attentiveness', free of anxiety, the mother allows the baby to create, for itself, a feeling of being real within its own body and a sense of life being worth growing up for. The 'good breast' is how Winnicott describes the good enough mother whose undemanding presence allows the baby to build up what he calls 'the basic stuff of the inner world that is personal and, in fact, constitutes the self' (Winnicott 1958a: 101). The baby brings to this state of 'meaningfulness' between itself and its mother what Winnicott calls its primary potential for being. Rather than seeking sexual pleasure, the baby clamours above all for intimacy, sociability and a relatedness which goes beyond the satisfaction of instinct suggested by

Freud. Winnicott always sees instincts within the context of the relatedness between the baby and its mother. The Freudian baby's phantasy of sexually penetrating the mother is transformed, in Winnicott's account, into the idea of the baby's wish to emotionally penetrate the mother who, if she can be good enough, is ready and willing to be emotionally penetrated.

For Winnicott, the baby, from the very beginning, has an innate awareness of its 'true self'. It makes this available to the relationship with the mother if the mother can take a positive role in the baby's desire to find it. By keeping the world she presents to the baby simple, the mother gives it the capacity to move freely between its inner and outer worlds. So, in Winnicott's version of the formation of identity, the baby is seen as an agent in its own creative development who longs to be understood and recognized, and waits for acknowledgement in the mother's face which, through its capacity for responsiveness, he argues in 'Mirror-role of Mother and Family in Child Development', like a mirror, reflects a self back to the waiting baby (Winnicott 1971a). Drawing on Freud's theory of narcissism, Winnicott argues that it is the quality of the mother's responsiveness that endows the baby with its identity. The child sees itself mirrored in the mother's gaze and voice, in the way she holds it in her mind as well as in her arms, in her touch and in the quality of unspoken understanding and empathy she brings to her responses to the baby's needs and the way she communicates to it that it is lovable, full of potential and a person who gives joy and pleasure to the beholder. Any serious interruption or disruption in this relationship – the baby waits too long for the mother, becomes traumatized and gives up hope – interferes with the baby's lifeline, what Winnicott calls its 'going on being' so that it loses its sense of coming into existence, its sense of a continuous self. This is replaced by feelings of deadness rather than aliveness (feelings we associate with depression) and, in its extreme form, psychosis. For Winnicott, it is this primitive pain of excessive deprivation, of a kind of emotional blackout, that leads to serious disturbance in later life and even serious physical illness. For him, the unconscious is not 'another scene' common to all of us but the place where these early deprivations are kept.

In Winnicott's conceptual world the mother provides the creative opportunities for the baby's *illusionment* (what Freud called phantasy) that it is omnipotent before its later confrontation with reality or *disillusionment*. Winnicott's emphasis of the importance of the baby's capacity for illusionment draws directly on Freud's description of the baby's ability magically to conjure up a phantasy or hallucination of the mother's breast before it 'eats' it. In 'Primitive Emotional Development', Winnicott (1988) focuses on how the good enough mother can make this act of personal creativity possible for the baby. The baby imaginatively conjures out of its desire for the mother an idea of the breast it wants and, at the same time, crucially, the mother is 'waiting to be found'. Winnicott suggests that by doing this she allows the baby actively to create its own good breast and realize its phantasy of control and possession. Winnicott sees phantasy, or what he calls 'illusion', as existing earlier than reality and argues that the experience of illusionment allows the baby to enrich its phantasies with positive experiences from the real world as it does when, apparently magically, it conjures up the breast it desires. By complete adaptation to the baby's needs, the mother fosters the illusion of its omnipotence which Winnicott considers is necessary before it has to adapt to the reality that it is not all-powerful. Phantasy is not a substitute for reality but provides, in the context of the mother's care, the means of finding it. Later, phantasy may be used as a way of escape from the inner world, sometimes in day-dreaming.

Disillusionment

After providing the vital opportunity for illusionment, Winnicott argues that the mother must then, gradually, create the opportunity for disillusionment. This involves her adapting to the baby less exactly so that it gradually confronts the fact that it cannot omnipotently control the world. Winnicott argues that the task of the good enough mother, at this stage of 'relative independence', is to allow the baby creatively to resolve its gradual separation from her through her ability to contain its ruthless tendencies. The baby and child's aggression is viewed as creative and vital to making the crucial distinction between 'me' and 'not me' (see Minsky 1996: 116–17). Winnicott sees the child's transition from phantasy to reality as a means to self-realization and growth rather than a painful confrontation with the loss of the mother as it is for Freud. As Adam Phillips (1988: 132–3) suggests, in contrast to Klein, Winnicott takes the view that the survival of the baby's aggressive tendencies, what Winnicott calls its 'primitive, ruthless love', is what creates the subject and not the baby's reparation to the mother. The mother must also survive and be resilient, but in a non-retaliatory way.

The false self

Winnicott's influential idea of the *false self* emerges from his concern with the consequences of a failure in the child's 'holding' environment, that is, of adequate maternal provision. In most of the examples

Winnicott gives this takes the form of the depressed mother who, instead of responding to the baby's needs, demands reactions to her *own*, forcing adaptation and compliance from the baby. The result of such a situation is that the baby's creativity is distorted into a compulsive attempt to establish the nurturing environment it needs, but which the mother cannot provide. This means it unconsciously tries to nurse its mother's needs into health so she can then care for it more adequately. This essentially amounts to the baby trying to mother the depressed mother as if she were the child in order to keep the mother emotionally alive. At the same time, the child may seek to make reparation to the mother for something it does not understand and has not done. Ultimately, for Winnicott, the false self (existing to varying extents depending on the degree of deprivation) represents a denial of its real self which has been split off or dissociated into the unconscious. It is a smoke-screen behind which the child and later adult attempts to cope with life without a viable sense of identity. This is similar to what Freud calls a narcissistic identity which builds an illusory self on the basis of reflections from other people or objects in the external world. These may include consumer objects which appear as independent, self-reflecting beings which seem to have life of their own. However, as Jacobs (1995: 59) argues, at one level the false self is a natural part of development built on compliance. Although it is inherently defensive, leading to a 'social manner' and a 'compromise' of the true self, in a healthy adult it can be given up when anything important is at stake and overtaken by the true self. It may sometimes be sublimated in a career in acting or in intellectual work.

Winnicott stresses the danger of the child having to live reactively to keep the mother cheerful rather than the other way round. Only when the baby does not have to react can it begin to 'be' for its 'self'. Winnicott argues that at the beginning the child has so little identity that every reaction to the needs of the mother results in a loss of identity. The idea of *compliance* is central to Winnicott's theory of the false self. If the baby is forced by its separation anxiety out of its own natural mode of creativity into one of compliance with the moods, needs and reality of the mother, it will feel a sense of estrangement from its own self and its body which, as we have seen, Winnicott always sees as constituting a psychosomatic unity which have to be felt in relation to each other. A mother whose own needs make it impossible for the baby to penetrate her – in the sense of allowing the baby's psychical being or presence to enter her reality – denies the baby her appreciation of its 'realness', of its existence, not only for herself but also itself. The baby is constantly confronted by what is incomprehensible and the mother is unable to make either the world, or itself, intelligible. The false self always lacks its own creative originality and hides the baby's and later adult's 'core self' which has to be protected from the ultimate catastrophe of annihilation. Where, for Freud, castration is the ultimate disaster, and for Klein the overwhelming of the psyche by hate, for Winnicott it is annihilation of a central essence, authenticity or core. But the essential defence of the fragile inner core by means of a false self may exact a severe price. 'When the false self becomes exploited and treated as real there is a growing sense in the individual of futility and despair' (Winnicott 1965b: 133).

When compliance remains the predominant way of relating in adult relationships, the unconscious alienation from the self continues and, if an emotional relationship breaks down, neurotic illness may ensue because the individual, by too much compliance, has sacrificed too much of the self to the other, made too many life-denying compromises and concessions in the interests of maintaining the relationship. Sometimes, in a desperate bid to break out of this inhibiting need to please an often elusive other, an individual may unconsciously go into reverse so that nothing a partner asks can be complied with. Both of these ways of coping, first with the fear of loss of the relationship and, later, with fear of loss of the self, are potentially destructive of relationships and identity. Our determination to survive and maintain a good relationship with those more powerful than ourselves is one of the major characteristics of childhood. As children we all learn to make concessions but, if we have to make too many, this denial of our own potential for development may leave a residue of severe loss of self, unfulfilled longing and, in some men, the desire for revenge on women. Of course, in a woman, the desire for revenge may be expressed in relationships with men but this does not take place within a context of cultural acquiescence as it often does for men.

Another, different problem may arise if the baby is compelled to develop a false self by having to react to the mother too much. In later life, as an adult, it may need constantly to surround itself with impinge-ments, a continuous round of demands and situations to which it has to react, in order to make itself feel alive. In 'The Mind and its Relation to the Psyche-Soma', Winnicott (1958a) argues that the child needs to get to the stage where it can mother its own self with its mind. But if the mothering has been inadequate because of the mother's depression or emotional deprivation the child may develop a phantasy of self-sufficiency which means that it can live *entirely* in its own mind. In this situation the mind is used not to continue the mother's care but to displace it altogether. The child's psyche tries to neglect and disown the body which is felt to be a persecutor. (This tendency seems to be a feature of much modern and post-modern theory.) What Winnicott calls excessive mental functioning, thinking as a substitute for feeling, may be the baby's, and later the adult's, way of dealing with the problem of unreliable mothering. An excessive interest in thinking and knowledge for its own sake is a form of splitting off part of the psyche which has been inadequately nurtured, what Winnicott calls *dissociation*. Retreat into a mechanical world of the intellect or work becomes an attempt to deaden and blot out painful feelings associated with loss and depriva-tion. Men may, again, be particularly prone to this kind of defence because of their enforced early separation from the mother experienced as deprivation. Within a Freudian context, we could describe this same phenomenon as a form of narcissism. We unconsciously take an identity from something outside our self, as a substitute for the lack of a self gained through a successful relationship with the mother in childhood. Winnicott (1986: 60) writes 'a person with rich intellectual endowment in terms of grey matter can function without much reference to the human being. But it is the human being who, by an accumulation of experiences duly assimilated, may achieve wisdom.'

Winnicott's false self describes the child whose potential aliveness and creativity has gone unnoticed. As a result, it may painfully withdraw from the world, concealing an empty, barren internal world behind a mask of independence and self-sufficiency. As an adult, it may only be able to survive by means of this defensive false self, and women, in particular, may be perceived, like the mother, as a potential source of psychical death which has only just been avoided.

Transitional phenomena

Winnicott was fascinated throughout his life by the question of how the baby makes the transition from dependency to relative independence. In the process of answering this question, he developed two of his most original concepts, the ideas of the *transitional object* and the *transitional space*, or what he sometimes calls the *potential space*. The *transitional object* is the special piece of rag, fraying wool, cushion or any object which becomes, for the child engaged in separation from the mother, of particular value and significance because it is both a symbol of her, its own self and the external reality it wants to see objectively. It symbolizes the child's negotiation of the transition from what Winnicott calls subjec-tivity to objectivity, from an inner world to an outer one from which its projections and phantasies have been removed. The crucial ingredient of the transitional object is that it is the child's own creative choice, that its status is never challenged, and that it is never interfered with or altered, for example, by washing, by anyone else. It represents for the child the state of its psyche in a delicate and fragile balance between intimacy and separation.

In parallel with the transitional object, Winnicott also developed his most crucial concept, the *transitional* or *potential space*. This is a psychical space, a place between the baby and its mother, which represents a bridge connecting the subjective to the objective, the inner world to the outer world where the relationship between phantasy and reality can be explored and negotiated. This replaces Freud's idea of the penis as the same kind of potential connection. Through a quiet, spontaneous playfulness and mutual participation which is pre-verbal, the transitional space offers a creative opportunity for the exploration of what Winnicott describes as 'what life is, itself, about' (Winnicott 1971b: 116). The strength of the transitional space, compared with language, is that it is creative because it is *provisional and inconclusive* like artistic experience.

Winnicott became suspicious of people using knowledge as a defence against emotional pain or as a substitute identity. Always wary of too much interpretation in analytical sessions, he rarely writes about knowing in the formal, non-intuitive sense. He saw much interpretation, however clever or insightful, as potentially an invasion of the patient's core self, of his or her capacity, given time, for making his or her own creative sense of self, and he writes of 'those who fear to wait and who implant' (Winnicott 1965b: 100). In describing the ideal condition for awareness, he writes enigmatically: 'The object must be found in order to be created' (Winnicott 1965b: 189). The mother's, and later the therapist's, relationship with the subject is founded on the mutual involvement in illusionment in which the baby or the patient participates in the creation of his or her self. Winnicott continually emphasized the intuitive rather than the theoretical knowledge which Klein valued so much. Winnicott's conception of the self became increasingly one of a 'hide and seek self', always ultimately unwilling to be known. He describes invasions by the mother or the therapist as 'impingement', as thefts of the child's and patient's creative ownership of their own knowing, in their own time. The paradox of both wanting to communicate and wanting to hide lies at the centre of Winnicott's idea of the true self or core of our identity (Winnicott 1965b: 179–92).

Playing and reality

The role and significance of the *play* shared by mother and baby comprise one of the most striking aspects of Winnicott's work. In a characteristically mischievous moment, he describes psychotherapy as being, in part at least, 'to do with two people playing' (Winnicott 1971b: 44). It is through play, he suggests, that the child – and the patient in therapy – go through the process of finding out through pleasure what interests them. Winnicott takes the view that the make-believe of children's play represents a negotiation of the inner world of phantasy with the 'reality' of the external world; he thought that both artistic imagination and enjoyment of art take place in the same psychical space, what he calls 'intermediate experience'. For him, the artist is the one who most completely embodies the desire for authenticity rather than a false self and the kind of personal integrity that he values most. Describing artistic ability, he writes: 'Through artistic expression we can hope to keep in touch with our primitive selves whence the most intense feelings and even fearfully acute sensations derive, and we are poor indeed if we are only sane' (Winnicott 1958a: 150). There is an account of how Marion Milner applies Winnicott's ideas to artistic creativity in chapter 9.

Winnicott belonged to what is known as the British School of psychoanalysis which was represented by the Middle Group within the British Psychoanalytical Society. (The other two groups were the supporters of Freud and Klein.) Winnicott's group were in favour of an eclectic approach within a more empirical tradition. Its members emphasized observation, empathy, the provision of a 'holding' environment, a confidence in people's ability to make themselves known and to be understood. They distrusted too much abstraction, interpretation and dogmatism. Fundamentally, they believed that the most certain aspect of the construction of human identity, including the capacity for each sex to have access to both its 'masculine' and 'feminine' dimensions, was its gradual development and that it would happen spontaneously given the right kind of maternal environment.

4

Lacan: the unconscious as language

With Lacan we move away from a direct involvement with the unconscious dynamics of the mother–baby couple central to Winnicott's work
to a theory of identity and the unconscious which is based on language.
In a dramatic re-modelling of Freud's theory, Lacan transfers all Freud's
major concepts away from the family and bodily experience into culture.
Identity becomes the subjectivity we find in using language; repressed
unconscious desire becomes the driving force and energy behind the
continual search for meaning in language; the symbolic father becomes
the constraints and possibilities of language, what Lacan re-names the
'place of the father'; the actual penis as the first sign of sexual difference
becomes the powerful symbol of the phallus and the basis for all the
other meanings in language also distinguished by difference; and psychoanalytic theory itself is transformed into the study of the construction
of the subject in language.

For Lacan, the unconscious is accessible only in speech and writing.
Building on Freud's earlier interest in symbolization in *The Interpretation
of Dreams* (1900) and on the clinical technique of free association in a
more elaborated way, Lacan argues that the unconscious is structured in
the same way as language. Lacan draws on modern Saussurean linguistics to re-conceptualize the unconscious as part of an endless chain of
unconscious meanings which we can re-find only in language in the
spaces between the conscious meanings. Lacan adopts Saussure's concept of the *sign* (a physical object which has meaning like a word) which
consists of two interdependent parts, the *signifier* and the *signified*, to
construct his model of language as the retreat of the unconscious as well
as the public face of conscious thought. The signifier is the physical part
of the sign, such as a mark on paper or sounds in the air, and the
signified is the meaning attached to the signifier. However, characteristically, Lacan alters these linguistic concepts for his own theoretical
purposes, making the signifier much more powerful than the meaning
itself which can change (for example, a thumbs-up gesture, a sigh, the

expression to 'run out'). Lacan argues, using his own version of Saussure's structural model of meaning, that all meanings, including those which are unconscious, can be represented as a continuous signifying chain in language. These extend down from the rationally chosen words of consciousness into the deepest recesses of our unconscious which reveals itself within language as gaps, slippages, blunders, sighs, hesitations or silences, all of which, words and gaps, interdependently, endow each other with meaning based on being different. No signifier can signify independently of other signifiers (for example, 'test' depends for its meaning on not being 'vest' and 'waste' on not being 'waist') and, in Lacan's view, where meaning and signification come to a standstill there is nothing except the intractable, unsymbolizable quality of 'the all' or totality, the materiality of the world, trauma, psychosis and death. This is what Lacan allocates to the realm of what he calls the Real. Again drawing on concepts from structural linguistics, Lacan transforms Freud's two major unconscious symbolic processes described in *The Interpretation of Dreams* – displacement and condensation which he used to interpret the meanings of dreams – into the linguistic categories of *metaphor* (an identification of two knowns, for example, in the substitution of 'stars' for 'eyes' or 'piercing' for 'emotionally painful') and *metonymy* (a part stands in for the whole in a sequence, for example, 'new blood' or the 'muesli belt'). These, like the unconscious displacement and condensation we experience in dreams, organize and connect the signifying chains of conscious meaning and make the structure and cohesion of language possible (see Minsky 1996: 28, 138–40).

For Lacan, the subject can only come into being within the endless strings and loops of interconnecting meanings that we find in the rational categories of language. Identity becomes nothing more than the endless accounts of the world and ourselves that we can create as personal narratives within the structures and meanings of language. The subject, no more Freud's ego built out of identifications, is always inhabited by what Lacan calls the Other, those others who lie outside the self within the inter-subjectivity of language. The subject, always imbued with the Other, has no substance of its own in the form of personal traits, aptitudes or dispositions nor a distinctive personality. Nor is it, as object-relations theory argues, like a container which waits to be filled by its objects, that is its relationships with other people. At its bleakest, it is a series of events – signifying processes – within language of which the individual is a part. For Lacan, these events are the procession of alternating meanings through which we are compelled to perceive the world which stands before us. Our view of the world can never be uncontaminated because of the deluge of pre-existing meanings which seep into our minds in the very act of perceiving it. Lacan argues that language always silently mediates and directs how we think about any aspect of reality. Language 'speaks us' rather than expressing our inner self derived from somewhere else. So we are subjects without any padding or filling of our own; hollow creatures who can only be brought to life by the energy of our own repressed desire which, re-located in language, drives our search for knowledge and the ultimate 'truth'. This view of an identity and sexuality which can exist authentically only in language has been popular among academics but very controversial among many analysts and therapists.

In Lacan's structural theory, sexuality no longer exists as the pursuit of pleasurable bodily experience. Lacan eroticizes both language and the linguistic concepts we use to analyse it by linking their meanings to the body and sexuality. Language becomes the means by which repression is achieved by driving our unconscious desire underground into the spaces between words and using its energy to propel us from one meaning to another. This is what makes inter-subjectivity possible. The child's discovery of the meaning of the phallus based on sexual differ-ence in the family becomes the blue-print for all the other meanings in the system of language which also depend for their meaning on being different from others. Identity and language are inevitably created as a form of emotional mastery of the loss and lack of our mother which the discovery of sexual difference inevitably sets in motion. Language is dependent for its meaning, like the meaning of the phallus, on arbitrary signs. For Lacan, it alone represents the father's symbolic castration, that is both the castration and curtailment of total fulfilment that each child must accept before it can become a human subject. But, at the same time, language, in its fullest, poetic rather than rational form, offers to the subject an infinity of richness and potentiality of meaning with which to interpret experience. For Lacan, this linguistic source of plenitude, con-sisting of unconscious as well as conscious meanings, brought together in the free-play of the unconscious, is the only genuine form of freedom, sexuality, identity and 'truth' we can ever expect.

The Imaginary and the Symbolic

In striking contrast with object-relations theorists, Lacan rejects the idea that our identity can ever be relatively coherent or authentic. He argues that all our identifications lead only to a *sense* of identity, not an actual identity and this sense of having an identity is always unjustified and based on a misrecognition. Lacan hangs his structural theory on three fundamental conceptual pegs: the Imaginary, the Symbolic and the Real. We create our selves, in different ways, only in the realms of the

Imaginary and the Symbolic. Let's begin by looking at what Lacan means by the Imaginary.

Drawing on Freud's theory of narcissism, he thought that, as babies, after initially existing in an undifferentiated soup of sensations, drives and emotions, we first begin to take up a position, a sense of having a distinct self with definable boundaries in what he calls the realm of the *Imaginary*. But this identity is always based on an image of ourself which is reflected back from someone else, like the reflection from a mirror. (In fact, he called this the 'mirror stage'.) The person, with whom we first 'identify', as a whole person, is usually our mother. Lacan calls this early and very fragile kind of identity an Imaginary one because, although it feels real to us, and makes us appear to ourself as coherent, as something with edges when we still feel emotionally and physically all over the place, it unconsciously depends on someone or something outside our selves. This self or ego is never our own because it depends on our identifications – it is always fused with other people or things in the external world such as, for example, lovers, film stars, clothes, cars, knowledge, and these become a part of who we are. (For a fuller account of the 'mirror stage', see Minsky 1996: 144–6.)

However, Lacan argues, we also establish another kind of identity – what he calls subjectivity – when we begin to acquire language in what he calls the realm of the *Symbolic*. Here, the apparently fixed meanings offered us in language give us an alternative, ostensibly much more stable *sense* of identity, a psychological place where we can discover what appears to be the 'real' meaning of who we are. Through our identification with, that is, investment in the certainty and coherence that these meanings seem to represent, we can gain a sense of having an integrated identity. We feel defined and buoyed up by these meanings which we experience as 'real'.

However, Lacan argues that, even in the Symbolic, all is not as safe and coherent as it appears. Language both places us and displaces us as subjects. We can never get a sure footing in it. The unconscious desire for our mother reappears in the language we speak where it is returned to us in the spaces between words, in the hesitations and stumbles which frequently give the lie to the meanings our words try to convey though never where we can know it directly. For Lacan, the phonetic relationships between words are more important than the semantic ones. For example, the meanings of the signifiers 'patients' and 'patience' belong to different contexts or loops of meaning. Their unconscious significance exists in the space between their conscious meanings. In a psychoanalytic session, a patient may say to the therapist 'If I leave you may run out of patients.' The unconscious rather than conscious meaning of this statement, existing in a space between the words, may be that the patient thinks that the therapist is running out of patience and is going to 'run out' on him or her. This may be connected with an early experience of rejection or death which has led to the patient finding it difficult to trust anyone.

So our identification with language, which at first sight seems so seductively stable, is always open to being de-stabilized by our unconscious desire and loss. It is the part of us where a sense of longing still lingers, an emptiness lying like a shadow behind the confidence of the 'I' we use in our sentences which may sabotage our conscious intention. Lacan argues, therefore, that our conscious identity, expressed through the rational categories of language with which we parcel up the world, is always bogus and false. Ultimately, he suggests, the identity we achieve in language in the Symbolic – consciousness and culture – is only another reflected identity without substance, like that with our mother and all subsequent identifications. It is no different in structure from the one we gained by looking into our mother's face (or Lacan's mirror) in the Imaginary. The crucial difference between these two reflected identities is that the Imaginary one is part of the personal, bodily, pre-Oedipal world we shared with our mothers, and is pre-verbal, whereas the Symbolic is part of the social, cultural world where we are supposed to be able to achieve an authentic identity and become independent, speaking human subjects. With this kind of argument, Lacan's theory sets up a challenge to all identity and the meanings we build on them in the knowledge we create. His stress on the importance of the fictional element in both the Imaginary and the Symbolic (the fact that we psychologically invest in false images of ourselves) and on the role of language in the formation of adult identity derives directly from Freud's theory of narcissism and Freud's stress on language as a form of mastery of loss. The crucial difference between Freud and Lacan is their view of the ego. For Freud, the ego has the capacity to develop from narcissism into a self which is relatively coherent, autonomous and self-reflective. For Lacan, the ego is always false because it is based only on reflections in the Imaginary from the external world.

So Lacan replaces Freud's three-cornered structural model of identity based on the id (unconscious), ego (consciousness) and super-ego (conscience) with his own system of concepts which represent not so much opposing parts of the self within identity but determining, inter-subjective structural 'orders'. His three realms of the Imaginary, Symbolic and Real position us in a field of interacting forces and thus retain the possibility of the analysis of both the ordinary construction of identity and the therapeutic treatment of neurosis and psychosis.

For Lacan, the drive or desire is no longer biological but the searching movement of language, an endless appeal to the Other for the meaning to end all meaning. Having lost access to the mother's body during the Oedipal crisis, we are, henceforth, caught up in a constant search for linguistic substitutes for it, words with which we try to paper over the cracks, plug the gaps at the core of our being, never able to regain the paradise of unity and self-completion which we phantasized with our mothers in the Imaginary. Civilization rests, as Freud first suggested, on the impossibility of our desires. Lacan, too, thinks this is the essential human predicament, part of what distinguishes us as human subjects. Symbolic castration by the father, represented by the symbolic constraints in the world of language, sets limits to our phantasies and desires created in the Imaginary by coercing us into culturally acceptable behaviour and conventional meanings. At the heart of both the place of the father and language is Desire, 'the power of pure loss'. In language, we can find our subjectivity but will never be able to find an ultimate meaning from which all meanings flow because in language we are permanently cut off from the object of our Desire (the mother and later substitutes for the mother) which, for Lacan, exists only in the realm of the Real, the third of Lacan's determining psychoanalytic domains along with the Imaginary and the Symbolic. By the *Real*, Lacan refers to everything which lies outside or beyond the symbolic process, the superseding power of totality, the 'all'. This is not the same as 'reality' as it is usually understood in psychoanalysis which refers to the external world outside the mind. For Lacan, the Real exists in both the mental and physical worlds. It includes the inexpressible pre-Imaginary moment of excess and impossible plenitude to which both the Imaginary and Desire refer (but which they cannot bestow). This moment lies inviolate and out of reach of both Imaginary identities and the subjectivity offered by the language in the Symbolic order (perhaps in the womb we once inhabited when we *were* part of our mother – the 'lost object', what Lacan calls the 'object a', for which we are always yearning). For Lacan, as well as the idea of impossible, super-abundant plenitude, the Real also includes everything else which cannot be symbolized. This includes the materiality of actual objects, the experience of trauma when we are thrown back into the baby's earliest experience of helpless speechlessness, the state of psychosis where the controlled perceptions available in the Symbolic are rejected so that subjectivity collapses into phantasy completely, and finally death, the triumph of the Real, which puts a physical end to subjectivity and meaning.

But while language, unlike the Imaginary, cuts us off from the objects of our Desire (our mother and substitutes for her), at the same time it returns Desire to us as we move, with a new sense of identity as a human subject, from one meaning to the next in a life-long search for a perfect fit between language and our phantasy of plenitude. In this way, for Lacan, it is our entry into language which becomes the transformative site for the Oedipal crisis rather than the actual father. Language becomes the Other, the symbolic 'place of the father', which insinuates itself between us and the objects of our Desire and makes Desire insatiable by continually de-stabilizing and moving these objects so that they always elude us. Ingeniously, Lacan ties the individual's repressed desire and yearning into the very stuff of language and inter-subjectivity. Language, says Lacan, 'is what hollows being [Imaginary] into desire [Symbolic]'. Contradictorily, although it revolves around emptiness and absence, language *articulates* the richness and fullness of the Imaginary and the idea of total oneness with the mother.

The father and the place of the father

Lacan, elaborating on Freud's concept of the father, distinguishes between the actual, what Lacan sees as Imaginary father, and what he calls the 'paternal metaphor' or 'the place of the father'. These last two terms refer to what the father represents to the child symbolically rather than the Imaginary, idealized father with whom Lacan thinks the Symbolic father is easily confused (Mitchell and Rose 1982: 39). Lacan argues that even in the absence of an actual father, the child experiences the place of the father and the Oedipal crisis through cultural substitutions, that is, primarily through language and other systems of representation. These symbolically represent an intrusion by culture into the fused, bodily world of the mother and child and, crucially, a severing of the child from the object of its Desire. The law of the 'name of the father', of what meanings are permitted in language, takes up the space left empty by the loss of the mother. The rational categories of language represent the cutting off (castration) of the child from its phantasies but they also represent the conversion of the child's need (to be the phallus for the mother) into Desire (which can never be satisfied) but which subsequently provides the searching, dynamic energy for knowledge and 'truth' which characterize language and reason. For Lacan, the only 'truth' is that lack and Desire, the division between what we are and the 'want to be', underlie and undermine all identity and knowledge.

The phallus: the first sign of difference

As we have seen, at the same time that the child is transformed into a subject of language and history through its obedience to the law of the father, as well as becoming a split subject with an unconscious, it also becomes a gendered subject. It is the child's ability to recognize sexual difference through the visibility of the phallus which allows it to take on a sexual identity for the first time. The father, or the Symbolic father, signifies this sexual difference by means of his association with the phallus. The phallus, a sign of power within patriarchal societies which is not to be confused with the visible penis (although this is presumably what the child does at one level), is the central term in Lacan's theory. It symbolizes to the child that there is a division between the sexes, and later that those who 'have' rather than 'lack' it are privileged. It also, crucially, signifies another division within identity in the formation of the unconscious. The need for the unconscious as a container for the loss of the mother and the desire associated with her is provoked by the recognition, in both girl and boy, that they do not or cannot have the phallus the mother wants. The girl has nothing that visibly compares with the phallus and the boy phantasizes the loss of his at the hands of the father if he pursues his desires. So the phallus symbolizes both desire and loss. The child has probably been dimly aware of sexual difference before the onset of the Oedipal crisis. But, once the crisis is in full swing, sexual difference and the sexual identities based on it operate like a law and the child is required to line up behind the phallic meanings of 'having' or 'lacking' in order for its construction as a culturally 'masculine' or 'feminine' human being to be completed. The phallus represents the moment when the father's prohibition of the desire for the mother must function. It signals to the child that having a viable identity can only be achieved at the price of loss (of the mother) and that being human can only come about as the direct consequence of a division (into consciousness and the unconscious) (Mitchell and Rose 1982: 40). It is at this point that Lacan introduces his most original (and controversial) re-working of Freud's Oedipal drama through his introduction of the dimension of language.

Language and the Symbolic

With the entry of the father onto the scene, the child is precipitated into a crisis. For Lacan, the crucial thing the child has to recognize is that identities which are not fused with the mother in the Imaginary can only come into being in language, the Symbolic, as a result of the perception of sexual difference. The phallus represents this difference. The father, or what Lacan refers to as the 'name of the father', symbolized by the phallus, legislates to the child that it must take its place within a family which is defined by sexual difference. In future it must acknowledge that it is different from some people and the same as others. But the difference represented by the phallus also entails, as part of its meaning, exclusion (the child cannot be its parents' lover) and absence (the child must give up its relationship with the mother). So, in Lacan's theory, the child's identity as a viable human subject, capable of operating within the family and in society, significantly depends on its unconscious recognition of difference, exclusion and absence.

At this point Lacan makes the vital link between the sexual world dominated by the phallus and the Symbolic world of language. At about the same time that the small child discovers sexual difference, it acquires language. And in the discovery of language the child unconsciously learns that the units of language only have meaning because they are different from other units, and that signifiers in general, like the phallus, can represent things that are absent. Words stand in for objects, and in this sense they operate like metaphors. This is perhaps the central moment in Lacan's theory. As the child learns, unconsciously, about the meaning of sexuality – in the discovery of sexual difference and exclusion from the mother – it is also learning about meanings based on difference and exclusion in the cultural domain, especially in language. Through its recognition of the pre-determined cultural fact that meaning depends on difference and exclusion, the child is able to move from a bodily world of sexual phantasy into the cultural world of language and symbolic systems. So, the recognition of the law of the name of the father or the meaning of the phallus in the sexual world anticipates the recognition of the law about what means what in language and of symbolic representation in the world at large. The phallus becomes the first, 'pilot-boat', signifier which leads the way to our understanding of all other cultural meanings.

The intrusion of the third term (father, phallus, the Symbolic) into the child's world turns out to be, in Lacan's theory, the law of how we perceive the world within language and culture. The third term which divides the child from the mother is at the same time both the father *and* the cultural meanings which pre-exist us in language. Both these acquire their meaning through the operation of difference, initially 'me' and 'not me', and have the power to set limits to our phantasies. They achieve our symbolic, if not real, castration by cutting us off from what we most desire but at the same time, by allowing us to enter culture, they make it possible for us to become fully fledged human subjects. In this way Lacan manages to link the sexual, psychical world with the social dimension of language and culture. In the same way, momentously, culture, perception and thinking become both sexualized and gendered.

So the child unconsciously recognizes the phallus as a sign (as something which bestows meaning) like the signs in language. Words can be seen as a chain of empty signifiers which, like the phallic signifier, in spite of their arbitrariness and emptiness, convey meanings which are vital for the achievement of our humanity. Our subjectivity is woven into these chains of meaning. For Lacan, the phallus is the first sign which the child encounters, whose meaning, if understood, allows the child access to all the other meanings symbolized in the same way in language. The recognition of the power of the phallic signifier within the context of the fear of castration – picked up and made significant by the undeniable visibility of the penis as the only mark of significant difference between the little girl and little boy – facilitates the acquisition of language by operating in the same symbolic way. By means of this joint entry into language and at the same time sexual ordering and identity, the small child gains an identity and becomes a human being capable of identifying with, seeing itself reflected in, the 'I' of language. ('He', 'him', 'she', 'her' are positions which pre-exist and lie in wait to receive the child when it 'steps into' language.) The child finds the idea of its gendered self awaiting it within language and can then identify with that sense of coherence and self it bestows, just as it did with the image in the mirror in the Imaginary. Although children of both sexes become adults, Lacan's theory suggests that only boys can become human subjects because the apparently gender neutral 'I', and the phallus on which it is based, is associated with the male body. This means that women are irretrievably consigned to being the sign of lack.

However, Lacan insists that there is always a *misrecognition* in the perceived power of the phallus as there is a misrecognition of the mirror image (Lacan always refers to the 'seeming' value of the phallus). The meaning of the phallus is, in this sense, always bogus and, since the phallus is the first signifier on which all other symbolic meanings are built, what follows also involves a misrecognition of the identity within language which the child puts on, almost like its symbolic clothes, to cover the pain of its loss of the mother. These clothes, however, turn out to be full of holes. Lacan insists that the power symbolized by the phallus can never be justified because it is based on *symbolic castration*. He reminds us that, within the sexual sphere, sexual difference, our gender, is achieved only at a devastating price for the boy, the one who possesses the phallus. This is the acceptance of symbolic castration by the father who humiliatingly retains the desired and desiring mother.

Fundamentally, the actual meaning of the phallus is therefore not power but powerlessness, that is defeat by the superior power of the father and the loss of the mother as an object of desire as well as of identification. Likewise, the girl's achievement of her gender identity is only gained at the price of a catastrophe – the acceptance of the lack of what her mother wants and what bestows cultural/social identity and power. The girl therefore, as the sign of the lack, is constituted, as it were, as a negative. Both children lose their sense of union with the mother's body – the 'object a' of what Lacan calls Imaginary Desire – but the girl also loses all sense of the validity of her own body and being since she lacks the legitimizing primary signifier, the phallus. For the boy, the pain of the loss of the mother and symbolic castration, and for the girl the loss of her mother and her sense that she has already been castrated, is repressed into the newly formed unconscious at this moment of sexual division.

Lacan suggests that at an unconscious level we understand the bogusness of the phallus and the falseness of all the identities based on it. It is from this that he – and several writers following him such as the French feminists Hélène Cixous, Julia Kristeva and Luce Irigaray – derive Freud's original idea that there is a drive from the unconscious which continually de-stabilizes and subverts the intended meanings and rationalities of language.

Language, therefore, has an ambiguous status in Lacan's work. It forces the abandonment of the full, passionate world of the Imaginary, but it is also the best source of identification that the child has yet had apart from the mother. It receives the post-Oedipal child exhausted by its loss and unsatisfied desire, picking it up and putting it on its feet by constituting it as an apparently convincing human being both to itself and to other people who will recognize it as such. By means of this entry into language, the child can achieve some mastery over its otherwise unbearable emotions of desire, humiliation and loss of the loved object. It does this within a pre-existing system of meanings which, although they represent emptiness, absence and loss compared with those associated with the mother, also offer rationality, objectivity, coherence and meanings which the child perceives as fixed certainties – as linguistic hooks on which it hangs its identity. Through the reassuring anchorage of language and understanding, the child can identify itself with the apparent stability it finds there. Language serves to cover the nakedness of painful experience with its rational linguistic clothes. Ironically, in Lacan's theory we need to be recognized as precisely what we are not. However, from the point of view of gender, for Lacan, the task for the little girl is much more complex and difficult than that of the little boy, for it may be that, in patriarchal societies, she has no connection with these linguistic clothes, they don't fit her properly. However, she has to try to live in culture with her unconscious lack of the phallus as if her lack of any significance, of her capacity to be a human subject, were her natural destiny. Lacan would argue that this destiny is entirely socially constructed. It is because it is *so* easy to confuse the most obvious sign of difference for the child – the visible, physical penis – with the phallus, the cultural sign of power, that the construction of 'femininity' can never be on the basis of anything other than lack, of 'not having' and therefore 'not being'. (For a fuller account of woman as the lack, see Minsky 1996: 158–61.)

For Lacan, the phallus seems to offer the only possibility of grounding an endless longing and yearning for completion, for the lost object of desire which he locates in language. It functions as a structural concept which is an absolute guarantor of all meaning. But, in fact, as Lacan recognizes, the phallus has no status in reality, certainly not in the actual male organ. He sees it as an empty symbol of castration and loss, a sign which has the power to insert us into the symbolic, phallic order of language, but which only gains its meaning from the fact that in patriarchal societies those who bear the sign of the phallus represented by the penis have the power to define all other meanings, and therefore the material power to dominate women. Lacan's focus on the extreme fragility and precariousness of cultural 'masculinity', which is quite contrary to the patriarchal myth, is perhaps one of his most important and enduring contributions to psychoanalytic theory.

In Lacan's unconscious there is a constant sliding and concealment of meaning like the confused meanings we encounter in dreams. He describes the unconscious language of free association as a 'sliding of the signified beneath the signifier', as a constant dissolving and evaporation of meaning (Lacan 1977a: 154). (The idea of the constant evaporation of meaning has been very influential in the interpretation of literary texts where Desire, the veiled unconscious meanings which set up a challenge to the surface meanings, is explored and made explicit.)

Quite clearly, if language and consciousness really reflected this turbulent, chaotic, enigmatic unconscious directly to us, we would never be able to communicate with anyone. It is because Lacan is trying to mirror his own theory in his writing, to uncover the unconscious in his own language, and avoid mastery that much of his work is unclear and difficult to understand. However, in conscious, everyday life, in our relationships, in the whole body of consciousness which is represented by the different disciplines, scientific and humanistic, it could be argued that through our identifications we do manage to achieve some aspects of our identity which are coherent and unified, and some values and valuable bodies of knowledge which reflect this centredness. But Lacan maintains that all this is purely at the level of the 'Imaginary ego'. If we believe in any stability and 'truth' in language and knowledge, we have simply made another Imaginary identification with an image of ourselves reflected back to us from words whose meanings are as fleeting and illusory as the identities we build on the basis of them (Lacan 1977a: 70–7). In this context all our theories become like psychological lifeboats to which we are tempted to cling to avoid being submerged by desire.

There is, therefore, a radical split in our identity between what we are and what we take ourselves to be in consciousness. When we say 'I will have another glass of wine', the 'I' that is the subject of the sentence is an immediately accessible and understandable point of reference (in linguistics it is called the 'I' of the enunciation). But this 'I' veils the shadowy outlines of the much more precarious 'I' who is doing the speaking (the 'I of the enunciating'). In the normal process of speaking and writing these two 'I's seem to refer to one unified self, but Lacan argues that this unity is still only of an Imaginary kind. The subject of the enunciating – the psychological person trying to communicate in language – is impossible to represent; there is no sign which can sum up my entire being. Most of what I am can never be expressed in language. I cannot 'mean' and 'be' at the same time. To emphasize this departure from Descartes' famous equation of consciousness and thinking with identity, Lacan re-writes the well-known 'I think therefore I am' as 'I am not where I think and I think where I am not'. For Lacan, the subject is always constructed through a series of paradoxical, fantastic inversions. But, what is crucial for becoming a viable human subject is the transfer from the illusory world of the Imaginary, where identity has been based on the search for the same, to the Symbolic where subjectivity is based on difference. This is a transfer from the world we see, of the senses, to the world we speak, of the signifier, from the domain of the specular to the domain of the social.

Masquerade and *jouissance*

How can women cope with their catastrophic predicament as the lack? Lacan argues that since 'woman' within patriarchy is constructed only with reference to the male sign, the phallus (while her hidden womb is left out of symbolic account), her life is lived as a *masquerade*, playing the part man has assigned to her – the 'not man', 'the lack', a fictional complement to himself (Lacan 1977a: 290). So, according to Lacan, what society takes to be 'natural' 'feminine' behaviour is an acting out of the role of what patriarchal societies require of women: wife, mother, housewife, mother-in-law, baby doll, *femme fatale*, scarlet woman, iron lady, shrinking violet, blue-stocking, bitch, bimbo. Women, therefore, can represent male phantasies, but never themselves, and cannot exist as subjects within the patriarchal social order even in the bogus sense in which men can. In Lacan's world, where no one has a genuine identity, woman represents a double lack – her own lack of the valued phallus, and as a projection of male lack produced by his symbolic castration by his father. So women are deemed doubly powerless.

Building on Freud's concept of penis-envy, and what he called secondary narcissism which can develop in the girl at the time of the Oedipal crisis, Lacan's notion of the masquerade may illuminate something of the ways in which women 'package' themselves as objects in response to the demands of male phantasy. In their desire for a phallus – for the power to be a human subject – they make their whole body and being over to attracting an 'Other', through whom they think that they may become potent and whole. In this masquerade, determined entirely in relation to phallic desire, women effectively annihilate any possibility of a self of their own. In an attempt to suggest a more positive role for women, Lacan develops the concept of *jouissance* (an untranslatable French word signifying sexual bliss) to suggest a form of sexual pleasure peculiar and specific to them. He describes *jouissance* mysteriously as being 'something more' – what escapes or is left over from the phallic function, and exceeds it (Mitchell and Rose 1982: 147). Here he refers to other forms of pleasure not 'summed up' and subsumed in phallic activity which, he thinks takes place only in the pre-Oedipal realm. These are sources of pleasure which, like the unconscious meanings which exist between words, lie beyond the reach and meaning of heterosexual physical satisfaction based on the phallus and are perhaps those forms of pleasure which are associated with the search for an alternative identity through the re-union with the mother, the originator of all Desire.

Lacan's work has been welcomed as a theory of how patriarchal ideology is perpetuated in the deep structure of a gendered and eroticized language and thought and has been widely taken up, particularly by the French feminists Hélène Cixous, Julia Kristeva and Luce Irigaray. I have given a fuller account and discussion of Lacan's work and feminist development of it elsewhere (Minsky 1996: 137–76) and in chapters 4 and 10 of this book.

Part II

Control or Containment?: Making Sense of Experience

5

Difference: the fluidity of gender

All human individuals, as a result of their bisexual disposition and of cross-inheritance, combine in themselves both masculine and feminine characteristics, so that pure masculinity and femininity remain theoretical constructions of uncertain content.

Freud, *'Some Psychical Consequences of the Anatomical Distinction between the Sexes'*

During the past three decades gender has been a subject of intense cultural interest largely as a result of feminist interest in the meaning of 'femininity'. The first debate about 'femininity' had been conducted largely among psychoanalysts in the 1920s and 1930s and centred mainly around the controversial issue of Freud's concept of penis-envy. Women analysts such as Karen Horney, Hélène Deutsch, Melanie Klein and Joan Riviere, supported by Ernest Jones, argued that 'femininity' and 'masculinity' were mostly biologically determined but that womb-envy was of far more unconscious significance than penis-envy in the small child's psychical life. Much later, in the 1970s and 1980s, theories of gender construction initially centred mainly around sociology and socialization theory which emphasized the cultural construction of gender in the family, education, media and other cultural institutions. However, this did not shed much light on why some men and women fail to conform to the cultural stereotypes of 'masculinity' and 'femininity' despite their elaborate socialization. For this reason, interest in psychoanalytic theory intensified, particularly among feminists who recognized the need to explore unconscious as well as conscious processes in the formation of gendered identity. In 1975 Juliet Mitchell attempted to convince feminists of the importance of Freud and Lacan's work to women in her book *Psychoanalysis and Feminism,* and in 1978 Nancy Chodorow drew attention to a more object-relations centred approach in her book *The Reproduction of Mothering.* Since that time, interest in psychoanalytic ideas on gender has focused increasingly on Lacan's re-interpretation of

Freud's theory and on the work of Jacques Derrida and the French feminist writers Hélène Cixous, Julia Kristeva and Luce Irigaray. These feminists, although critical of Lacan, have drawn heavily on his interest in language and the idea that this is the only place where we can have access to the repressed 'feminine' as unconscious desire. Although the work of each of these feminists is distinctively different, they all make the repressed 'feminine' into a positive theoretical category, at the same time stressing the idea of fluidity and multiplicity of identity and meaning rather than binary gender divisions and unified, fixed categories which they associate with a distorted, cultural 'masculinity' which denies difference and turns women into split-off dimensions of men. More recently, Judith Butler and Kaja Silverman and others have attempted to develop a theory of identity in which the concepts of 'masculinity' and 'femininity' play no part. Individuals are defined simply on the basis of being different from each other, this difference depending on the pattern of their early identifications.

Psychoanalytic ideas have been crucial to our insights into the unconscious processes which underlie the construction of 'masculinity' and 'femininity'. They have also been important for our understanding of the role of language and representation in the historical silencing of women and the 'feminine' within culture. Since gender and its relationship to culture are central to both Freud's and Lacan's work, their ideas will form the main focus of this chapter and reverberate through subsequent chapters. I shall postpone discussion of post-Freudian and object-relations approaches, which raise other important issues in relation to sexual difference and gender, until chapter 6.

Culture and the father

Culture plays a crucial part in Freud's ideas about the unconscious construction of our identity. As we have seen, for Freud, the moment when culture becomes a central component of who we are is the time when, through the process of identification, we internalize the father as the powerful symbol of the world beyond the body of the mother, at the end of the Oedipal crisis. For Freud, culture first enters our mind in the shape of the father's presence as a rival in love for the mother. The father breaks into the fused psychosomatic, mutual reverie between the child and the mother, and it is through our subsequent identification with him that we internalize the laws and values of culture which the father symbolically represents. From this time on, the symbolic father, now ensconced in our inner world as the super-ego, presides over the rest of who we are and attempts to set limits to the demands of our unconscious desires. Freud thought that the girl identified with the father less than the boy because, feeling herself to be already castrated, she had nothing to fear from him. Freud suggests that this makes women's moral sense less rigid and uncompromising than men's because they do not internalize the father's cultural authority to the same extent. So for Freud, it is the father, as different and separate from the mother, who compels children of both sexes to exchange unrealistic, omnipotent phantasies about staying with the mother for ever for the relative 'reality' of culture and symbolization. But although the symbolic father cuts us off from our phantasies, Freud argues that he also allows us to identify with culture sufficiently to enable us to become relatively self-reflecting, coping human beings. As Weatherill suggests, in both Freud's and Lacan's theory, it is the father who situates us as a subject, as a separate self, in relation to the world. It is the father-based component of our identity who will 'help us tolerate a certain unbearable sense of separateness, loneliness and isolation which follows on from his interdiction and which we will never totally accept as reality. We will always feel that we are missing something' (Weatherill 1994: 89).

For Freud and Lacan, it is this symbolic castration of who we are up until the Oedipal crisis which, ideally, allows us emotionally to come to terms with loss and accept that we can never find total satisfaction or the ultimate 'truth' and that life in culture is always about ambiguity, contradiction and ambivalence. It is this recognition which allows us to discern the difference between reality and phantasy when we glimpse the emergence of a self through which we can look at the world with some confidence that it is, in some important sense, 'really' there.

Bisexuality and the rejection of 'femininity'

Contrary to what is often thought to be Freud's emphasis on biological drives, his central concepts of the unconscious and bisexuality radically free sexuality and gender from a dependence on biology. (However, he wisely never entirely rules out what he calls 'constitutional' factors.) Freud suggests that gender arises out of what the child 'makes' unconsciously of its passionate sexual/emotional entanglements with both its parents in early childhood in the context of cultural constraints symbolized by the father. These initially result from the child's drives but are transformed into unconscious symbolic meanings in the mind of adult men and women which have a dramatic bearing on who they are able to be (examples of extreme outcomes would be a castrating woman

unconsciously dominated by male-envy or a misogynist man unconsciously dominated by castration anxiety). We need to keep in mind that,
for Freud, unconscious phantasies, like myths and fairy-tales, are impossible to fit into rational ways of making sense of the world which is why
many of his ideas, like penis-envy and castration anxiety, appear mostly
unrecognizable to our consciousness. Although Freud spent his lifetime
trying to discover how the traditional gender identities of 'masculinity'
and 'femininity' come into existence, he ended up concluding that since
most children identify with both parents, the pure categories of gender
rarely exist. Even when they appear to be pure it is only because
unacceptable dimensions of gender have been firmly repressed into the
unconscious, that is, lingering penis-envy in girls and castration anxiety
in boys. So, whatever Freud's preferred views and feelings about gender
which seem, at times, ambivalent, defensive and over-influenced by the
cultural assumptions of his time, the over-riding impact of his theory is
that the pure, biologically determined binary identities of 'masculinity'
and 'femininity', historically purveyed by culture, are largely non-existent
because children of both sexes are bisexual. They both fall in love with
and identify with both parents and, to differing extents depending on
family dynamics, as well as culture subsequently express or repress those
desires and identifications as adults in culture. So, in Freud's theory, what
culture calls 'masculinity' and 'femininity' emerge as forms of identity
which refuse to be confined inside the boundaries of male and female
bodies, leaving men and women as inherently bisexual mixtures of
gender. Each of us is a product of a range of desires and identifications
which make us different individuals across the dualistic divisions of
'masculinity' and 'femininity' and activity and passivity.

Importantly, Freud's theory also suggests why, within culture, traditional gender categories are so often allied with superiority and inferiority which have such a surprising capacity to masquerade as natural and
'given' properties of men and women. Freud's theory powerfully suggests that this is because they match up with many children's earliest
unconscious phantasies in relation to their parents and their emotionally
driven hierarchical perception of sexual difference. In other words, in
these early childhood phantasies, having a penis seems, incontrovertibly,
to symbolize the mother's desire and acceptance (making it superior),
while the lack of one symbolizes her rejection (making the little girl
inferior). Retrospectively, in the context of the meaning of the symbolic
father, this then gets translated into cultural power and presence ('masculinity') and cultural inferiority and absence ('femininity'). So this means
that, before its massive reinforcement by culture, it is likely that, for the
little girl, the idea of superiority is powerfully connected with the idea

that the mother desires the male father (or a substitute), that is someone *unlike* rather than like herself. This means that the little boy, although he has to give up the mother, sees that he at least has the kind of body that the mother desires even if she is culturally out of bounds and the wrong generation in relation to him. The little girl, of course, discovers that she is completely out of the running because she lacks the kind of body the mother desires.

Freud thought, controversially, that conventional gender positions provide the best defence the individual has against painful and inhibiting neurotic symptoms because they fit with the requirements of culture; they are therefore more comfortable to live with. In this sense, if not in any other, he could argue with justification that anatomy is destiny if individuals repress what is unacceptable to culture. Freud took the view that it was largely cultural prohibition in the form of the internalized father which causes our need for the repression of unacceptable desires (the girl's 'masculine' identification with the father and desire for the mother and the boy's 'feminine' identification with the mother and desire for the father).

So Freud's theory suggests that the ideals of gender within patriarchal societies consist of splitting human attributes potentially common to all of us into two complementary ways of being human, one of which is apparently universally valued more than the other. Each sex then re-presses the culturally unacceptable dimension of their identity which then forms the basis of their unconscious. Ironically, from a psychoanalytic point of view, it seems to be the *mother* who first helps to confer special value on the penis by apparently wanting one in the form of the father. Little girls unconsciously want what they perceive the mother desires so that they can fulfil their phantasy of having exclusive possession of her for ever. The small girl's initial wanting to have and be what the mother *desires* rather than what the mother *is*, may, along with the wound to her narcissism, suggest part of the reason for the inferior status of 'femininity' in the unconscious minds of some, perhaps many, women as well as men. Children of both sexes may unconsciously reject 'femininity' because the mother wants something different from rather than the same as herself.

Fluid identities

Freud's concept of bisexuality, so central to his theory, enables us to explain differences among men and women as well as between them – the reasons why many people, for a variety of reasons, fail to resolve their Oedipal crisis entirely in accordance with cultural demands. This means that they fail to repress all their culturally unacceptable sexuality so that they end up as complex and varied *amalgams* of what patriarchal societies designate as 'masculinity' and 'femininity'. Active women and passive men, and many positions in between, clearly exist as possible gender positions despite their continuing unpopularity within many cultures. The unconscious identifications and desires for both our parents which we felt as small children are often expressed unconsciously in our adult relationships, both heterosexual and homosexual. 'Masculine' women often unconsciously choose 'feminine' men as heterosexual partners and vice versa. This means that children may then identify, unconsciously, with a more 'masculine' mother or 'feminine' father which might explain the variety of homosexual as well as heterosexual identities. Lesbian women and gay men may be 'masculine' or 'feminine' identified or any position in between. Sometimes, appearance may confound reality even further when a 'masculine'-identified woman adopts an unconscious compensatory ultra 'feminine' style. As many feminists have suggested, it seems helpful to talk about 'masculinities' and 'femininities' or 'difference' rather than 'gender' to reflect this situation.

In the context of the mixture of conscious or unconscious 'masculinity' and 'femininity' in us all, which Freud's work makes so apparent, Marie Maguire suggests that many girls' difficulties with achieving some autonomy from the mother seem to be related to difficulties with identifying with paternal qualities of assertiveness and active sexuality in the father. But she argues that, in most actual families today, the mother does much of the work of preparing the girl for independence, while the father may well provide some maternal emotional containment for the infant. She argues that, ideally, children need to be able to identify with 'masculinity' and 'femininity' in both parents so that neither is seen as the exclusive possession of one (Maguire 1995: 68). She also stresses that girls need to identify with the active sexuality of their father and other paternal figures (Maguire 1995: 8). The difficulty, as Maguire observes, is maintaining the capacity for intimacy and sexual passion in a situation which blurs 'masculinity' and 'femininity' across the frontiers of the body. This raises the issue of the extent to which passion depends on the repression of aspects of our gender so that our passions are ignited only by finding what we have unconsciously repressed in ourself, in the other. This clearly happens in both heterosexual and homosexual relationships and forms the basis of romantic love. Perhaps the most optimistic response to this problem in the context of specifically heterosexual relationships may be that sexual feelings are likely to be inspired at least in part by the recognition of bodily difference as well as gender difference. It may be that in gay and lesbian relationships, where there is a desire for bodily sameness rather than difference, opposing gender and other differences are more important.

In the case of what Freud calls fetishism within heterosexual relationships, sexual difference is both recognized and denied at the same time. Something on the body of the female loved object stands in for the penis (fur, high-heeled shoe, satin underwear), reproducing the mother as she is first perceived by the pre-Oedipal child. At this time, before the cultural impact of the father and the phallus, she appears to the child as all-powerful and therefore as a phallic mother. Importantly, at this time, her identity is also still fused with that of the little boy. So the fetishist, in that he chooses a female lover, straddles two opposing desires. He wants, at one and the same time, both to recognize sexual difference and the need to separate from the mother and to deny it so he can remain fused with the mother's identity for ever and not have to grow up. Laura Mulvey's work in film theory has suggested that the glamorous image of female film stars of the Hollywood era (tight, 'slinky' dresses, high-heels, fish-net stockings, shiny crimson lipstick, diamonds and expensive jewellery) represents a partial refusal of women's difference which is fetishistic and constructed for the visual pleasure of the predominantly male gaze (Mulvey 1991: 14–26). Later work, however, which emphasizes Freud's insights into the fluidity of gender, includes reference to the female 'masculine' gaze which involves women as well as men in the pleasures of looking.

The victimization of the 'other'

For Freud, the castration complex in children of both sexes is central to his understanding of what the child does with its discovery of sexual difference based on the visibility of the penis/phallus and the child's eventual separation from the mother. It offers a further explanation for the cultural denigration of 'femininity' in addition to the mother's usual preference for a male body. In Freud's theory, crucial repercussions often follow from the child's identification with the father, and particularly in the case of the boy who has an emotionally or physically unavailable or over-severe father. As both children, but especially boys, internalize the father as the feared potential executioner, their identity may subsequently become one which consists of part victimizer and part victim of symbolic castration based on the loss of the mother to the father. To capitalize on the power of the father as a source of power and moral authority, and to avoid the painful feelings involved in the idea of being a victim, both children, but again particularly the boy who identifies most with the father (because he has the most to fear and shares the same kind of body), may succumb to a destructive unconscious solution. In the context of his recent discovery of sexual difference and the existence of a physically different 'other' in the external world, the boy may discover the psychical opportunity of projecting the painful 'victim' feelings of humiliation and vulnerability onto this newly discovered other. This means he is then able to disown those painful feelings which interfere with his newly acquired sense of power and identity gained through making an identification with the symbolic father. By expelling or externalizing the part of himself he finds intolerable, the small boy may find a way of achieving a sense of stability and power at the cost of making a psychical victim out of 'woman', now defined as different and therefore contemptible and 'bad'. This means, subsequently, that women, 'femininity', or passivity wherever it exists, may be hated, denigrated and feared because it represents a despised, castrated part of the man's self. He remains consciously unaware that his fear of women, who now embody split-off parts of himself, is responsible for his urgent need to control and dominate them. Some men, with significant parts of themselves now dangerously located outside in the external world, are likely to feel that women are constantly trying to attack and undermine them. This unconscious dependence on women may lead them, through the mechanism of paranoia, to undermine or attack women as a means of defence against the threat of psychical annihilation. Women, as the different 'other', become the symbol of potential psychical castration.

At this point, we should also remember that some women, for similar defensive psychical reasons, project unacceptable parts of themselves onto men as the denigrated 'other' who then represent their 'stranger within'. We shall explore the nature of women's projections onto men in more detail in chapter 6. In this context, Julia Kristeva (1981) warns feminists not to fall into the seductive trap of transforming women into the new 'truth' and turning men into the despised and denigrated 'other' in an unconscious reversal of the patriarchal equation.

Fear and dependence

So, Freud's theory suggests that patriarchal cultures, characterized by the social reinforcement of the unconscious construction of the pure, binary, hierarchical categories of 'masculinity' and 'femininity', may perpetuate potentially destructive unconscious perceptions stemming from early childhood: the idea that 'femininity' is the identity the mother rejects and also the identity that frequently 'carries' what the man cannot bear to acknowledge in himself. This does not bode well for relationships between men and women. From this perspective, even successful relationships between men and women who broadly identify with traditional categories may often contain elements of sado-masochism, victim and victimizer, as Jessica Benjamin (1990) has argued. (However, we should not forget that in the case of 'masculine'-identified women and 'feminine' men the situation may be reversed.) But if paranoid phantasies based on the 'other' as a split-off part of the self do underlie patriarchal cultures and many of the relationships between individual men and women, it would help to explain the persistent need, historically, to demonize and dominate women. The widespread extermination of women branded as witches in seventeenth-century Europe, who did not conform to cultural norms about what women were supposed to be, can be seen, from a psychoanalytic perspective, as a systematic attempt to destroy those who refused male projections of castration, dependency and lack. Those designated as witches may have been unconsciously perceived as psychical attackers and therefore their eradication experienced, at one level, as self-defence. In refusing men's projections of their 'other', they threatened many men with the very real prospect of psychical annihilation. In more recent times, domestic violence against women and, in extreme cases, the rape and the killing of women, and the popularity of representations of violence against women in film and video may stem from the same paranoid mechanisms in some men.

Klein's development of Freud's ideas emphasizes that many of us project good and bad phantasies of ourselves onto the same people, objects or ideas at different times so that those who have been initially idealized may subsequently become hated and despised. Women are idealized by some men as angels, goddesses and Madonna figures but also denigrated as whores and witches. Men have been idealized by women as heroic, godlike 'knights on white chargers' and protective father figures but also, more recently, denigrated as violent, controlling monsters, rapists, potential murderers, wife-beaters, child abusers or wimps. But psychoanalytic knowledge suggests that all these projections or phantasies, which so often appear in cultural representations of men and women, blind us to the reality of what individual men and women are like underneath the aspects of ourselves we have super-imposed on them so we cannot see them. This then prevents us from realistically confronting and appreciating the otherness of other people and our own unconscious, internal 'other'. As I suggested earlier, in the therapeutic session, projective identification is often crucially important because it allows the therapist to 'experience' how the patient feels and draw this to the patient's attention. But, in ordinary situations, we may not be so skilful at becoming aware, at any moment, that our feelings belong to someone else who has unconsciously projected them onto us. We may mistake them for our own rather than being able to use them to communicate with the other person's unconscious.

Marie Maguire's clinical experience supports the implications of Freud's ideas about gender. She suggests that many men, in contrast to women, assume a stance of pseudo-independence while projecting their passivity or dependence and vulnerability onto women who then, without being aware of it, feel men's feelings of helplessness and dependence on them, and, in addition, are forced painfully to confront their own (Maguire 1995: 2). She argues that many men feel a contradictory mixture of both longing for and dread of women because of the presence of both the idealization of women as the hidden but most authentic part of the self and their denigration. But some women may sometimes experience themselves as caring, loving victims of men's destructiveness through the mechanism of projection which prevents the emotional 'working through' of earlier frustration and disappointment in relation to the mother. Perhaps it is this kind of destructive projection on the part of some women which has been unconsciously involved in a recent disturbing tendency to denigrate and devalue the role of fathering. This may, in the context of positive changes in women's position which confound male projections of vulnerability and dependence onto women, leave many men, who are already plagued by a mixture of guilt, envy and longing, with no 'masculine' psychical place to go. This often takes place in a context of low economic and social status, insecurity or unemployment. The increase in suicide in young men between the age of fifteen and twenty-four is likely to be related to cultural deprivation and the social injury of unemployment (Hawton and Fagg 1992). But, in some, it may also be linked to widespread feelings of imminent psychical annihilation stemming from a very real crisis of 'masculine' identity. We shall explore this theme further in chapter 6.

Feminized 'others'

Freud's work, whatever its omissions in the light of later theoretical developments, seems crucially important to our understanding of some of the unconscious factors which may be in play in the subordination of women and, by extension, all those considered as 'other' and different

which follow on from the small child's first discovery of sexual difference. It suggests that the unconscious rejection of 'femininity' by most
children of *both* sexes in early childhood (the view of the girl as castrated
and the over-valuation of the penis/phallus as a result of symbolic
castration by the father in boys and penis-envy, or longing to be what the
mother desires, in girls) may underlie not only the historical and global
domination of women but also of others who have been 'feminized' by
patriarchal men (although not all men are patriarchal and not all women
experience penis-envy). Freud's work offers insight into the roots of
racism, classism, tribalism, homophobia, violent forms of nationalism,
religious persecution, ethnocentrism and intolerance of difference generally as forms of 'feminization' stemming from an unconscious hierarchical and destructive response to difference. Implicit in all these is a notion
of the despised 'other' as the means to maintaining an idealized self.
Quite often this is allied to a preoccupation with purity and cleanliness
and the omnipotent need to order and control exemplified in the fascist
preoccupation with racial purity and the need to control and destroy the
'other' perceived as 'dirty' and contaminating. This suggests that some
individuals never abandon the defensive, sado-masochistic behaviour
characteristic of what Freud describes as the anal stage of our pre-
Oedipal infantile sexuality. Here, he suggests, we establish and maintain
a sense of identity predominantly on the basis of control which involves
both sadistic and masochistic elements. As the sociologist Max Weber
recognized, these anal, sado-masochistic features are also characteristic
of all the control implicit in hierarchical, bureaucratic systems.

So Freud's work suggests that early childhood observations of the
apparent superiority of having the penis/phallus and inferiority involved
in the lack of one seeps through individuals into culture, so that having
the phallic sign/penis comes to represent activity, potency, superiority
and authority (associated with culture, mind, purity, whiteness, lightness
and the 'human') and the lack of one, passivity, inferiority and powerlessness (associated with nature, body, dirt, 'blackness', darkness and the
sub-human or animal). Freud's insights powerfully suggest that, as adults,
many of us may live in the destructive shade of the very small child's
narcissistic, anal and phallic-dominated perceptions of the meaning of
the body, as it struggles to discover who it is and how it can fit in. Some
of the most striking forms of the control and denigration of the 'other'
within culture seem to entail an unconscious re-configuration of elements involved in early, primitive ways of establishing and defending
identity. We shall return to the sado-masochistic dimension of difference
and the idea of 'feminization' of the 'other' in later chapters.

Cultural change

Freud's work suggests that many men, if they want to conform to the cultural ideal of 'masculinity', have to give up the emotional dimension of who they are by identifying with the cultural 'masculinity' of the father and cut themselves off from the emotional, 'feminine' world of the mother in early childhood. Women, on the other hand, in order to conform with cultural norms must, ideally, try to cut themselves off from their active, assertive feelings in relation to the mother, including their anger and active sexuality, and, instead, accept an identity rooted in a sense of lacking what it takes to participate fully in culture. Traditional gender roles therefore cut both men and women off from half of what they potentially are. But recent developments in many Western countries have seen significant social changes in the position of women and public, if not always private, attitudes to gender. It has become much easier in some circles, at least, to express dimensions of ourselves which have previously been repressed. These changes have been powerfully influenced by the gradual acceptance of feminist ideas within the culture at large since the early 1970s, even if some women still find it difficult to describe themselves as feminist. For these women, despite agreeing with many of the ideas associated with it, feminism may still smack of just too much 'masculinity' and therefore threaten some women with the loss of the 'feminine' identity they value in spite of its limitations when divorced from the more active, 'masculine' dimensions of who they are. This is an example of one of the contradictions within which many women (and men) live. Similarly, many men trying to come to emotional terms with their 'femininity', without losing the 'masculine' qualities which they value and which they feel make them attractive to women, face the same kind of contradiction. Finding a gender balance (if our unconscious childhood experiences allow us any options which frequently they do not) without losing the capacity for sexual intimacy in heterosexual relationships is, as has been observed earlier, perhaps a problem men and women face if heterosexual passion, as Freud seems to suggest, is based on at least a degree of gender 'opposition'. Legal, social and economic change have benefited some women, often middle-class, particularly in the Western world. Many women are now confronted with a hitherto unknown range of choices and have become increasingly active and assertive in cultural areas traditionally associated primarily with men. These women have often managed to withdraw projections of their strength and assertiveness from men without losing access to culturally 'feminine' strengths and attributes. However, we need to remember that this is made easier in cultures where becoming more like a man often raises a woman's status because of the privileged position of 'reason' and 'masculinity' whereas a man who consciously owns more of his 'femininity' by acknowledging emotional vulnerability and nurturing capacities may lower his social status in many social situations.

Perhaps the most important single factor to bring about a change in women's position in the West has been the development of increasingly reliable forms of contraception stemming from the early part of the twentieth century. This has allowed women to control their fertility and for many women this has led to greater sexual independence as well as social freedom. Indirectly, this has no doubt contributed to the increased incidence of family break-up and single-parent families in the last decades of the twentieth century. Central to this development seems to be many women's increased unwillingness to tolerate unrewarding relationships. It is likely that women are more likely to leave their partners than men largely because of their higher expectations of what mutually emotionally fulfilling relationships should involve. This has meant that many women now try to fulfil the role of the father as well as the mother for much of the time, especially when estranged partners move away and, in almost half the cases, after two years lose contact with their children. On the other hand, many men, in a cultural climate more sympathetic to new forms of male identity, have felt able to express the more culturally 'feminine' dimensions of who they are and have come under increasing pressure to do so from women dissatisfied with husbands and partners still wedded to traditional, patriarchal ways of being men which they find inhibiting and damaging. There has been a dramatic rise in the number of people who have chosen 'living together' as an alternative to marriage and, increasingly, men have become more emotionally as well as practically involved with the needs of their children in both single- and two-parent families, although the absence of change in social organization involving such issues as paternity leave, state nursery provision and genuinely equal pay in many Western countries still makes full role-sharing difficult to achieve. However, as Maguire (1995) comments, even as some men are more able to enjoy the emotional rewards of an increased share in family life, where there are two parents, they still retain their cultural position of privilege and many have difficulty recognizing the vulnerability which changes in women's position have exposed in them.

In parallel with the social changes outlined above, there has been an increasingly widespread cultural acceptance of homosexual and lesbian identities, largely as a result of political pressure from these groups themselves. But patriarchal societies, as well as provoking homophobia, damage homosexual and lesbian as well as heterosexual relationships by producing many men who are incapable of emotional intimacy because they have to make such a damaging break with the emotional world of the mother. In the context of all these changes, Freud's ideas, which make culture so central compared with other psychoanalytic perspectives, suggest that previously unconscious aspects of gender and sexuality may not have to be repressed in the future to the same extent, since women and men will represent a more diverse or fluid culture.

Gender and biology

However, the notion of the fluidity of identity does not allow us to do away with conventional gender expectations altogether. However unfashionable this view may be, there may well be some aspects of conventional gender distinctions which represent genetically determined psychological differences associated with sexual difference which we need to recognize as such and take account of, in spite of the fact that they may have been exploited in the interests of power and domination. Although we may not be able to control such characteristics (to date), psychoanalytic theory suggests we need to confront them rather than denying them. It seems more important to work out cultural strategies which will allow these 'essences', if they exist, to be used creatively instead of destructively, rather than disclaiming them simply as 'essentialist'. For example, if most women were discovered to have a tendency to be more emotionally empathic than most men and this was shown to be connected with a hormone linked to their biological capacity to feed and care for very young, helpless babies, this could still never justify their confinement to mothering and nurturing roles when they also, self-evidently, possess many other talents and aspirations shared with men. This can be compared to confining men exclusively to jobs demanding aggression and physical strength because there might be a tendency for men to have greater aggression and muscular strength than women due to the presence of higher levels of testosterone. Men tend to be more interested in the building of bridges and towers than most women which may have as much to do with biology as culture but this need has no connection with the subordination of women. It seems important to acknowledge that there are differences between groups and individuals which may be based on biological as well as cultural and unconscious factors and that we need to find ways of working against an unconscious temptation to use the existence of any difference destructively and negatively in order to feel better about our 'selves'. Anatomical differences between the sexes make men and women different in some respects and they influence the way we live our lives. They affect our anxieties and phantasies, physical and sexual capacities and our experience of sex, reproduction and life as we live it consciously and unconsciously. They also affect our responses to adolescence and mid-life. As suggested above, if it should turn out that there are some aspects of our identity which are biologically determined, we need to acknowledge this consciously as one of the aspects of 'reality' which lies beyond our control. From a psychoanalytic point of view, this is about giving up what Freud calls the baby's omnipotent phantasy that it is in control of everything. As Maguire (1995) observes, this means facing up to the fact that the most important facts like our sex and death are out of our control and the recognition that even those we love are essentially separate and unpredictable.

Degrees of gender precariousness

In welcoming the relative fluidity of gender which Freud's theory of the unconscious makes visible, it is important to recognize that there are situations where extremely painful and damaging experiences in childhood result in gender identities which are so precarious that they result in severe neurotic or even psychotic disturbance. In this context, it seems more realistic to think about identity in terms of relative degrees of precariousness rather than using 'precarious' as a blanket term covering very different kinds of identity. For some, living with precariousness is about ordinary creative, adult living, whereas for others it is about living extremely painfully with a high degree of anxiety and inhibition, a sense of futility and emptiness which frequently makes it difficult to cope with life. Clearly, some identities are significantly more precarious than others in spite of individual attempts to conceal this from themselves and others. Freud distinguished clearly between neurotic unhappiness stemming from internal conflicts which he thought could be alleviated by psychotherapy and ordinary human unhappiness which has its sources in external and conscious rather than internal and unconscious circumstances. Experiences which might lead to severe neurotic disturbance and a sense of extreme precariousness are infinitely variable but some of the most common might include sexual and other forms of physical and emotional child abuse, which may have cut the child off from any possibility of a comfortable resolution of its Oedipal crisis or even from being able to enter the Oedipal phase. These kinds of experience, and the context of desires, identifications and anxieties in which they take place, frequently manifest themselves in a complex of neurotic or psychotic symptoms of confusion, rage, inhibition, psychological or physical illness and painful feelings of gender confusion. This kind of gender precariousness, which often involves a high degree of splitting and projection, is clearly of a different order from the precariousness of identity we associate with the idea of the ordinary divided self potentially always open to sabotage from the unconscious but subject to ordinary rather than severe neurotic or psychotic unhappiness.

Symbolic castration and loss of a 'feminine' identity

Both Freud's and Lacan's theory suggest that the boy's symbolic castration by the father amounts to the symbolic annihilation of one of the best forms of identity the small boy has had so far – the fragile and illusory identity bestowed by the pleasure involved in phantasies about winning the mother for himself. But the small boy has to repress this sense of psychical mutilation of who he thought he was and, ironically, spend his life pretending he has a natural and exclusive right to cultural power on the basis of an identification with phallic phantasies of control and power which he unconsciously knows were thwarted by his father. In Lacan's re-figuration of Freud's theory, this pretence based on phantasies of omnipotence lies at the centre of the patriarchal man's being and constitutes the bogusness of the phallus as a source of meaning and knowledge. In addition, the boy has to give up his identification with the 'feminine' and the powerful emotional world the mother represents. Sometimes the small boy experiences his separation from the mother as her rejection of him. This confusion may subsequently leave a large and painful residue of pain, rage and loss which later, as an adult, is projected along with other bad feelings, onto women. This means it may express itself in a variety of controlling and dominating behaviour and an underlying fear of his continuing unconscious dependence on women. In extreme cases this might take the form of, for example, a generalized misogyny and, in more extreme cases, wife-battering, rape and violence against women.

The need for separation

A boy's or girl's inability to separate from the mother and identify with some aspects of cultural 'masculinity' may be just as damaging for later relationships as a too early or too radical separation. In Freudian terms, if the child of either sex has any impression of having won the Oedipal battle in terms of taking the place of the father, by, for example, being the mother's main or secret confidant(e), he or she may not experience symbolic castration. This failure to set a boundary on her or his desires prevents the child's progress from the unreal enticements of phantasy to the real demands and opportunities in the external world. If the child has the sense, perhaps unknowingly fostered by the mother or father, that it has replaced the father in the mother's affections because of the actual or emotional absence of a father, or the mother's evident dissatisfaction with the father, then that child, as an adult, may be prevented from having successful emotional relationships. It remains locked in a love-affair with the mother which appears to have substance in external reality. It has no sense of there being a satisfied sexual/emotional couple already in existence from whom it emerged. It is this real immovable obstacle which confronts the child with the painful reality that it has to separate sufficiently from the mother to eventually allow it, as an adult, to become part of a new sexual/emotional couple. Symbolically, to remain the mother's exclusive emotional partner means that the child will have a sense of having broken the incest taboo. According to Freud, it is this taboo which opens the way to the possibility of a relatively autonomous identity in the domain beyond the mother's body. As well as possibly having damaging effects on future close relationships, this situation may cause the adult to be stuck in a perpetual phantasy of potential castration and guilt because the Oedipal crisis has never been adequately resolved. Lacking the experience of intervention by the father, he or she may remain trapped in phantasy and unable to engage with the demands of the external world. This may be characterized by a high degree of anxiety, confusion, anger or false hopes, an often destructive and self-destructive inability to recognize the need for any boundary on phantasy and a compulsion to repeat rather than learn from experience. As Maguire argues, in Freud's and Lacan's theory, the mother seems to represent unboundaried narcissism and a regression to archaic early experiences from which the child must separate. However, she argues, if the child is brought up in a one-parent family with perhaps only the mother, how the child develops heavily depends on the mother's own relationship to her internal male aspects, including her identification with her own father and the 'masculine' and paternal qualities of both her parents. If she can make this 'masculinity' available to the child, as well as her 'femininity', the child will be more likely to be able to separate. The boy will feel less fearful of his 'femininity' and the girl will not feel she is the only 'masculine' principle in the mother's life. As Maguire also points out, the father's capacity for cultural 'femininity', emotional containment and for mothering is also under-emphasized in Freud's and Lacan's theories (Maguire 1995).

If the boy fails to resolve his Oedipal complex, Freud's theory suggests that he may feel intense unconscious hatred and contempt for women provoked by his unresolved castration anxiety. His misogyny may make him feel terrified that he will lose his 'masculinity' and become like the women he hates and dreads because he remains identified with her and she appears castrated. If the girl's Oedipal crisis remains unresolved she may, Freud's work suggests, unconsciously identify largely with her father, retain her mother as a phantasy love-object and experience considerable penis-envy. This may make her hostile and contemptuous of men and, like the misogynist man, she may have difficulties maintaining close relationships. However, unconscious awareness of her predominantly 'masculine' stance may make her present herself as traditionally 'feminine', even as a *femme fatale*, as a form of compensation, just as the 'feminine'-identified misogynist man might need to present himself as ultra 'masculine' or macho.

Heterosexuality

As we have seen, Freud's theory of bisexuality raises some fundamental questions not only about the status of the cultural categories of 'masculinity' and 'femininity' but also about the nature of heterosexual desire. Patriarchal cultures see heterosexual relationships as involving unequal opposites who are propelled towards each other in a search for the other, complementary part of themselves embodied in someone of the opposite sex. Here, sex and gender adhere to the boundaries of the bodies. The view of heterosexuality suggested by Freud's work is rather different. In this version, heterosexuality, although mainly representing genital (as opposed to oral, anal or phallic) sexuality which Freud thought was the final, potentially most mature and satisfying stage of sexual development, seems fundamentally to represent a return to the mother for both sexes, but in a culturally veiled and non-explicit form.

Freud's papers on femininity written in 1931 and 1933 suggest that, for 'normal' women, heterosexuality has at least two different and apparently conflicting meanings, one of which forms a kind of sub-text to the other. It represents two forms of desire simultaneously, one of which is a vehicle for the other. The first is the culturally acceptable passive form of women's sexuality as an object for men. The other, at the level of unconscious phantasy, is the active form of women's sexuality in the form of imaginatively 'becoming' the penis the mother desires through acquiring a share in one with a male partner. Lacan also argues that the woman becomes the phallus (the substitute for the lost mother) in the sense that her desire for the man creates its power. Freud's concept of widespread penis-envy, taken to one of its logical conclusions, suggests that the apparent passivity involved in heterosexuality is unconsciously experienced by many women, very actively, as the phantasized route back to the mother, but this time temporarily equipped with a share in the penis women lack. She can gain access to a penis only vicariously by means of a male partner and the capacity to phantasize. However, Freud also thought that some women's penis-envy was so powerful that it could cause frigidity and did not operate in the interests of heterosexuality.

So, in relation to women's involvement in heterosexuality, conscious appearance may conceal unconscious reality. Freud suggests that for what he thought was the majority of women, unconscious envy *stands in for* the penis. Envy represents the symbol or metaphor for women's forbidden active desire for their mother. As we have seen earlier, apart from expressing itself positively in heterosexual relationships, Freud thought it could also be expressed, like men's womb-envy, as hostility and contempt for the opposite sex. He thought that most women suffered from varying amounts of unconscious penis-envy, the degree depending on their particular unconscious and social circumstances.

In the last part of his lecture 'Femininity', Freud reiterates his view that the powerful pre-Oedipal love for the mother, which he thought continually resurfaces in many 'normal' women, also powerfully influences the character and flavour of women's subsequent relationships with men in many important ways (PFL 2: 167–9). But, he stresses that this relationship with her mother, which is so frequently transferred onto her relationships with men, is almost always ambivalent. As suggested earlier, it contains, as well as love, substantial quantities of hostility for all the deprivation associated with the mother in the past. Freud suggests that because of this hostility directed towards her husband, a woman may only be able to really love her son who can represent both the mother she loved and with whom she identified and the penis she coveted. Freud also thought that women often choose a male partner narcissistically as a reflection of a woman's self love – he represents the man the woman would have liked to have been – and is therefore idealized until reality breaks in and he is despised or dropped. Of course, this also frequently happens the other way round. Freud's suggestion that women's love tends to be more narcissistic than that of men stems from his belief that women have more difficulty internalizing the super-ego because their lingering, symbiotic love for the mother prevents them separating from her sufficiently. They therefore remain stuck in a merged, narcissistic way of loving which is based on loving the self in the form of the other who, in loving, confers on the woman a self. Nowadays, modern psychotherapists suggest that penis-envy is an un-conscious feature of some but not most women as Freud suggested. Significantly, as many have suggested (Klein, Horney, Lomas, Irigaray, Maguire), there is considerable clinical evidence of womb-envy which raises the issue of the extent to which Freud may sometimes have been projecting his own envy of his mother (reputedly beautiful, emotionally powerful and only twenty when her first son, Freud, was born) onto women in his theory. Since he was the inventor of the theory and practice of psychoanalysis he was compelled to rely on *self*-analysis to free him from his own projections which, as anyone who has experi-enced psychotherapy knows, was unlikely to reveal many aspects of his own unconscious. But certainly, nowadays, many psychoanalytic thera-pists acknowledge that some of the main reasons why women seek psychoanalytic therapy stem from difficulties in the area of dependence and separation from the mother. As a consequence, they have problems in achieving a sense of relative autonomy and emotional independence. Clearly this may often be reinforced by cultural assumptions about gender but sometimes it may stem as much from unconscious as directly cultural factors.

Freud's work as a whole suggests that many women are able to become in phantasy the subjects of their own desire for their mothers only when they become the objects of men's desire. This really means that the desire of many women to be the objects of men's desire embodies another, deeper, more primary desire for the love of the mother as well as the father. In a parallel but inverted way, men's involvement in heterosexuality also entails, as well as their acknow-ledged desire for the mother expressed overtly in their attraction to women generally, the unacknowledged phantasy of a return to the mother as a form of identity. This is a return to their primary emotional identification with the mother (their homosexuality) which they have had to deny so emphatically since early childhood. Freud suggests the idea that women as well as men tend to 'marry' their symbolic mothers. Women consciously acknowledge their deepest emotional identifi-cation with their mothers in early childhood but unconsciously disown their desire for her (their active 'masculinity'). Men consciously own their sexual desire for women, their mother substitutes, but disown their primary emotional identification with their mothers in early childhood (their passive 'femininity'). In this context many men and women may be seen trying unconsciously to reclaim the homosexual part of themselves which culture, up until very recently, has demanded they deny.

So, in the context of Freud's work, within patriarchal societies, hetero-sexuality is more than it seems. Women have to deny half of their sexuality (their active sexuality) to conform to cultural demands and then try to regain it through their heterosexual relationships. Men, on the other hand, have to deny half of their identity (their feminine identification) to conform to these same demands and then try to regain this through their heterosexuality. This suggests, ultimately, that although men and women need each other, men's need for women is greater than women's for men because men need to gain access, in phantasy at least, to their primary identity. As suggested earlier, it is this sense of vulnerability or dependency on women for access to their primary emotional identity which is consciously denied in men's patriarchal ideal of 'masculinity'.

Homosexuality

Freud's view of homosexuality seems to have been highly ambivalent. Sometimes, especially in his earlier work, he regards it as a perverse and immature form of identity which has got stuck in the phallic stage in a 'feminine' identification with the mother (PFL 14: 143). For Freud, this indicates that the Oedipal crisis has not been adequately resolved with its accompanying focus on genital rather than oral and anal sexuality associated with infantile sexuality. However, at other times in his work he suggests that homosexual identities are not perverse or 'abnormal' but simply represent an alternative form of identity stemming from the child's bisexual desire for both the parent of the same as well as the opposite sex in early childhood (PFL 9: 384–6, PFL 10: 206–8). Although some modern analytical therapists still regard homosexuality as immature, many take the view that since neurosis is evident in all kinds of relationships, heterosexual, homosexual or bisexual, and is not the prerogative of any form of sexuality, there is no basis for thinking that homosexual or bisexual identities are more or less neurotic than many heterosexual ones. A largely 'feminine', mother-identified man may choose a male partner or a more 'masculine' woman and a predomi-nantly 'masculine', father-identified woman may choose either a female 'femme' partner or a more 'feminine' man. There seems to be no way of predicting whether individuals whose gender significantly crosses the boundary of their body will be bisexual, heterosexual or homosexual. On the whole, both Freudian and object-relations psychoanalytic theory suggest that what is important in human existence is, all other things being equal, the capacity for creative self-reflexivity, for relative autonomy but also intimacy and love, and the ability to be happy in whatever form of gender and sexuality allows this to be possible.

Lacan: a gendered language and culture

Let us move now to Lacan's distinctive and influential re-formulation of Freud's theory and its striking proposals about the relationship between culture and gender.

In an attempt to re-build Freud's theory using modern linguistics, Lacan makes the claim that our identity exists only in language and that the very thought processes through which we speak are both gendered and eroticized. In other words, culture and all identities within it are gendered 'masculine' and fuelled by unconscious desire. Paradoxically, Lacan argues that the part of who we are which is hidden, that is, our repressed desire for the mother, is itself to be discovered within language along with consciousness, so that 'masculinity' (consciousness and subjectivity) and 'femininity' (the unconscious and lack of subjectivity) become two sides of the same signifying coin. In this striking re-figuration of Freud's concepts, Lacan makes a dramatic link between the bodily, sexual world of the Oedipal crisis and the cultural world of language which includes the reassuring body of knowledge it makes possible. If the binary divisions of meanings in language are understood in the same way as the meaning of the phallus as the first sign of (sexual) difference that we encounter, rational thinking and subjectivity become effectively 'masculine'. The 'feminine' in language becomes what is absent and lacking because the mother is repressed and women lack the powerful phallic sign. Women therefore represent the lack of meaning and subjectivity in culture and can exist only in the spaces between the rational categories in language through which we sculpt out a meaningful, though unpredictable, existence. In this sense, 'masculinity' and 'femininity' are unequal and complementary in language pre-figuring traditional gender categories. So, for Lacan, gendered identities exist only in the inter-subjectivity of language where we bring ourselves into cultural existence through the narratives we speak. Since the meanings of language have no direct links with the external world they describe, and are based only on the arbitrary sign of the phallus because this is the first sign of difference the child encounters, all identities in language and all knowledge they produce are also shifting and precarious. Lacan sees all identity in terms of what Winnicott would see as a 'false self' created by rational language. Lacan, using Saussure's linguistic theory of signification, shifts all meaningful life into language which, at the same time, both constrains and empowers us. As a consequence, Lacan argues that since our repressed desire is accessible only in language, the sexual relation can take place creatively only within the context of the recognition of the difference implicit in our use of the Symbolic. It cannot happen in the sameness of the Imaginary (that is, heterosexual love). It can occur only within the poetic text and not in what he sees as the sterile relationships between embodied men and women where the object of our love can never be more than an empty substitute for the lost mother. For Lacan, the heterosexual relation is an Imaginary farce based on reflections of sameness rather than difference. Here, each partner offers the other that which neither possesses because the man's phallus is symbolically castrated and the phallus which the woman offers to the man is only her desire to be the phallus vicariously through the man (this harks back to Freud's idea of penis-envy). So Lacan replaces embodied heterosexuality with the pleasures and transgressions of artistic experience which can disturb the apparent certainties of a 'masculine', phallic language and culture. Here the 'masculinity' of the words of consciousness can embrace the 'femininity' of unconscious desire, freed up in the playful activity of free association in a poetic form of intercourse which disturbs all settled meanings. Inconveniently, for our understanding, Lacan attempts this in his own writings.

Crucially, Lacan distinguishes between idealized forms of the lost mother in the delusory identifications of the Imaginary which lead nowhere (consuming 'causes', popular celebrities and icons, consumer goods, romance) and 'femininity' as the repressed unconscious Desire in language where it fulfils its proper subversive, creative function. For Lacan, when we can manage to articulate these unconscious meanings in the free play of meaning in poetry, 'femininity' comes to represent the only worthwhile source of the 'truth' of who we are, the 'truth' of the unconscious. But 'masculinity' always fluctuates between potency and castration because the phallus has been symbolically castrated in its first incarnation in the family. Thus, for Lacan, as we have seen, sexuality becomes the ambiguous, provisional artistic 'truth' of the meeting of 'masculine' and 'feminine' in poetic language within the text. The embodied experience of gender and sexuality is superseded by the meanings of art. The mind and the body remain irrecoverably separate.

So, Lacan, with great originality and theoretical panache, paints a gloomy picture of a patriarchal 'reality' in which we are all imprisoned. Those who ally themselves with phallic rationality (mainly men) are offered cultural power but this form of 'masculinity' is always fragile and precarious because it is rooted in loss of the mother and symbolic castration (by the father). Women, on the other hand, seem to be irretrievably locked in absence and lack within language from which they can escape only temporarily through their involvement in the creation of poetry and *jouissance* within texts. Lacan rules out the possibility of finding some symbolic power for women in the powerful pre-Oedipal mother. This, he argues, can only leave women in the unsignified realm of the Real, in the clutches of hysteria and psychosis. This means that Lacan's theory offers no hope for change outside the literary text. Since all positions in language are equally arbitrary and precarious, no point of view can have more value than any other. This rules out any basis for human values or consideration of the different outcomes which result from different positions. This suggests that the avoidance of cruelty or the alleviation of suffering does not count as justification for the privileging of one point of view over another. Democratic ideas carry no greater moral weight than totalitarian ones.

Lacan always argues that we have no choice about identifying our-selves with the conscious meanings of culture, at some level, because it is only through our entry into the constraining, pre-existing meanings of language that we can become coping human subjects. Lacan insists that Freud's conception of the symbolic meaning of the father has been dangerously neglected by object-relations theorists' preoccupation with the mother. For Lacan, the father is crucial for setting boundaries to the child's unbridled desires for the mother which prevent it experi-encing both the constraints and the creative opportunities offered by culture.

Lacan's de-centring of all identity presumed previously to be power-ful and relatively unified has been a powerful component in the post-modern enterprise. The 'feminine' as repressed unconscious desire, permanently ensconced in language, always has the potential to disturb the settled, surface meanings of any text. Through equating the uncon-scious and the disruption of meaning exclusively with the 'feminine', Lacan's work has played a major part in the influential post-modernist work of Derrida and French feminist writers such as Julia Kristeva, Luce Irigaray and Hélène Cixous. These writers, although critical of what they see as Lacan's phallocentrism, have each, in their own distinctive way, used his idea that the unconscious is directly accessible in language to build new theories emphasizing difference, fluidity and multiplicity of identity and sexuality. Building on Lacan's idea that the unconscious and desire can be located only in language, they re-position Lacan's negative view of 'femininity' as the lack or absence of meaning into a positive force for change. What they see as the bogus certainties of patriarchal rationality can be subverted and challenged only by using what has been repressed in language, the lack, a 'feminine' space capable of creating a revolution in language. In each of the theories of Cixous, Kristeva and Irigaray, the pre-Oedipal mother, though she is used to different effect, is seen as the site of potential meaning which pre-exists the patriarchal reign of language based solely on meanings associated with the father and the phallus. Only poetic language which works by turning established categories and syntactical structures inside out and upside down can reflect the world of the pre-Oedipal mother and challenge the often false certainties of the law of the father.

Cixous (a creative writer and literary theorist), Kristeva (a professor of linguistics and later practising psychoanalyst) and Irigaray (a philosopher and later practising psychoanalyst) argue, from significantly different perspectives (they cannot be considered as a group), that culture stands in need of a new kind of discourse which reflects the little girl's phantasies around the mother, the female Imaginary currently repressed in language. Cixous and Irigaray emphasize the need to undermine and eventually supersede current language based on male phantasies in the Imaginary. They argue that the latter is characterized by false, excluding binary distinctions in which woman always occupies the inferior, negative term and by a desire for sameness rather than difference which effectively denies the meaning of embodied women and the origin of men in women's bodies. They want a new discourse, what Cixous calls '*écriture feminine*' in which the erotic mother–daughter relationship is symbolized and thus incorporated and, as Irigaray puts it, given symbolic 'shelter' in culture. Kristeva, concerned to avoid any hint of a feminine essence, argues that culture requires a double discourse which symbolizes both the meaning of the father and the need for law and boundaries on phantasy and the subversive meaning of the mother and unconscious desire. Emphasizing the castration implicit in all identity and therefore the existence of the 'other' or 'stranger' within us all, she warns feminists against the dangers of idealizing 'woman' as the absolute 'truth' and denigrating 'man', thus perpetuating the destructive projection implicit in the false idealization of power based on the phallus and the denigration of women. Kristeva's work, in particular, has been very influential in the field of literary studies where she has emphasized the need to seek the disruptive, subversive elements in writing by locating the desire concealed in the text. (For accounts and discussion of the work of these three writers, see Grosz 1989, Jardine 1985, Minsky 1996, Moi 1985, Tong 1993.)

The rejection of experience

Lacan's theory, particularly in relation to its focus on language and meaning, on the precariousness of cultural 'masculinity' and the underlying gap within us all between what we are and what we want to be, is immensely powerful in many ways, particularly in its intriguing multidirectional quality. But the problem is how can we tell how much of it is 'right', or rather 'right enough' to lead us in positive directions. Theories, like ourselves, can be very suggestive and illuminating about some things but wrong about others. In many ways, Lacan's antihumanist theory seems dazzlingly coherent and inclusive. As he himself claimed, everything seems to be accounted for in his three over-arching structural orders of the Imaginary, the Symbolic and the Real. But beguiling as Lacan's theory might be, should we question whether *all* identity is a fiction, a delusion, a false self, an empty narrative with which we stuff ourselves? Are we all completely 'hollow' men and women? Can there really be no 'heart' or substance at the centre of ourselves or culture because we, and what we care about, are created only through the arbitrary meanings of language originating in loss and lack? Can we accept that nothing exists outside language, that there is no part of our experience which is not mediated by culture? Is the discovery of the possibilities of the free-play of desire in texts really the only thing we can aspire to? Is language more exciting than life or the expression of desire in embodied relationships? Has something crucial about human existence and the basis for value been missed out in Lacan's theory or is this question fuelled only by the desire to fill the gap, the want-to-be, for Imaginary satisfaction?

Lacan has been accused of phallocentrism by feminists. But, in fact, Lacan makes it clear that he is not trying to justify the rule of the phallus in culture but rather to unravel how its power is derived. Rather than celebrating its power, he exposes the fragility and vulnerability of 'masculine' identity, knowledge and culture but at the same time argues that we cannot do without it. We cannot live in a sea of unconstrained longing for our mother even though the meaning of the father who impedes us seems to evaporate before our eyes. In this sense Lacan's theory is 'realistic' in that it always points in two directions at once. Life and reality are characterized by ambiguity, ambivalence and contradiction. More controversially, Lacan suggests that we need to conform but also not put any trust in our conventions, subverting them when we can with the poetic 'truths' of the unconscious. This presupposes that nothing we articulate in ordinary rather than poetic language derives from intuitive forms of knowledge gained outside language which contain their own versions of 'truth' or wisdom. From a more object-relations-based perspective, Lacan's insistence that all identity and experience outside language is delusory, and his conviction that the only 'authentic' sexual relation exists in poetic language in the free-play of the unconscious involved in free association, does cause problems. The neat connections Lacan makes between the social and the psychoanalytic, culture and sexuality, consciousness and the unconscious are theoretically enticing but, from a more eclectic standpoint, his theory leaves out all the existential ways of being and knowing based on the intuitive experience which often occurs outside conscious knowledge or language. The object-relations work of Klein, Winnicott, Bion and Bollas suggests that the way we 'learn from experience' is emotional and that those who cannot 'learn' from experience suffer from an emotional disturbance. Focusing on the early relationship with the mother, object-relations theory suggests that a vital dimension of our identity emerges intuitively and empathically within the emotional containment which characterizes our earliest pre-verbal relationship with the mother. This part of our identity is not delusory although it may take place within the same space as narcissism. This experience prepares the child not only for its entry into the meaningful creativity offered by the symbolic but also into the intuitive dimensions of relationships which form a crucial component in the capacity for emotional intimacy in relationships and creative living. This is another level of thinking or knowing which may not be 'thought' in language and which goes beyond desire. The absence of this dimension in Lacan's theory means that we have no way of grounding feelings: for example, the intuitive feeling that certain kinds of outcomes which lead to the oppression and suffering of others are unacceptable and morally impoverished. Without the experience of emotional insight and the capacity for some emotional integration, we have no basis for value or a sense of moral purpose. Lacan is able to argue that no position is more valuable or 'moral' than any other because his theory leaves out the dimension of human experience which gives most of us the kind of information we need to generate values. At some level, many of these lie outside the arbitrary grasp of language and culture. When we express the desire for some notion of 'decency' in government or revulsion at the cruelty of genocide, object-relations theory suggests that we refer back to a quality of experience and knowledge which may pre-date language but which is not a delusion. In taking an uncompromising anti-humanist stance which sees effective identity as solely the subjectivity constructed within language and the Symbolic, Lacan pays little attention to the intuitive, empathic language of feeling which lies outside texts. The rationality of the Holocaust triumphed in the absence of certain states of feeling or empathy. The devastating effects of the arms trade, environmental pollution, the economic relationship between rich and poor can be rationalized only when they are separated from emotional insight. Psychoanalytic theory as a whole suggests that it is the capacity for the integration of emotion and thought rather than a splitting off from feeling which endows us with a reliable sense of what is morally or humanly acceptable and what is not.

For Lacan, in the psychoanalytic session, insight emerges solely in the conversion of what he calls 'empty' speech into 'full' speech or in the bringing together of the conscious and the unconscious in speech. In contrast, object-relations theory, and especially Winnicott's and Bion's work, suggests that emotional change in the analytic session occurs as much as a result of the emotional texture of the empathic relationship between patient and therapist and the emotional containment and digesting of the patient's anxiety, impulses and phantasies by the therapist as it does through interpretative insight. Bion's object-relations theory suggests powerfully that rational thinking does not operate within a vacuum of identity. We do not enter language naked and empty of anything of value with an identity based only on narcissistic delusion. (There is a brief summary of Bion's ideas in chapter 8.)

So from the perspective of other important psychoanalytic approaches (Freud's and object-relations), Lacan's theory, while fascinating and useful in some ways, seems to leave out a lot of what is important about being human. Freud's and object-relations theory suggest that creativity and sexuality are about living in relationships with people as well as in texts. Individuals communicate intuitively and empathically as well as through signs. From a psychoanalytic perspective, Lacan's theory suggests a splitting off or defence against the painful emotional and sexual aspects of those pre-verbal dimensions of existence it leaves out. This is not entirely different from what may be seen as the grandiosity and denial of difference involved in the old 'grand narratives' and some modernist views of the world where empirical experience counts as the only form of 'truth'. Here, only certain experience, stripped of all its intuitive and feeling components, is legitimized as science and reason. Lasch's work, among others (Frosh, Irigaray, Weatherill), as well as much art and literature, prompts the question of how much contemporary Western culture rests on almost pathological levels of emotional denial and defence which have traditionally been defined as cultural 'masculinity' and reason. To what extent can Lacan's work be entirely excluded from such a cultural scenario? Chapter 10 contains further discussion of Lacan's work in the context of other psychoanalytic perspectives and explores why his work has been so appealing and persuasive.

6

Womb-envy and women as 'too much of a good thing'

Against the faith men had in the institutions they, not women, had shaped, women upheld some other principle of selfhood in which 'being' sur-passed 'doing'. Long ago men had noted something unruly in this. Women simply enclosed the space men longed to penetrate. The men's hostility was aroused.

Ian McEwan, The Child in Time

Change and psychical survival

Freud made penis-envy, and the little girl's longing to be what her mother wants, a central component of his theory of 'feminine' identity. But he largely bypassed the issue of womb-envy and the little boy's discovery that he can never be like his mother, although initially, like the girl, he shares a merged identity with her. Womb-envy is an idea that was taken up very persuasively by Freud's female contemporary Karen Horney, and by his follower Melanie Klein.

Within the context of contemporary culture and the notion of a crisis in male identity, the concept of male womb-envy is very suggestive. It poses the question of whether changes in the social position of many women, in Western countries at least, may mean that women are being increasingly experienced by some, perhaps many, men as 'too much of a good thing' – as a 'good thing' which is 'getting out of hand'. In the past twenty years women have increasingly moved into areas traditionally associated with cultural 'masculinity', generally experiencing an increase in status as they do so. However, when men have entered areas traditionally associated with cultural 'femininity', such as shared child care, house-keeping and become more emotionally nurturing and open, less patriarchal or 'laddish', they risk a decline in status because of the continuing low cultural status of 'femininity'. If, as some have suggested, there is a perceptible crisis in male identity, a sense of confusion about what 'masculinity' is really about, often mixed with considerable guilt, then psychoanalytic theory as a whole suggests that it may be closely related to women's changed social situation. This, crucially, often includes women's withdrawal of their unconscious projections of the active, assertive, strong dimensions of themselves onto men. This means that as women re-own these previously split-off, unconscious aspects of themselves, they can no longer represent the traditional 'feminine' attributes of only passivity, vulnerability and lack. Psychoanalytic perspectives suggest that access to bisexual dimensions of ideality is frequently associated with creativity and emotional growth. Of course, this kind of psychological development must be set alongside social and economic changes in the Western, industrialized world. Increasingly reliable methods of contraception but also higher levels of male unemployment, job insecurity, low pay and other forms of social damage have changed the balance of power between men and women. Women no longer need to be in men's care and protection as much as they used to be because they have fewer children, but many men have lost access to the work which allowed them to offer that economic protection.

The concept of womb-envy suggests, at its starkest, that for some, perhaps many, men, as a result of very early experiences of envy of the mother's physical and emotional richness and power, which remains emotionally unresolved, the subordination of women in some form or other is the only means of maintaining psychical survival. In a culture where many women no longer collude with many men's view of them as predominantly passive, lacking and vulnerable, many men suddenly find themselves without women onto whom they can project their own unconscious lack, loss and envy and may feel overwhelmed by feelings they never knew they had. Unfortunately, culture, by undervaluing emotional ways of thinking and knowing, cuts many men off from the very thing they need to help them – the emotional means of resolving and coming to terms with feelings of envy, loss and vulnerability in a creative way. Most women, unlike men, are not required by culture to cut themselves off from the emotional, intuitive world of the mother. They tend to turn to intimate conversations with friends, counselling or psychotherapy in search of emotional containment and intuitive ways of learning and change, whereas men often tend to attempt to obliterate emotional pain through work and social camaraderie which often involves heavy drinking. For increasing numbers of men, especially young men, the psychical protection of work, job security and the camaraderie associated with these has been lost.

Womb-envy

The existence of womb-envy was specifically recognized, though in different ways, by both Freud and Melanie Klein. However, Freud regarded it as much less important than penis-envy in the unconscious construction of identity whereas Klein regarded it as of central importance. But it was Karen Horney, a follower of Freud, who first took issue with his theory and proposed the idea of womb-envy. She produced the first full-blown critique of Freud's theories in the late 1920s and 1930s. However, although she opposed Freud's view that penis-envy was central to the construction of 'feminine' identity, she acknowledged the existence of penis-envy on the basis of her own clinical experience. 'Every little girl who has not been intimidated displays penis-envy frankly and without embarrassment' (Horney 1967: 133).

Horney thought that the importance Freud attributed to penis-envy sprang from male narcissism and, most importantly, envy and fear of women's physical capacity to reproduce. She thought that under normal circumstances penis-envy was not the result of a phantasy of being castrated and that the little girl, motivated by both a clitoral and vaginal capacity for pleasure, moved happily towards her father in the context of the idea of the penis as a source of pleasure. Horney took the view that penis-envy only persisted in the little girl in the case of severe disappointment such as rejection by her father. In such a situation the little girl, caught up in a phantasy that she is being castrated, identifies with her father instead of her mother and regresses back to the pre-Oedipal stage in self-defence. This means that she then returns to a 'masculine' stance in relation to her mother and the resulting penis-envy is a secondary rather than primary development which results from what Horney calls 'wounded womanhood'. Horney, unlike Freud, believed in an essential, biological 'femininity'. She argues that the little girl's sense of injury to her 'womanliness' is a projection which stems from the little girl's inability to tolerate her own desire for the father. This re-formulation of Freud's ideas began a famous debate about the construction of 'femininity' which came to be known as the Jones–Freud debate in which Ernest Jones and Melanie Klein were involved in disputing Freud's idea of penis-envy. In her paper 'The Dread of Woman', Horney (1932) argues that men are deeply envious of women's capacity for motherhood and are subject to womb-envy. She suggests that the loss of identification with the mother is something from which many men may never be able fully to recover. In this paper she argues that male envy of women is as powerful as their desire for them and that this is evident in the widespread existence of myths and legends, folk-tales, fairy stories, poems and religious stories which contain warnings and cautionary tales of what happens in relations between men and women. Horney argues that men's unconscious dread of women inspires not only denigrating or idealizing phantasies of them but also homosexuality. This arises from a fear of castration during penetration as a result of a phantasy of the vagina as a *vagina dentata* (which appears in the Native American myth of the toothed vagina). Horney writes 'Only anxiety is a strong enough motive to hold back from his goal a man whose libido is assuredly urging him on union with the woman' (Horney 1967: 137).

Melanie Klein agreed with Horney's ideas and argued that she was the first person to explore the female castration complex from inside the Oedipal crisis rather than as something which precipitated it. In the context of her own theory in which the mother's rather than the father's body is the major preoccupation of the child (the mother's body initially contains the idea of the penis [father] as something of secondary symbolic importance), she argues in her paper 'Early Stages in the Oedipal Conflict' that boys mask and over-compensate for their womb-envy by both an over-estimation of the penis and a displacement onto the intellectual plane (Klein in Mitchell 1986: 75). She writes that what she calls the 'femininity' complex in men goes with an attitude of contempt and 'knowing better' and is highly asocial and sadistic. (Here, 'knowing better' suggests the over-valuation of knowledge and reason within culture and the devaluation of the intuitive and emotionally creative levels of existence which prevent reason being sterile and arid.) Klein took the view that women's main unconscious preoccupation is the fear of damage to her internal organs as a result of projection and a paranoid expectation of attack from the mother rather than penis-envy. She emphasizes the child's envy of the mother rather than rivalry with the father as the major obstacle to psychical development and change.

Freud thought penis-envy was more important than womb-envy because it explained something he found difficult to elucidate without it – the little girl's dramatic transfer of desire from her mother to the father in the Oedipal stage of early childhood. The little girl, Freud suggests, crosses over to the father initially in the wild hope that he will give her a penis with which to captivate her mother. However, although evidence for womb-envy, a phenomenon which parallels penis-envy, is central to Freud's view that all identity is inherently bisexual, Freud still considers clinical manifestations of womb-envy to be structured in relation to the phallus, indicating homosexual desire for the father rather than bisexuality. The male desire to have a baby must then suggest an attempt to stave off fear of castration by the father just as regression to an earlier pre-genital stage of anal eroticism might also be. Freud, perhaps unconsciously protecting his own 'femininity', perceptive as he was, seems blind to other perceptions of womb-envy.

Two discoveries of sexual difference

If we keep in mind the powerful experience of physical and emotional creativity the child has of the mother from birth, it seems very probable that children of both sexes have another, perhaps earlier experience of sexual difference than the one described by Freud. Here, when the little boy discovers that he is not the same as his apparently powerful, creative mother, it is he who feels he is lacking rather than the girl. The conversation might run like this:

> Boy: Mummy, when I grow up I'm going to have a baby like you.
> Mother: But you won't be able to because boys can't have babies.

After this momentous discovery, the small boy has to repress his envy and loss of the powerful physical and emotional meanings of the mother in favour of the cultural power associated with the father and the phallus. Psychoanalytic theory suggests that this denial of the mother's *being* as much as the loss of her as a potential *lover* may be a major factor in the construction of 'masculine' identity. Let us imagine the experience of the small boy in the throes of Freud's Oedipal crisis.

For the small boy suddenly faced with the reality that he is not his mother, or even like her, and with a terrifying sense of potential psychical disintegration, an identification with the cultural power of the phallus, however unjustified, must appear as the best option available. Having assumed in his so far short life that he will be like his mother in every way including her ability to have babies, he suddenly has the devastating realization that he is not and never will be. At this moment he is compelled to give up his original 'feminine' identification with his mother and urgently seek another identity. In the father he finds someone who he discovers has the same kind of body as himself and who also seems to have won the loyalty of his mother. The little girl, as Klein suggests, may also initially envy the creative power of the mother but eventually, and usually, she discovers that she can identify with it, in a way the boy never can, because she has the same kind of body as the mother.

The experience of lack, loss and castration in relation to the mother may well pre-date or occur around the same time as the small boy's recognition of sexual difference based on the presence or absence of the penis which Freud makes central to his theory. In Freud's version the little boy sees the little girl, rather than himself, as the one who is lacking. As Silverman argues, Freud's failure to acknowledge that the small boy will have already encountered a variety of losses or castrations (which include the loss of the mother's breast and other part-objects) before the discovery of sexual difference, which is based on the presence or absence of the penis rather than the womb, may be an unconscious defensive manoeuvre on Freud's part (Silverman 1988: 14–17). The assignment of lack to the girl conceals both Freud's and the small boy's unbearable sense of loss and lack on two counts: in relation to the need to separate from the mother's body experienced as part of the self (initially children of both sexes exist in a state of symbiotic shared identity with the mother) and the loss of the mother as the object of desire. Perhaps the most devastating of the boy's losses, together with the loss of and separation from the mother as a love-object, is his necessary loss of identification with his mother in order to enter culture and language. He can neither be the mother nor possess her. This first loss is loss of the only sense of identity he has ever had up until that moment, or feels he ever wants. It also represents the illusion of Imaginary wholeness which the girl may be said also to want in her desire for a penis. She wants to be everything, her father as well as her mother, both male and female at the same time. In the moment the little boy realizes that he cannot *be* his mother, before or at around the same time that he has also to recognize the other harsh reality that he cannot *have* the mother to himself either (a realization shared by both sexes), he has to relinquish his original identification with her, as we have seen, and find something else to be. In this situation the phallus and the girl's apparent lack come to his rescue. The little girl, although she knows she is the same as the mother, at another level may operate within the cultural realm of meanings which, resting on the denial of womb-envy, prefers sight and reason to insight, intuition and empathy. Within culture, as Freud and Lacan argue, she may give up the powerful creative meanings of her own and her mother's body but at the same time, as an adult, she can usually, privately and in the company of other women, still take for granted these self-evidently valuable meanings. The same cannot be said for most men who must separate from the mother as an object of love and shared bodily identification, with all the envy and loss this often entails.

Sight and in-sight

If we think about the powerful meaning that the mother's body has for the baby, it seems very strange that it does not function as an equally powerful symbol in culture. As many have observed, Western culture largely denies, or is highly ambivalent about, the value of the mother and all she represents. If we build eclectically on the ideas of Klein, Horney, Freud and Lacan, is it possible that in early childhood, during what Freud calls the Oedipal phase, a form of emotional knowledge associated with the small child's *in-sight* into the powerful creative potential and significance of its mother, derived from its experience of her emotional handling as well as its phantasies, is unconsciously repressed or denied in favour of the *sight* of the visible, palpable phallus? One form of recognition of sexual difference based on the mother's body is overshadowed or eclipsed by another based on the male body and the visible presence or absence of the phallus. This scenario suggests that the child discovers difference in two ways: one in relation to wanting, desiring to be what the mother *is,* and the second in relation to desiring to be what the mother *wants.* This unconscious denial of the insight into the creative and containing meanings of the mother may have momentous consequences. It may mean that a vital form of emotional knowledge, underlying perhaps what we commonly refer to as wisdom rather than reason, is not generally available to the child or culture as an alternative form of consciousness and knowing. The child denies in-sight (in-visibility?) into the powerful creative meaning of the mother in favour of the sight or visibility of the phallus which is subsequently discovered to signify cultural power. The effect of this may be that, in the small boy, in particular, unbearable feelings connected with early multiple loss, envy and lack may never be integrated within the self. Instead, they can only be dealt with in culturally approved ways which cut him off from the very emotional as opposed to rational capacity he needs to resolve his feelings. They can be mastered through work and the status and substance provided by what Lacan sees as the seductive fullness of patriarchal 'masculine' culture and knowledge – the apparent certainties and truths encapsulated in the dominant forms of technological rationality and science – or they can be unconsciously projected outwards onto others, most obviously women. This may mean that women then contain both the boy and later man's two losses, his double lack: the loss and envy of his identification with the mother's body and the meanings associated with it (an apparent castration by nature) and the loss of his mother as a love-object (symbolic castration by the father or culture).

Male and female projections onto the 'other'

As we have seen, Freud's theory suggests that women may be the first major focus of many men's unconscious projections because the small boy discovers difference *at the same time* as he feels potentially over-whelmed with a sense of lack and loss. He's lost his mother as a love-object, he's been turned into a victim of symbolic castration by his father. But he also finds he can't have babies like the mother as the girl can, although at first he assumed he could. However, it is the father or culture with whom the boy now has to identify, even if highly ambivalently, if he wants the chance of having any viable identity at all. So, the small boy's new identity, which must substitute for his earlier 'feminine' identity, contains both his phantasized father, now internalized as a cultural authority, but also himself, now phantasized as the hapless victim of symbolic castration. But, as we have seen, the newly discovered other, 'woman', provides him with a psychical waste-bin into which he can externalize what still threatens to overwhelm and 'unman' him. By becoming the symbol or carrier of the despised male unconscious lack and envy, the idea of woman as vulnerable and lacking allows many men to feel potent and in control. As Kristeva reminds us in 'Women's Time', in the Oedipal crisis the small boy may often internalize a father who is, in phantasy, both victim and executioner *at the same time* as he discovers sexual difference (Moi 1986: 209–10). In the context of having to face his painful loss of identification with his mother (one kind of symbolic castration) and his symbolic castration by the father, 'woman' provides the perfect 'other' (with whom he has already shared a fused identity) for these projections. This predicament of psychical depend-ence on women may then set the scene for women's denigration and dread of women (and hatred of dependency generally) but at other times also the idealization of woman as the lost part of the man's identity to which he secretly longs to regain access by becoming her lover and, in phantasy, regaining access to the womb. Male phantasies of women testify to this swing from idealization to denigration: angel, goddess, Madonna, earth mother, wise woman from the mountains, 'my other half' but also evil witch, slag, bitch, whore, slut and, less attacking but still denigrating, battle-axe, bimbo, bit of skirt, little woman, doll, pet, chick, baby, ''er indoors' (this last vividly suggests the need to confine the 'feminine' part of the male internal world which has been split off into women).

Although the small boy's loss of the mother is based largely on an unconscious *phantasy* of total goodness and plenitude and unending bliss, this doesn't make the loss any more bearable. Phantasies are powerful because they feel entirely 'real' when we are under their sway. The problem for individual men and women and the cultural meanings they produce may be that, as a consequence of early, infantile phantasies, women, who are suddenly discovered as the 'other', may perversely come to represent male loss and lack, particularly, as a result of unconscious womb-envy, for the very reason that they are experienced as so full and present. When pregnant with a male baby, they may appear as the symbol of total plenitude, the ability to be both sexes at once. As we have seen, in both Klein's and Winnicott's versions of object-relations theory, the mother, in the small child's experience and phantasy, has usually been experienced as potentially overwhelmingly powerful, as the 'good breast' positively brimming with goodness and emotional riches, the fount of all life, comfort, wisdom and identity itself. This may have little to do with the mother's actual feelings about herself. However, as Kristeva points out, the problem is that, for both sexes, the opposite sex or 'other' may come to represent what she calls 'the stranger within' us all – our own otherness, the part of our identity we don't want to acknowledge which has been pushed out into the external world (Kristeva 1981).

In the context of this 'stranger within', we need to recognize that women also project things they find painful about themselves onto the opposite sex. Freud came to the conclusion, late in his career, that some women habitually project onto men their anger with the mother for all their losses in childhood such as weaning, toilet training, prohibitions on masturbation but particularly for not giving her a penis. However, as we have seen, according to Klein, women project envy onto men as a result of initial envy of the mother's breast which is subsequently transferred to the penis. Still envious of the mother, they turn against men in order to spoil them as love-objects for the mother. Marie Maguire argues that because women often project their unacknowledged, unconscious, active, assertive, aggressive dimensions onto men, it encourages those women to see themselves often as objects and victims rather than as active, powerful subjects of desire (Maguire 1995: 2, 103). These women, then, may feel under attack from men for reasons which have nothing to do with the men as individuals. For such women, all men, rather than some, may be seen as potential attackers and abusers. However, these projections have been significantly less culturally far-reaching and destructive in their effects than men's projections of loss and lack onto women. Some men's rueful assertion that women don't really want a 'new man' who likes looking after babies if they can have one who prefers riding a Harley Davidson has some truth in it. The contradiction between our conscious and unconscious wishes is one of the complications we all have to deal with. Maguire argues that, to overcome this, women need to be helped to identify with the 'masculine' components of the mother and the father just as men need to be able to identify with 'feminine' nurturing qualities in the father and mother (Maguire 1995: 8, 39, 68).

A further factor in the visual dimension of the boy's response to the penis is the visual perception that the body of the little girl is so different from the mother's (it lacks breasts and never becomes pregnant) which distances the idea of the little girl's (female) lack from the powerful meaning of the mother's body. So the little girl's undeveloped body perhaps shields the little boy from his awareness that he lacks what his mother has (and the little girl will have) and that in future he is barred from the emotional world she represents. By representing lack in relation to a different part of the body and zone of experience, the little girl in seeming to be nothing makes the disappointed little boy feel as if he might still be 'something'. He needs the power conferred onto the father, and those who possess the penis, and the father to fill the gap left in his identity by his mother. An inflated view of the value of the penis in the context of what he now may unconsciously regard as his biological and emotional inferiority in comparison with the mother is, of course, reinforced by culture.

So, to achieve separation, both children suffer losses in different ways. The little boy suffers the loss of the mother as an object of desire and his identification with her. The little girl also suffers the loss of her mother as an object of desire and the loss of what it apparently takes to be her mother's lover, subsequently translated in culture as being defective as a full human being. But, in addition, the little girl, paradoxically, as well as representing the lack of what the mother wants, also has to carry a third lack which denies any value to her special capacity to reproduce herself. Through the mechanism of projection she seems to come to symbolize exactly what she is not – the male unconscious – that is, male lack of being what the mother (and she) is. This reversal, achieved through projection, brings about what looks like an astonishing unconscious conjuring trick in which women, who are so self-evidently present, magically come to represent absence and the lack in culture.

Sexuality and identity

As we have seen, penis-envy, stripped of Freud's unconscious over-valuation of the penis, seems, predominantly, to be about the small girl's unconscious envy of what the mother apparently desires more than the girl herself. Little girls phantasize that they can't possess the mother for ever as a lover because they lack the right kind of body, but they can be *like* her. So the little girl gives up her original form of sexuality but not her identification with the mother. On the other hand, culture doesn't require the little boy to deny his original form of sexuality. He can eventually love someone *like* his mother, although not his mother, but culture does require him to deny his first *identification* with her. However, although culture compels him to give up this initial 'feminine' identification with the mother, at a further level, so does biology. Even if he manages to hold on to some or all of his 'feminine' gender, for the boy, having babies is permanently and uncompromisingly ruled out. So, in Freud's theory, at the end of the Oedipal crisis, even if things go smoothly, paradoxically children of both sexes may unconsciously yearn to be what they are not, or rather, more than they are. Penis-envy and womb-envy, in different degrees, linger respectively in both sexes, as a result not only of cultural prohibitions in relation to gender but also, in another sense, biology. So, in the perception of the little boy, anxiously in search of an identity, women are biologically endowed with a powerful and seductively creative identity which he can never share. Although 'femininity' and 'masculinity' exist across the boundaries of the body, up to now at least, the capacity for motherhood remains exclusive to women whether or not they choose it and whether they achieve it through reproductive technology or naturally. 'Feminine'-identified men cannot have babies but 'masculine'-identified women can and do. In this particular sense, biology is, uncomfortably, destiny and this may have a major bearing on some men's perception of women (see figures 1 and 2).

Women as 'too much of a good thing'

So, psychoanalytic theory as a whole suggests that, in a very real sense, boys lose both their primary sense of being and their first object of desire in early childhood. This can be seen symbolically as a double castration in the unconscious. Girls have to sustain the unconscious loss of a part of their sexuality but not their identification with the mother but carry men's unconscious sense of lack and vulnerability. But, despite these layers of conscious and unconscious undermining and denial, most women do recognize the value of the powerful creativity of motherhood even if culture denies their insight into this power. One of the major conflicts many women have to cope with within culture is that, in relation to the creative potential of their mother's body and what this entails *and* their ability to use rationality in the symbolic even if they do

	[Sexuality]	[Identity]
Boy	*Retains* first main disposition to *heterosexuality* because mother is female	*Denies* first *identification* with mother and the emotional world she represents
Girl	*Denies* first main disposition to *homosexuality* because mother is female	*Retains* first *identification* with mother and the emotional world she represents

So both children *deny* half of what they are:

    The boy *denies* part of his identity
    The girl *denies* part of her sexuality

May lead to: Boy ⟶ womb-envy
               Girl ⟶ penis-envy

Figure 1   Freud's Oedipal crisis

Two encounters with sexual difference:

1 **Insight** by girl and boy into mother's capacity to reproduce

    Girl: powerful sense of identity because same as mother

    Boy: feels lacking (womb-envy) because different from mother

2 **Sight** by girl and boy of visible penis

    Girl: feels lacking (penis-envy) because different from father

    Boy: powerful sense of identity because same as father, reinforced by culture

Phallus represents the rescue from the lack

Figure 2   Extended version of Oedipal crisis

not fully identify with it, they frequently *feel* powerful despite culture's denigration of them. Sometimes a sense of their power leads some women to play themselves down in relationships and in the workplace. High unemployment among men may only compound this problem of playing themselves down. At the same time, the unconscious rejection of 'femininity' by many women as well as men, as Freud's theory suggests, expressed in some women's unconscious envy of men, has made them very vulnerable to collusion with the cultural reinforcement of the idea of women's inferiority. In Britain, women are almost twice as likely to suffer from depression as men.

In this kind of context, the problem of difference may stem from the unconscious perception, in many varieties of 'masculine' men, that most women do not have to *struggle* as much for psychical survival as they do. Their perception may be that, however much culture may deprive women of a cultural identity, the creative and powerful identity of the mother is usually always available to them, in addition to, at least potentially, the other identities available to men. (This perception is independent of whether women avail themselves of this procreative identity or even value it themselves.) The identity of the mother is, of course, intimately involved with the crucial and delicate business of making an eventual identity possible for her children. For many men, in the context of their two major unconscious childhood losses, their unconscious perception of women may be that, in spite of women's difference and their persistent cultural denial and subordination in many quarters, most women *still* emerge in possession of what seems to them (the men) to *really* matter. This seems to take the form of at least one emotionally authentic and creative and usually guaranteed source of identity and pleasure (all other things being equal) which is not based on the small boy's phallic myth of control and omnipotence – the biological capacity literally to double themselves and, subsequently, in most cases, the emotional capacity to be what Winnicott describes as 'good enough' mothers. Being 'good enough' consists, fundamentally, in being able to respond creatively to another human being's helplessness and need to organize and establish an identity, before their own; Bion describes this as the mother's capacity for emotional containment. Julia Kristeva describes the common maternal capacity to respond, not as masochism or a fitting in with a cultural requirement for women habitually to sacrifice their own needs, but as the suspension of narcissism: 'the slow, difficult and delightful apprenticeship in attentiveness, gentleness, forgetting oneself' (Kristeva 1992: 206). This is not the same as the mother treating the child as an extension of herself which Freud argues *is* narcissistic and potentially damaging to the child because it demands compliance, is not emotionally containing and denies the creative involvement of the child in the formation of its own identity. Winnicott, a paediatrician as well as a psychoanalyst, thought that this capacity for creative response-ability in handing her power over to the child and helping it make the crucial transition from phantasy to reality was characteristic of most mothers, even though a minority undoubtedly feel uncomfortable in this role. Some women may not find mothering appealing because of early difficulties with their own mothers which remain unconscious and unresolved.

The envy and hostility that object-relations theory suggests might be provoked in some, perhaps many, men by their childhood insight into women's creative capacity for motherhood would help to explain the ambivalence of patriarchal culture towards motherhood and its unconscious need to make it as difficult as possible for women to achieve much success in anything except motherhood. History testifies to the need to keep women out of both the cultural sphere and high-status professions or jobs. Even today, if a woman is allowed to have uninhibited access to *both* her potentially fulfilling, powerful and pleasurable identities – as a mother *and* in a rewarding job or career or other activity perceived by many men as part of the male domain – she may begin to erode many men's sense of themselves. An active, speaking woman, who refuses the position of being only the lack, effectively throws the lack back onto men which may then threaten some of them (through the mechanism of paranoia) with psychical death. Irigaray has emphasized how women symbolically represent castration and the death of male identity for many men. In male phantasy, women's power threatens to run out of control as soon as she seriously enters culture as if she too is a subject and demonstrates her intellectual and creative as well as physical and emotional capacities. Crucially, then, in some men's *phantasy* women may be seen as not just men's equals but substantially *more* than men. They threaten some men with being 'too much of a good thing' – sexually attractive, emotionally literate and capable of intimacy and containment, capable of having babies if they want to and intellectually and creatively clever and effective in what was previously considered the male sphere. Increasingly, such women are becoming more visible in culture. In many men's phantasy, a creative mixture of activity and passivity, there seems to be something 'real' about women with which the culturally accepted phallic version of 'masculinity' cannot compete, which does not seem to rest on the need for power and control. Because this kind of patriarchal 'masculinity' is such a distorted form of masculinity, motherhood is bound to smack of an *authentic* source of creativity and power whereas, as Lacan has suggested, the status of patriarchal 'masculinity' feels unconsciously bogus because it actually rests on symbolic castration by the father. The existence of womb-envy suggests it also rests on the denial and concealment of envy of women. Of course, in 'reality' rather than phantasy, the capacity to have emotionally and sexually fulfilling relationships, to be a good father, to get satisfaction from creative work, what Freud called the crucial indicators of psychical health, the capacity to love and work, are realistic, authentic ways of being a man. But, the *phantasy* in many men, derived from childhood, may be that lack of the power to reproduce leaves men irretrievably deficient. Culture may then offer the only way of making good this lack, together with the control and domination of women. Within the social sphere, unemployment is a multiple disaster for many men in that, as well as depriving them of economic substance, it also deprives them of the substance of a viable identity often, these days, in relation to wives or partners who are in work, even though this work is often part-time, unskilled and low-paid which may, perversely but unconsciously, be some consolation to some men. In such circumstances, even women who feel they have very little may be experienced as 'too much'.

So envious feelings in relation to the notion of women 'having it all' and being 'too much', together with the association of the mother with the unlimited control over them as helpless babies and small children emphasized by Winnicott, may reinforce sufficient unconscious envy in some men to make it a major feature of their relationships with women in the private, public and institutional spheres. Cruelty towards women and the continual unconscious spoiling and exclusion of women's potential power within the social, cultural and political spheres function, perhaps crucially, as the means of preventing some men's sense of psychical annihilation. Klein suggests that the young baby sometimes attempts to spoil the mother or 'good object' by biting the breast so that it no longer provokes its envy. The continual unconscious spoiling and exclusion of women's potential power in the form of paying her 70 per cent of the male wage in Britain where women form one-third of the total workforce, the 'glass ceiling' put in place by many men's dislike of working under a woman, may still operate as the means of preventing 'masculine' psychical damage. Winnicott argues that men would be less likely to take revenge on women through cruel cultural customs and social exclusion if they could acknowledge their dependence on women. He links men's tendency to seek danger, for example, starting wars, to envy of the risks women are exposed to in childbirth.

The womb as such has historically possessed predominantly negative cultural connotations of instability, hysteria, madness and disease. More recently, it has specifically connoted various forms of women 'going wrong', including the need for increasingly technological male management of birth and the need for hysterectomies to maintain women's health. Given that we might expect the over-riding connotation of the womb to be physical creativity, these meanings may well be symptoms of historically and culturally mediated manifestations of womb-envy (Lomas 1966). Bruno Bettelheim, Karen Horney, Peter Lomas and many others have suggested that culture resonates with what look very much like cultural signs or symptoms of womb-envy. The Christian idea that Eve was created out of Adam's rib and the idea of Eve as the idealized virgin before the fall only to become, afterwards, the whore whose seductive presence drags men into sin and misery, the ancient belief that Zeus gave birth to Athena out of his head (mind), the female muses who are said to inspire male poets, Plato's view of the productions of philosophers as metaphorical 'births', the widespread practice of clitorectomy, the male fear in some primitive societies of contact with women during menstruation in case it leads to their death (perhaps this symbolically refers to the death of their identity or psychical death or castration), the idea of the castrating woman in Medusa's withering phallic look which turns men to stone, the ancient oriental practice of binding women's feet, couvade rituals in some cultures in which men simulate labour pains, 'lie in' after their wives' deliveries and go on special diets, ceremonial male initiation rights which produce the 'birth' of man in adolescence, the male control involved in reproductive technology as well as the management of modern childbirth, the attempt to control women's right to decide who they may marry, whether their female babies should be allowed to survive, whether they can have abortions – these are just some of a vast and diverse collection of cultural ideas and practices which smack of the male need to control and limit women's power or try to appropriate it for themselves. Eva Feder Kittay (1986) gives an extensive and persuasive account of anthropological and historically situated material which seems to provide convincing evidence for the widespread phenomenon of womb-envy and the need to appropriate women's power to procreate. Irigaray, in her critical analysis of both philosophy and psychoanalysis, has emphasized the persistent historical absence, denial, denigration and appropriation of the 'feminine' and particularly the denial of the mother and the womb as the point of origin in the realm of knowledge as well as in the social world (Irigaray 1993a: 39–40). As has been widely documented, historically and globally women have persistently been designated as irrational, ultra-precarious and particularly prone to madness. As Irigaray sees it, women have been compelled to live in a state of cultural dereliction without a symbolic shelter for their raw experience (Irigaray 1993b). Psychoanalytic theory generally suggests that this has been a psychically necessary

unconscious manoeuvre by many men to sustain their idea of themselves, and culture, as rational and objective – and to protect them from
recognizing their unconscious dependence on women.

Robert Stoller (1975) argues that early anxieties about giving up an
initial identification with the mother, rather than about fear of castration
by the father, lead men to fear becoming female or homosexual. Stoller
argues that this gender confusion may result in the desire to return to a
fused relationship with the mother, a dread of the loss of identity which
would result and a longing to gain revenge on the mother for initiating
this painful conflict. This results, according to Stoller, in the cruelty,
misogyny and emotional withdrawnness characteristic of 'masculine'
men. This involves an idealization of cultural 'masculinity' and the father,
a failure to identify fully with authentic male strengths and assets and a
devaluation of the early experience with the mother.

Knowledge as a defence against womb-envy

Let us turn now to the effects that envy of women may have on what
culture counts as knowledge: the issue of womb-envy and the victory of
'seeing is believing' over 'intuition and insight is believing' in relation to
the small boy's (and some girls') identification with the phallus. This
occurs at a time in the child's early life when most children, although
they may be smitten by the discovery of difference, are also very keen
to know where babies come from. This question, according to both
Freud and Klein, becomes of crucial importance for the child during the
Oedipal crisis. Freud regarded this phase of almost frantic curiosity as the
beginning of intellectual curiosity which he saw as an unconscious
means to what he called 'mastery' – that is, control over overwhelming
feelings of loss in relation to the mother (SE 7: 197). This suggests that
after the discovery of the phallus, the boy, in particular, needs to
substitute his emotional insight with theoretical knowledge or intellectual
understanding which serves to shore up the pain of separation and loss.
The girl doesn't have to separate from her mother so radically and can
eventually re-identify with her in spite of gradually becoming aware that
her insight into her and her mother's creative, emotional power isn't
shared by culture. But perhaps we need to remember that, although
many women are subordinated in culture, most women talk about much
of their experience of motherhood with pleasure and describe it as a
major source of fulfilment in their lives despite the low status, frustrations
and disappointments it brings. In this sense, paradoxically, many women
themselves feel that their bodies and their capacity for emotional respon-

siveness, at one level, allow them to defy the attempts by male-dominated societies to control them. Klein also saw the child's initial forays into knowledge as an unconscious wish to discover more about the womb, that is, the contents and nature of the mother's body (which for Klein includes the phallus as well as other babies) (Mitchell 1986: 75). Modern Kleinians distinguish fundamentally between the desire for knowledge, including the desire for emotional insight, and envious curiosity involving a wish to gain power and control over others in order to deny feelings of vulnerability, loss or humiliation.

The fact that the phallic sign is so visible in the child's early body-preoccupied world might help to explain why observation-based knowledge has been so privileged within culture compared with intuitive forms of knowledge. But psychoanalytic theory generally suggests that academic, theoretical knowledge of all kinds, historically dominated by men, may be used as a flight from emotion, as a narcissistic defence against feeling. The fact that culture demands that boys have to try to separate from the mother much earlier than girls in order to become culturally acceptable 'masculine' men means that many men are cut off from emotional forms of knowledge and insight at a very early age. They may, therefore, remain more prone to making narcissistic, 'false self' identifications with exclusively rational forms of knowledge than women (see figure 3).

The concept of repressed womb-envy suggests that consciousness and culture may stand in for the loss of everything the small boy valued and desired at the beginning of his life and protect him from knowing anything about it. If, as Klein suggests, womb-envy is often concealed in

---

Unconscious womb-envy, inherent in male cultural power, which subordinates women

Unconscious penis-envy, inherent in female cultural subordination

Both involve denial of initial *insight* in favour of *sight* (visibility) in many men and women

Insight and intuition also denied as valid cultural knowledge in favour of *sight* – observation-based empirical knowledge (science)

Figure 3   Effect of extended version of Oedipal crisis on culture and history

men by displacement onto the intellectual plane, that is, onto reason and knowledge, then culture represents not only repressed desire *for* the mother but also a repression of the desire to be what the mother *is*. Culture then represents the male substitute for procreation when childbirth is not an option. As many have suggested, there are a declining number of emotionally containing institutions within culture and those which exist, such as counselling and psychotherapy agencies, are largely used by women and frequently denigrated by culture at large, particularly by the media. In recent years, women's cultural position has been improving in Western Europe but caring cultural institutions concerned with ordinary human need, in, for example, the old, sick, disabled, displaced or poor, have frequently been described in the language of dependency and the 'nanny state'. This might help to explain the maintenance of the stark equation between culture ('masculine', active and independent) and nature and the body ('feminine', passive and dependent). So language, science and rationality, when they are separated from feeling, dependency and vulnerability, become the defence not just against the loss of the mother as a love-object and symbolic castration, as Lacan argues, but also against womb-envy and the unconscious dependence on loss of the mother's creative, containing being. This would suggest why the mind must be kept so firmly insulated from the body along with the intuitive, empathic forms of thinking and emotional containment associated with the mother's body. A marriage between body and mind might risk breaking down the defences that the mind and culture provide against conscious knowledge of the powerful meaning of the mother's body. If Lacan is right, the phallus and culture protect against unconscious symbolic castration but also envy of the womb. The relationship between the sexes seems to be marred by a refusal by culture to recognize the power of women's procreative as well as sexual being.

In this context it is tempting to speculate on the recent popularity of the post-modern idea of identifying with 'feminine desire' or the repressed unconscious in the text and the theoretical project of 'writing the feminine'. This may be empowering and liberating at one level but when it elevates the 'feminine' in male rather than female bodies, it suggests it may be another cultural expression of womb-envy. As Irigaray (1987) has suggested, it may be an unconscious attempt to share in or even appropriate women's power while ignoring the reality that, however much some men may identify with the 'feminine', women's bodies are a dimension of women's identities that they cannot share. There is a difference between identification and identity, gender and sexual difference. In the matter of being heard, it still makes a difference whether one is speaking from a man's or woman's body. Suzanne Moore (1988) calls the academic fashion for men writing their 'femininity' in literary texts as a 'kind of gender tourism' because men can always return 'home' to male bodies which, all other things being equal, do make a real difference to their lives in terms of cultural power.

Intuitive, empathic ways of knowing

The work of French feminists such as Hélène Cixous, Julia Kristeva and Luce Irigaray, who have used some of Lacan's ideas to develop their own approaches, suggests that we all stand in urgent need of a new way of thinking and writing. As Kristeva (1992: 155–6) suggests, this would involve the conscious recognition of two powerful symbols of meaning, without denying the value for living of either: it would have to emphasize the creative, containing power of the mother or womb, symbolizing a non-rational, intuitive way of knowing and creativity as well as the rationality of existing language. The meaning of the phallus as male power would need to be balanced by the meaning of the womb and female power and creativity. If reason does represent a defence against unconscious dependency on the womb and women's creativity, this may seem like a lost cause. However, reason would be relieved of what many now see as its preoccupation with control because of the modifications made possible by access to insight and empathy associated with the new symbolic meanings of the mother. This way of making sense of the world would incorporate our need for reason and intellectual understanding but also our pressing need for more wisdom to go with it. More access to intuitive, 'artistic' forms of knowledge within the individuals and institutions that make up culture might begin to modify the seductive but often emotionally sterile rationality associated with commercially competitive and technology-driven cultures, frequently lacking intuitive insight or, for want of a better word, wisdom and the capacity for intuitively informed judgement. Perhaps the arms trade and global environmental pollution are two of the most striking examples of what we could define as the lack of a capacity for intuitive insight. The incorporation and valuing of more empathic, intuitive forms of emergence knowledge within culture generally might lead to the emergence of more creative, and at least partially integrated, identities which are neither dependent on power and control or under the sway of unconscious phantasies based on denial.

Winnicott (and Marion Milner in her work described in chapter 9) also suggest, from a more humanistic standpoint, that we need to make our knowledge more like an art than a science. They suggest that forms of unconscious, intuitive knowledge and experience associated with the mother are able to resonate with our conscious experience and generate a form of 'truth' based on emotional insight as well as intellectual 'cleverness'. The latter, without our awareness, often involves a danger-ous dissociation of feeling from experience. We know that most forms of what we describe as art are inspired by feeling rather than reason and yet have their own distinctive, intuitive mode of structuring reality. Winnicott regards this artistic process of shaping and patterning as an intuitive activity having more to do with finding an external form for our uncon-scious experience than rational or logical coherence. Working within what Winnicott calls the domain of 'the transitional space', Winnicott and Milner suggest that many creative artists are primarily involved with the negotiation of the relationship between their inner and outer worlds using the different physical media – sound, paint, stone, words, in fact anything in the external world – as the external means by which they give symbolic shape to their unconscious preoccupations.

So psychoanalytic approaches generally suggest that we need many of the conventional meanings and categories which we call consciousness but always underpinned by intuitive sources of meaning derived from our earliest experiences of being, relating and loving with our mother. These form our psychosomatic experience of her. This way of thinking does not imply a return to the phantasy of an Imaginary self which is unified and centred. It still entails the need to live with the notion of precariousness, in varying degrees in different people, in the context of identities which are always subject to the eruption of the unconscious despite their greater access to emotional insight and integration. The development of more intuitive forms of knowledge, which are able to draw on our experiences of both inner and outer 'reality' and do not deny and retreat from such experience, might allow us to humanize both reason and unconscious desire. Object-relations theory suggests that this seemingly potent combination must still be inadequate if it lacks the intuitive dimension of the mother's symbolic meaning. As well as its drives in relation to the mother, the baby learns both to 'be' and to relate to her intuitively through its love for her. Without the component of the capacity to 'be' as well as to 'do' our knowledge will inevitably lack the humanity to which much of it aspires.

Change and the withdrawal of projections

Inevitably the question arises of how change could take place on any significant scale when, for many men and some women, psychical survival seems to require the unconscious denial of envy and dependence on the mother and the emotional meanings and forms of knowledge associated with her. How can we address the widening gap between many men's increasing sense of uncertainty, if not crisis, and an increasing sense of integration, confidence and status in women as a result of withdrawing their projections of strength and assertiveness from men, often with the help of counselling and psychotherapy (see figures 4 and 5)? Psychoanalytic theory as a whole suggests that change in many men would require them to acknowledge terrifying feelings of loss, lack, emptiness and envy previously associated with women which would risk psychical collapse or breakdown. Although there have been signs of new forms of 'masculinity' in the Western world, there have also been signs of identity crises in men and a backlash against women.

Normally, the kind of changes which may need to occur in many men (and some women) can only be achieved in the containing environment of psychotherapy. Here, hostile and idealizing projections can be withdrawn from others and painful feelings of loss, lack and emptiness consciously experienced and mourned, while at the same time the patient is supported and protected from too great a sense of annihilation. Through gaining access to painful emotions through emotional insight and the emotional, intuitive texture of the relationship, a more authentic sense of identity can emerge. Since large parts of the self are no longer projected outwards onto others in the external world, these others do not need to be controlled or systematically attacked and spoiled. Clearly, mass analytical psychotherapy is not a realistic means of achieving

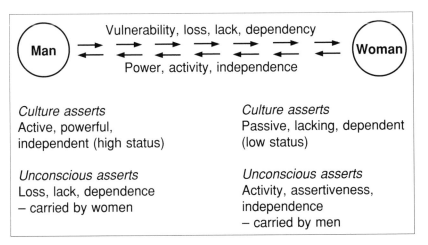

Figure 4   Projections and cultural change: traditional situation

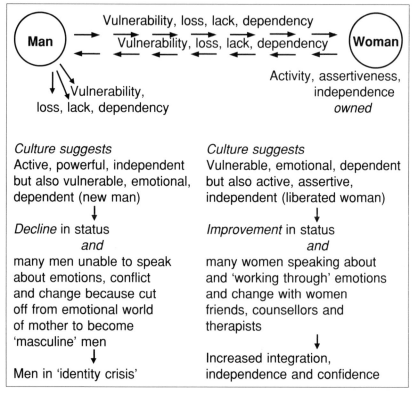

Figure 5 Projections and cultural change: developing situation?

change although many women are increasingly involved in it, but awareness within culture generally of the painful unconscious predicaments many small boys as well as girls face in early childhood may in the long term help to bring about change.

Containing the unthinkable

The question of how we could realistically achieve such awareness is a daunting one. Winnicott and Bion have emphasized the mother's role as an emotional container, not only literally as the womb which contains the unborn baby during pregnancy but also for the baby's earliest anxieties, impulses, sensations and emotions. Bion suggests that the mother, acting as an emotional mediator, emotionally contains, digests or metabolizes what initially confuses or terrifies the baby so that these feelings and sensations are made bearable for the baby. She makes it possible for the infant to begin to 'think' the unbearable through phantasy and later language. In this sense, the womb is a metaphor for containment. Although it may be women's changing position that is one of the main factors responsible for precipitating a crisis in some men's identity, perhaps many women, in the context of their association with the idea of emotional containment (which culture endorses), could help to produce a cultural climate in which the issues surrounding this crisis could be talked about more openly. Clearly, in a situation where gender crosses the boundaries of the body, some men, who have not split off from the mother so radically, could be and already are involved in this process. There are, of course, also some women who have split off from the emotional, containing dimensions of themselves. But if substantial numbers of men need to gain access to the emotional creativity associated with their bisexuality and their unconscious envy of women, then perhaps the role of women is very important since culture permits them to remain most in touch with intuitive forms of knowledge and a capacity for emotional containment through their longer association with the emotional world of the mother. Without idealizing this emotional world, or underestimating the difficulties some women have in separating from a merged identity with the mother and becoming more independent, perhaps many women are in a position to provide the kind of protective emotional environment necessary for some men close to them to confront their unconscious womb-envy. This might represent an important way of making it more possible for more men to risk allowing themselves access to potentially overwhelming emotions which often remain unconscious and externalized. However, this would mean that women may also need to confront issues they may not have been very aware of before. They may need consciously to recognize their capacity to provoke envy whatever they may actually feel about themselves (however unenviable they feel), and how this envy may relate to the vulnerability, dependence and the fragility of the dominant form of cultural 'masculinity'. And, since it seems both sexes sometimes envy the other, women would also need to acknowledge the envy some women project onto men even if this is not culturally reinforced. In recent years, a welter of articles with titles along the lines of 'What are fathers for?', 'Are fathers really necessary?' 'Men, who needs them?' seem to be less than helpful and to have the flavour of female envy. Psychoanalytic theory suggests strongly that fathers serve as a vital alternative space in the child's mind which is separate from the intensity of its fused relationship with the mother and which eventually allows it to separate. The capacity for emotional intimacy, creativity and the ability to be a good enough father as one half of the sexual couple is surely where an important part of the 'real', rather than phantasized, phallic 'masculine' identity lies. Women may also need to acknowledge consciously how much, in the past, if less so today, they have unconsciously projected the active, assertive, aggressive parts of themselves onto men for a variety of complex cultural and psychical reasons. As women increasingly own their own strength and assertiveness and remove these projections from men, it is not surprising that for many men the psychical effects may be devastating. Despite the danger of making some men's hostile projections worse, perhaps more awareness among women of these kinds of unconscious issues might mean that some women (and men who feel able) could produce the kind of protected, loving, containing cultural climate necessary for a more open, empathic, containing dialogue between men and women.

7

The psychical significance
of fathers

If, as seems probable given my sporadically fatherless state, part of my obsession with Arsenal was that it gave me a quick way to fill a previously empty trolley in the masculinity supermarket, then it is perhaps understandable if I didn't sort out until later on what was rubbish and what was worth keeping. I just threw in everything I saw, and stupid, blind, violent rage was certainly in my field of vision.

Nick Hornby, *Fever Pitch*

Cultural change

The second half of the twentieth century has seen significant changes in the perception of the social role of the father largely as a result of social changes in the position of women making many of them less vulnerable in a variety of ways. In previous centuries women were self-evidently frequently physically vulnerable at times when they were heavily pregnant, giving birth and when they were nursing and caring for babies and small children. At such times, their and their children's economic survival normally depended on support from the father who fulfilled the role of provider and protector. Until the introduction of contraception during this century, the times when a woman was economically and physically vulnerable extended over a large period of her life until the menopause (babies were often born at one- or two-yearly intervals if she survived childbirth). This 'real' rather than constructed vulnerability inevitably served to sustain conventional gender categories of women as vulnerable, needy and dependent and men as strong, powerful protectors whose physical viability remained unimpeded by pregnancy and childbirth. This justified attribution of vulnerability to women on the basis of one feature of their life seems, within patriarchal societies, to have been elaborated to include all dimensions of a woman's being. A conception of women as constitutionally vulnerable (and we need to remember many women died in childbirth) may well have contributed to the concealment of many men's sense of vulnerability and lack. But since the introduction of contraception, when women became able routinely to limit their fertility, the basis for the traditional role of the father as protector and provider has become increasingly difficult to sustain. Now that the very real vulnerability that accompanies pregnancy and nursing lasts for only relatively short periods of most women's lives, women have increasingly demonstrated that they also can be providers, especially when nursery provision, or good quality child-care is available to provide support. Without this support, many women's lives are still very inhibited. However, nowadays, for large parts of their lives, most women in Western countries work full or part-time (women now represent one-third of the workforce) and, increasingly, frequently fill the role of sole provider in single-parent families.

If, as psychoanalysis suggests, significant numbers of men project their sense of lack and loss onto women, the cultural peeling away of the need for men to provide for physically and economically vulnerable women risks exposing many men's own vulnerability for the first time. As suggested in chapter 6, in this new situation, it now seems very important to identify new forms of 'masculine' identity which can incorporate vulnerability and dependence and no longer depend on women having the monopoly on these human attributes. It also seems important to explore the unconscious as well as social significance of fathering.

In recent years, in the wake of feminism and significant changes in the position of women, ideas about the meaning of fathers and fathering have become increasingly confused. Sometimes, some women seem to have come to the conclusion that the only way a man can be a good father is if he recognizes his repressed 'femininity' and nurturing capacities and becomes a substitute mother. Certainly many men have become much more emotionally involved with their children and practically involved in their day-to-day care (despite lack of support in the workplace), but since 'masculinity', for a long time, appeared to rest unconsciously on the idea of being 'not the mother', 'not woman', it also seems important to discuss in what ways the psychical meaning of the father entails something more than simply sharing the role of the 'good enough' mother. To what extent is the unconscious meaning of the father for the child related to the father's difference from the mother in terms of the psychical space he takes up in the baby's mind?

Leaving aside for a moment Lacan's idea that language is the symbolic 'place of the father' rather than the actual father, psychoanalytic ideas about the unconscious meaning of the father suggest that, although he is usually not as crucial as the mother in the first weeks of the baby's life (where the mother is available), he is nevertheless very important to the development of the child for the very reason that he is qualitatively distinct from the mother. The baby has never lived inside the father's body so the sense of bodily connection is likely to be of a different order from that with the mother. The father smells different from the mother because his body is chemically different, he lacks breasts, possesses different genitals and feels generally different when the baby is held against his body. In psychoanalytic terms all this makes him admirably suited to symbolizing a dimension of existence which extends beyond the baby's sense of still having a merged existence with the mother's body, that is non-fusion and distancing. This is quite different from his symbolizing a radical break with emotional or intuitive ways of being and relating which has been traditionally implicit in the patriarchal conception of fathers. Marie Maguire, in the context of the fluidity of gender, suggests that among her patients there are men who are much more emotionally containing and intuitive than their more career-oriented female partners (Maguire 1995: 36). However, the child may still turn first towards the mother for emotional comfort because of its earliest bodily connection with her when she and it were indistinguishable. But psychoanalytic theory as a whole suggests that the father, as well as having the capacity to be emotionally nurturing, also crucially needs to symbolize the baby's eventual psychical move into a life beyond the comforts of the mother's body. In this sense, the father as the symbol of culture is everything that is not part of the magical sense of physical and emotional connectedness that the baby experiences with the mother before it begins to separate.

In this context, let's look again at some different psychoanalytic accounts of the unconscious meanings of the father, all of which emphasize the need for him to be experienced psychically as someone different from the mother. Let us begin with Freud's idea of the symbolic father. This is the Oedipal father who, crucially, sets boundaries to the child's so far unboundaried, phantasy-based existence with the mother so that it is able to cope creatively with the frustrations and pleasures of living in culture.

The symbolic father

For Freud, our early identification with the father at the end of the Oedipal crisis installs culture at the centre of our being. The father symbolizes the world beyond the mother's body which we eventually have to learn to inhabit in spite of the limitations it puts on our phantasies. Freud suggests that this identification is easier for boys than girls who have less to gain from such an identification, feeling themselves, according to Freud, already lacking. Their fear of the father is therefore reduced and so they have less motivation to identify with him fully. Little girls are also encouraged to make a secondary identification with the mother (one which is no longer fused with her) which is not open to the boy as an alternative in the same way. But for children of both sexes, to different extents, Freud's symbolic father, as the symbol of culture, represents the third term in the child's mind which breaks in on its phantasies of unending bliss with the mother. The father represents the reality of the world beyond the mother–baby couple and, importantly, one-half of the sexual couple which preceded the child from whose relationship the child must inevitably be excluded. He helps the child make the vital transition from a state of merged oneness with the mother to a state of twoness by converting the mother–baby couple into a triangle. This triangle crucially symbolizes the incursion of the laws and constraints of culture into the child's phantasies of continued merged bliss with the mother. Freud stresses that the Oedipal crisis always contains three people. But it is not only about the child's desire. It is also about the desire of and between the mother and father which, together with the discovery of sexual difference, sets in motion the Oedipal crisis and makes the child, in one sense, into an outsider. So, in Freud's theory, the father represents the reality principle, the boundary which permanently blocks and resists the child's omnipotent phantasy of total possession of the mother (the pleasure principle). The father confronts the child with a tangible cultural obstacle which produces the sense of loss which has to be repressed into the unconscious, what Lacan later calls the unobtainable 'want to be' that undermines, but at the same time enlivens, all identity. For Freud, it is the father who necessitates the loss that must be at the centre of all human identity and the child's eventual recognition of this loss enables it to form part of a new sexual/emotional couple also able to tolerate the addition of a child and the beginning of a new generation beyond their own. Freud suggests that if the child fails adequately to internalize this cultural block on its dreams of omnipotence and perfection the child may never be able to distinguish clearly between its desiring and murderous phantasies and the demands of reality. So Freud suggests that the boy simultaneously needs to identify with the positive strengths of the father and other men and face the fact that he will never possess the mother or have her reproductive capacities. At the same time he has to resolve his womb-envy by identifying with the mother's nurturing capacities as well as her psychical 'masculinity'.

Although the idea of the symbolic father and the notion of the super-ego have been interpreted by some as a prescription for the maintenance of the status quo, I think this is to miss the importance of what kind of status quo they refer to. Essentially, in Freud's theory, the symbolic father seems to stand for the following ideas: we cannot remain permanently in a merged state of being with our mother, dominated by phantasies, without destroying the possibility of 'growing up' in the sense of having satisfying, relatively un-merged relationships with other people; we can never achieve a state of wholeness, perfection and complete fulfilment because other people can never be entirely predictable so we have to learn to tolerate frustration; we have to submit to the law and authority of culture to the extent that we cannot have incestuous relationships with our parents and, in normal circumstances, we should not murder those people who stand between us and our desires; our anatomy is out of our control in the sense that it is unrealistic to hanker after a penis if we are a woman or a womb if we are a man. This suggests that without cultural inhibitions, we can, ideally, lead creative, fulfilling lives whatever sex we are. These ideas, taken together, seem to amount to a recipe for developing the capacity to cope creatively rather than destructively with both frustration and happiness, with which many of us would agree. In essence, they highlight the resistance that reality offers to our omnipotent childhood phantasies of incest, murder and the idea that nothing is ever going to stand in our way.

Some writers, among them Christopher Lasch (1980) and Bob Weatherill (1994), have suggested that modern Western cultures actively encourage an infantile narcissistic quest for the immediate satisfaction of desire. They suggest, controversially, that this is linked to unparalleled levels of violence in Western societies. They argue that this situation arises from a cultural failure to recognize the importance of the meaning of the symbolic father as the link which makes possible the development of our ability to move from a state of mind based on the fused mother–baby dyad to one more realistically based on a triangular relationship involving the father, culture and the idea of 'not me'. Without access to paternal boundaries, they argue, we are all abandoned to a meaningless 'maternal' soup of potentially unsatisfiable desire, psychically unable to move away from the symbiotic and impossible fused love for our mothers into identities that can find a creative rather than infantile outlet for our sexual and aggressive desires. In other words, like Freud, they are suggesting that it is our identification with the father and culture, and the guilt and inhibition of our desires that it provokes, which allow us to accept loss and achieve our human potential. It is the father who helps us to comprehend the gap between what we are and what we want to be so we can use it creatively. This is the alternative to what they see as the infantile delusion that we can fill the gap in our 'selves' through cultural substitutes for the mother such as, in today's Western culture, sex, drugs ('Ecstasy' as the phantasy of bonded bliss with the mother?), consumption of consumer goods and celebrities, religious and spiritual cults, political ideologies. These offer us the illusion of a completion they can never deliver, the loss of which the symbolic father represents.

However, modern culture also offers many people new opportunities and pleasures which are not backward-looking or regressive. Education and a vast variety of artistic forms of cultural enjoyment extend our horizons and deepen our experience as well as giving us pleasure. Such experiences, in contrast to narcissistic gratifications, often confront us with the painful domain of loss as well as joy, rather than encouraging us to deny it as do purely escapist forms of pleasure. In achieving a creative meeting of our inner and outer worlds, art, in whatever form, seems to be able to energize and change who we are. But although many regard Lasch's and Weatherill's view of modern culture as unduly pessimistic, its emphasis on the need for the symbolic father as that which sets limits to phantasy seems very important to keep in mind. As we shall see, psychoanalysis more generally suggests that if the constraining meanings of Freud's symbolic father (and, as Marie Maguire argues, the 'masculine' aspects of the mother) are not sufficiently internalized by the child, or are unavailable or actively rejected, the child has nothing to put the brake on its unrealistic omnipotent phantasy of unending pleasure with the mother or cultural substitutes for her. Without the boundaries of the binary oppositions the father represents, the child may lack the ability to find its place in the fluid, infinite space of culture. But, we should be careful not to confuse the idea of a symbolic father with a patriarchal or authoritarian father. It is widely recognized by contemporary psychotherapists and analysts that there is a strong correlation between authoritarian, violent and abusive fathering and criminal violence. If the father can be emotionally available to the child he will allow it to separate from the mother without too much sense of loss and anger because the father is ready and willing to support the child's need to come to terms with the 'reality' of culture. However, the reasons for violent crime cannot be laid exclusively at the door of a failure of children sufficiently to internalize the symbolic father's constraints on their violent impulses or of a violent father. We know there are also social roots to violent behaviour such as poverty and, more recently, relative poverty in the midst of others' affluence, new technology and labour market changes, unemployment, low pay, economic insecurity and poor conditions of work, bad housing, homelessness and social discrimination which often interact with individual psychical factors. All of these create societies of insiders and outsiders which breed frustration, despair and violence.

Lacan's re-development of Freud's theory withdraws from the world of experience and emphasizes 'the place of the father' as language, thought and culture, while relegating experience of the actual father to the world of phantasy or what he calls the Imaginary. For Lacan, Freud's symbolic father becomes specifically the constraints and opportunities offered by ordinary language and knowledge. But although these appear to endow men, at least, with power and subjectivity, Lacan argues that this power is riven with symbolic castration and loss (the father kept the mother, not the child). For Lacan, it is repressed unconscious Desire for the mother which drives our futile search for the ultimate 'truth' in language. He insists that only free association in language can harness this unconscious desire in the service of the provisionality, indeterminacy, fluidity and ambiguity of poetic truth. For Lacan, this is the only kind of 'truth' capable of subverting what he sees as the necessary but bogus law of the father enshrined in language which claims a certainty and authority which is never justified. For Lacan, without the incorporation of unconscious desire, the law of the father as culture can be only a fiction and 'reality' can never be more than a kind of cultural dreaming, divorced from the deepest 'truths' of our existence which can only be encountered in the challenge of the poetic. Although Lacan is not interested in actual embodied fathers, his ideas do deepen our understanding of Freud's notion of cultural substitutes for the symbolic father and their roots in distance and loss.

The father as an alternative psychical space

Klein's view of the father is distinctively different from that of both Freud and Lacan and, in its emphasis on inner states, is not much concerned with cultural issues directly. However, it is often illuminating and interesting. It springs directly from her ideas about how the ordinary baby initially relates to the mother through instinct-based phantasies of hate and envy as well as love. (Of course, as we have seen, Winnicott and many others take the view that Klein pathologizes the ordinary baby and that her theory of hate and envy only applies to babies who have suffered maternal deprivation.) However, this may include many people.

Klein argues that fathers are, at first, understood by the baby through its phantasies about the mother. Her idea of the symbolic breast contains the notion of the penis (father) and siblings who, in the background of the baby's mind, are implicated in the painful absences of the mother. Although this equation of the breast with the penis sounds rather an odd idea, in therapy with adults it is possible to meet individuals who have never learned to distinguish between the meaning of the breast and that of the penis, mother and father, so continuing oral needs for the mother become mixed up with the penis and sexuality. However, Klein thought that, in the early months, the baby often experiences the idea of the father as its ally who helps it to protect the mother from its destructive phantasies which the father sometimes is able to carry instead of the mother. The sense of the father diffuses the intensity of the baby's bond with the mother. But, as the baby enters the depressive position, it becomes increasingly aware that the father is another person who sometimes deprives the baby of the mother's presence. This gradually destroys its illusion of unity with the mother and provokes jealousy with which the baby has to learn to cope. The father may then directly become the container for the baby's hostile projections but he may also represent the baby's reparative and creative impulses which help it deal with its destructive ones. In this way the father may be the catalyst for new creative phantasies which can help the baby separate from its initial merger with the mother and, eventually, grow up and lead a relatively independent existence. Unlike Freud, Klein argues that the child eventually wants the father primarily as a love-object rather than a means to the possession of the penis and the power associated with it. But she also suggests that the quality of the baby's relationship with the mother often dramatically colours what is possible with the father so that the latter may be regarded with more or less envy or gratitude depending on the baby's overall attitude to the mother and life in general. If the mother is experienced as frustrating and depriving the child may seek revenge by turning towards the father. Julia Segal suggests that this may happen in a mild way after a time of increased separation from the mother such as her returning to work, weaning or the birth of another baby. If the child has had a good relationship with the breast, the baby is likely to feel love and concern for both parents, but if the child feels less secure or envious it may seek refuge with the father although this hatred towards the mother may emerge later in the relationship with the father. Indeed, the child may turn back to the mother, idealizing her in order to deny an underlying hatred. However, the bad relationship may continue to affect the child and may be played out in future relationships with men (J. Segal 1992: 48). In some circumstances the child may also turn towards the father because it perceives him to be as deprived as itself and this may lead to a perception of him and other men as lacking any power of their own. This may affect future relationships with men. The child's perception of the father as weak and needy may be confirmed or contradicted by the way the mother represents him to the child. If the mother continually denigrates the father, the child may never be able to see the father in any other light, whatever he is actually like. The presence of the father also provides an alternative model for the child or, if he is violent, weak or abandoning, someone who the child definitely does not want to be like. If the child actively tries not to be like the father it may be forced into a false, shallow way of being because the father's place in its identity is empty because it has had to be denied. This denial of a part of the self may be particularly likely where a family is split up and either or both parents denigrate the other. Because both parents are a part of the child's inner world of loved objects out of which it constructs its 'self' through its identifications, this represents a denigration of part of the child's identity. If one of its crucial internal objects is made to seem bad or worthless, the child may feel a corresponding unconscious sense of worthlessness and emptiness which it may have to split off and deny.

Klein's work suggests that the child may experience a violent father as expressing not only his (the father's) own destructive feelings but also, through projection, those of the child so the father's violence is denied. This may then set up a pattern of denial of feelings which have been split off so that later, as an adult, violent behaviour may suddenly erupt from nowhere because ordinary expressions of anger have been denied. This may cause bullying and violent behaviour towards other adults and children to test the recipient's capacity for violence and its damaging effects. Criminal violence such as murder and rape is frequently found to be linked, in men, with a history of a violent father.

In marked contrast to both Freud and Klein, Winnicott has very little to say about the father, always placing the emphasis on the self-sufficiency of the mother and baby couple. In his theory the father seems to hover in the wings as one whose role is primarily to offer sexual and emotional support for the mother so that she feels able to provide the child with the kind of 'good enough' mothering it needs. As we have seen, for Winnicott, the 'good enough mother', within the transitional space, through her own intuitive and empathic responsiveness, is able to allow the child, untraumatically and almost imperceptibly, to creatively play itself into an identity which is no longer symbiotically and erotically merged with her own. These days, however, most analytical therapists would challenge this rather isolating view of the mother and baby and argue that the father, ideally, should also be a part of the transitional space. But Winnicott distinguishes carefully between the capacity for 'being' in a state of merged oneness with the mother's breast and also the capacity, later, to feel 'at one' with others (what he calls the feminine) and 'doing', which involves active relating and passive being related to (what he calls the masculine) which *both* exist in all of us. This suggests that the mother can compensate for an absent or unavailable father by making sure she brings her own culturally 'masculine' qualities into the transitional space. However, Winnicott also suggests that male misogyny and the cultural need to control women may well be directly related to the child's early experience of the mother's overwhelming power, both in phantasy and actuality during infancy and childhood. He also suggests that the mother is associated with the baby's earliest chaotic potentially annihilating experience of its non-being. Using this kind of perspective, the feminist writers Nancy Chodorow (1978) and Dorothy Dinnerstein (1978) have argued that the father's presence and active involvement in child care helps to diffuse the mother's power and ultimately benefit women and men.

The third position

More recently, Kenneth Wright, in his book *Vision and Separation* (1991), has persuasively built on Winnicott's developmental ideas to generate a striking theory of his own about the psychical role of the mother and father. He argues that the father is central in both the structuring of identity or the self and in the development of symbol formation. He suggests that the third position (that is, when the baby first becomes an observer) begins to exist in the emerging space between the mother and baby pair as the baby begins to experience the mother as a separate, observing object rather than one always fused with itself. At this moment, the baby discovers that it is not only a subjective 'I', though one still merged with the mother, but also an object of the Other's look. Wright argues that the growing importance of the mother's smiling, resonating facial gesturing both endows the baby with a self through mirroring the baby to itself, but also, because it is primarily *visual* rather than dependent on touch, at the same time opens up the possibility of space and distance. The mother's face cannot be incorporated and possessed like the breast. Whereas the breast is the first object of the baby's drive, the mother's face is the baby's first 'not me' object which, because it is visual, suggests a distance between the mother and baby which cannot be totally captured and which is the harbinger of the baby's eventual need to separate. Wright argues that the opening up of this third position culminates in the triangular position with the father who is originally seen as outside the mother–baby pair. It is the firm establishment of this third position, for which the distancing meaning of the baby's visual perception of the mother's responsive face has been the vital preparation, which acts as the guarantee for this space as the eventual site for thought and representation. Wright suggests that the third position is an essentially 'looking' position created by the exclusion of the child from the separate space of the parental sexual couple during the Oedipal period. Here, the child experiences itself as an object of looking from someone with whom it is not merged. Here, in contrast to the fused relationship between the baby and mother, 'looking' means the father's looking at the mother–baby couple and the beginning of an absolute prohibition on touching or doing in relation to the mother. Although the visual nature of the baby's response to the mother's face had opened up the possibility of distance and separation, the touching and doing so central to the baby's earliest merged identity with the mother could remain part of the baby's psychical world right up until the onset of the Oedipal period. But, for Wright, the father's space in the baby's mind means the separation of a looking space from a touching, doing space. In this way it paves the way to the development of the vital space for symbolic representation where touching and doing, although implied in the experience which lies behind the meaning of the symbol, are at another level, banished by it. In this sense, the symbol, or word, empty of touch, becomes all that remains of the child's early, blissful attachment to the palpable mother's body which the baby believed to be a part of itself. But, nevertheless, it is something which allows it to complete the crucial exploration of the world for which the mother's body and face prepared it. In the context of the triangular position, Ronald Britton (1989), in his paper 'The Missing Link', emphasizes that the baby at this time also has to learn to differentiate between types of relationship. It discovers that the sexual relationship between the parents is different from the parent–child relationship and that, although it may still have a relationship with the mother, it cannot be a sexual one (Britton 1989: 85).

So Wright argues that the first stage of getting outside the self, of making a distinction between self and other, of becoming self-conscious, involves looking back on itself with the mother's eyes in the two-person position. The next developmental stage is that it has to move to a three-person position where it can see itself objectively in relation to the mother through the father's eyes.

Wright stresses the importance of the child's experience of the father as essentially different from the mother so that he will also be loved and hated like the mother but for different reasons. Crucially, Wright argues that, apart from smelling different and holding and handling the child in a different way, the father is experienced as radically different from the mother who still has an aura of remembered oneness about her. In this sense the father replaces the mother, standing for an unknown world away from her body and another dimension of experience. Wright argues that, rather than the father having a subsidiary role to the mother, the father stands for continuing progression and development and exerts a positive pull on the child drawing it away from what he describes as the 'regressive undertow of the maternal, merged identity'. This means that the absence of a father may mean that the child collapses back into a continuing state of merger with the mother. But Wright emphasizes that a father can be emotionally, if not physically, absent as is the case when there is a weak father who is not sufficiently separated from a dominating wife. He may strive to be a mother to his children so depriving the child of the experience of difference and, as Wright (1991: 114) puts it, 'a star to steer by'. Importantly, in the context of current discussion about the significance of the father, Wright argues that if the child turns the father into a substitute mother, it may try to recreate the fused state it once had, or lacked, with the mother. This means that the opening-up meanings of the father are obscured and the child may have only a fragile hold on separateness and difference. Wright suggests that for the little girl this situation might mean a blurring of the distinction between fusion and sexuality and, for the boy, there may be difficulty with homosexual longings for a substitute father. This suggests that another woman, such as an aunt or partner in a lesbian couple, may not be a satisfactory substitute for the father because she is also likely to become another mother figure with which the child becomes fused.

Wright suggests, like Freud, that in the Oedipal period the child is forced into the position of the outsider or third person, but in contrast to Freud he argues that the child feels threatened by the father not so much because of its sexual desire for the mother but because of its continual need for security. Wright argues, following Winnicott and Bowlby, that the most important issue is that it is the child's attachment to the mother which is being threatened.

Wright emphasizes that, although the space of the father represents a firmer, more absolute kind of boundary and distance than the one the child has known within its distancing experiences with the mother, this space is precarious throughout life and its boundaries can be relatively easily invaded by more 'embodied' rather than symbolic objects (like consumer goods, cultural icons or a romantic infatuation) that can attempt to fill it up and obliterate it. These are the same as the narcissistic objects in what Lacan calls the Imaginary which offer the phantom of blissful wholeness and completion with the mother and vie for control of identity with the precarious meanings of the Symbolic. So, for Wright (1991: 136), the father's space proclaims 'no entry' and 'no touching'. Wright emphasizes that it is only in such a space of radical separation from the mother 'that fully-fledged, representational symbols, such as those of language, can arise' (Wright 1991: 121).

Looking at Freud's concept of the father and mother as the ingredients for a new part of the ego (through the processes of identification and introjection which replace previous sexual desires), Wright considers the content of what Freud thinks of as the 'precipitate' or what is left after experience and loss. He suggests that in the case of a harsh father who the child fears and hates, in the process of identifying with him, the child will be compelled to take inside himself someone who feels like an external aggressor. This may, as we have seen, make him potentially capable of being a victimizer as well as a victim. But, if the father has been deeply loved, the child can reinstate in itself the lost sense of earlier closeness or fusion with the mother, but, importantly, this is a secondary identification and different from the *primary* sense of fusion it had with her. Wright suggests that the father identification, in representing both the reality of a taboo against incest together with earlier fusion with the mother, can be compared with Winnicott's transitional object (such as a piece of fluffy blanket), also used by the child as a way of negotiating a sense of loss and separation. But he argues that the extent to which the boundaries and constraints represented by the father are durable and lasting depends, as we might expect, on the actual experience of the father. It rests on whether they have been unwillingly or willingly accepted within the context of a loving relationship with the father and, integral to this, the overall balance of love and hate. This powerfully suggests that the quality of space for symbolization and self-aware thought rather than for rebellious, regressive 'acting out' or 'doing', which might, for example, entail violence or the blind following of authoritarian hero figures and causes, significantly depends on the experience of fathering.

So, for Wright, at first only the mother exists for the baby. The father may be there but only to support the mother or for 'stop-gap' mothering, not in his own right. As the gap of separation from the mother begins, the child begins to discover the mother as an 'other' and a captivating world is found 'out there' beyond its fused existence with the mother which demands to be explored and experienced. It is in the world 'out there' that the child encounters the father as different, as a beckoning counter-attraction to the regressive pull of the mother. Later, the Oedipal crisis threatens the child with the loss of everything it ever knew. This is what Wright calls the 'cruel space' in which the child, within Wright's new formulation, must learn to 'look' but not 'do', the moment that threatens castration. Once the child has recognized the crucial difference between its longing for things to continue as they are and the demands of reality, the way is paved for the symbol and language. In future the child, in a developmental process which exists in a continuum with the early visual experience of the mother, will, securely held in the arms of the symbolic, 'see' what you mean, gain 'insight', 'reflect' on experience, 'illuminate' a point, be 'blind' to some things, 'have its eyes opened' to others. Once the child has grasped or 'seen' the meaning of the name-of-the-father, the door created by the visual opens into the symbolic order.

So Wright suggests that actual fathers, who are clearly distinguishable from the mother, are vital in the psychical development towards the capacity to symbolize and think in language for children of both sexes. Freud and, to a greater extent, Lacan suggest that the father may be a symbolic position which culture can fulfil independently of an actual father. However, Freud suggests actual fathers are also necessary to young boys as a source of male identity, as someone who provides a reassuring sense of what they can become. He suggests girls also, to a lesser extent, identify with 'masculine' aspects of the father but also look to him for a sense of sexual otherness which confirms an important part of their developing sexuality. The boy, as Freud emphasized, has the same kind of confirmation of sexual otherness with the mother which may make it easier to separate than for the little girl who sees her as the same as herself. This is not an argument for traditional gender roles but one which takes the view that sexuality is an intrinsic part of how we experience who we are and that children need sexual as well as emotional confirmation from parents of both sexes. Since psychoanalytic theory as a whole suggests that we are all fundamentally bisexual, the child needs confirmation of both domains of its sexuality while at the same time learning that parents are sexually unavailable and, in terms of their generation, inappropriate partners.

The child's sexuality in relation to the father inevitably raises the fraught and painful issue of child abuse. The rise in child sexual abuse in the past ten years has, among other things, added another layer of confusion to the issue of fathering, leading to further distrust of men and a feeling, among some women, that children are better off without fathers. This argument tends to ignore the fact that some mothers are themselves involved in child abuse and that others collude with abuse by fathers, a matter about which there has been a significant cultural silence. Recently, in the context of child sexual abuse, there may have been a tendency to project all our anxiety about the safety of our children onto men so all men become potential monsters and abusers leaving women entirely untainted. As many have suggested, this seems to be an over-simplification which may seriously inhibit many innocent fathers' relationships with their children, particularly in a cultural context where men have traditionally denied their need for emotional intimacy. It is now generally known that child abusers have frequently suffered from abuse in their own childhood so that, as so often happens, the victim, having identified with the victimizer, becomes the new victimizer. But perhaps the apparent rise in the incidence of child abuse (though this may only appear so because of higher detection rates) may also be connected in some way to an increase in tensions in the relationships between men and women generally stemming from issues of power between them. One example out of many might be that a man may turn to a child because he cannot contemplate a more equal power relation with his partner. The child's powerlessness makes sexual intimacy less threatening and potentially overwhelming. Although the reasons for child abuse are complex and varied, it may be that children's lack of power, within a cultural context where power relations between men and women are often so problematic, is what makes them so particularly vulnerable. In Britain, both the Orkney and Cleveland child-abuse cases highlighted the powerlessness of the children compared with the power of the parents whatever the truth about the existence and extent of abuse. The rights of children have continued to remain subordinated to concern about the rights of men and women on whom they are so dependent for so long.

The baby in the father's mind

Christopher Gibson (1995) interestingly focuses on the meaning of the baby in the father's mind rather than the other way round. He argues that, for both parents, the positive decision to have a child, in spite of the loss of freedom and the change that this normally involves, requires the voluntary giving up of the narcissistic phantasy of omnipotence and indestructibility which lingers for so long in many of us. The decision to begin a new generation which will outlive us compels us to face up to our own mortality and the idea that one day we are going to die. Psychoanalytic theory suggests that we cannot live creatively and relatively autonomously or be generous, holding parents until we have been able to recognize the fact of our own mortality. It also suggests that our acceptance of this recognition is a continuing part of the process of separation from the mother which begins in childhood, and represents the final part of the transition from phantasy to reality. Gibson, focusing our attention particularly on the father's mind, reminds us that before the baby's birth the baby exists in the mind of the father as well as the body of the mother. After its birth, it continues to exist in the mind of both parents, not as an extension of the self but as an other who will carry the parents' biological 'line' through into the next generation. He cites Klein's theory, in particular, as suggesting that this awareness of the child in the father as well as the mother is communicated to the child non-verbally throughout its infancy and gives the baby a sense of a context which goes beyond the immediate merged relationship between itself and the mother. Klein's concept of the mother as containing the idea of the penis (and other siblings) as well as the breast reminds us of how the mother represents the father to the child non-verbally right from the beginning. But, a father who is unable to make a conscious decision that he wants a child may leave the mother soon after the baby is born or always feel hostile to the child because of his dread of facing up to his fear of death and loss of phantasized omnipotence symbolized by the arrival of the next generation. So, Gibson stresses that the willing father's involvement in the child's conception and the emotional process of anticipating and nurturing a child as someone distinctively different from the mother is, ideally, a vital part of the formation of the child's identity. It is also a crucial part of an authentic male identity which may, in some men, have been culturally obscured by an identity based on the over-valuation of the phallus as a symbol of power and control rather than generation and life, in some ways both like and unlike the repressed creative meanings of the breast and womb.

Finally, let us look at the phenomenon of physically or emotionally absent fathers and how, among other things, this can offer us insight into the meaning of fathers when they are present.

Absent fathers

Physically and, therefore, often emotionally absent fathers are now central to both culture generally (particularly in relation to the payment of maintenance) and to the concerns of psychotherapists dealing with some of what are seen as the psychically damaging effects of absent fathers. In the context of a dramatic rise in the number of single-parent families in recent years, most often headed by mothers, a recurring question among women has been about how necessary fathers are in the development of their children's identity and, if so, in what ways children may be affected by physically or emotionally absent fathers. Many divorced fathers see their children frequently, but an almost equal number become increasingly absent and eventually lose contact with their children altogether. In this cultural climate, feminists have tended to emphasize the importance of the mother, but there has also been a climate within psychoanalytic psychotherapy which has tended to favour mother- rather than father-centred approaches, although the tide is now turning. This question, sometimes posed anxiously and at other times more defensively, has formed the basis of numerous articles in the press in recent years. As we have seen, Freud's theory suggests that fathers perform a vital role in compelling the child to give up its phantasies about the mother and cope with the 'realities' of life within culture, whereas object-relations approaches stress the father's importance as an alternative space in the child's mind which also prepares the child for symbolization and representation. But, importantly, Freud also suggests that there are ways in which children can compensate for an absent father through access to substitute symbolic fathers. These may be male friends or relatives or male teachers but they may also include powerful cultural institutions such as the church, political parties, companies or other cultural organizations. Let us look, for a moment, at Freud's idea of the existence of cultural substitutes for the symbolic father within the contemporary context of widespread male unemployment in much of Europe, especially among young people.

As we have seen, Freud thought that psychical health lies, essentially, in the successful combination of the capacity to love and work. This suggests that work may often function as a cultural substitute for the symbolic father, especially among the young. In such a context, high unemployment, especially among young men, may be a particularly psychically as well as socially damaging phenomenon. This may be especially true when it is combined with high levels of single-parent families and absent fathers. In this situation, jobs cannot substitute symbolically for these absent fathers.

At a Council of Europe conference on adolescence in Vienna in 1997, almost every country reported a rise in divorce and a growing proportion of adolescents living in single-parent families. Research in Britain and America suggests that between 40 and 50 per cent of fathers lose contact with their children soon after divorce. Freud's idea of cultural substitutes for the father suggests that, for young men without the emotional and psychical support of a father, a job can act as a crucial psychical as well as social entry into the adult world of culture. A job offers a sense of

148   *Making sense of experience*

achievement, self-respect, social camaraderie, contact with a generation of older, more experienced workers and boundaries in what may, up until then, have been experienced as a lonely, unsupported, atomized, boundary-less world. Recent research shows that many young people in Britain, many of them men, are still living at home and have never been economically independent. Psychically and socially, they are trapped in the prospect of a perpetual adolescence. Dr John Coleman, Director of the Trust for the Study of Adolescents, comments, 'Fifteen years ago, some 50–60 per cent of sixteen year olds went into work; now it's 7 per cent and 50 per cent of young people aged 21–24 are still living at home' (quoted in Watts 1997: 2). As Helena Kennedy argues, on the same theme, 'They become marooned in an adolescence that goes on for ever. There are no rights of passage for these young men as there were for working-class men like my uncles, who moved into the world of work through apprenticeships, among older men' (quoted in Watts 1997: 3).

Psychoanalytic as well as social theory suggests that a situation in which new technology has created moral and economic anxieties and uncertainties, and two-parent family structures have crumbled, is likely to breed a climate of vulnerability, alienation, frustration and despair. Tom Whylie, of the National Youth Agency argues:

> We risk having a status zero population – a group of 200,000 young people living in the outer rings of major cities who are not in education, training or employment, and have no stable place to live, viable income or secure adult identity. I don't call them 'disaffected' because it's a label, and in some cases they are right to be disaffected. So they have closed themselves into a ghetto mentality, in music, dress, speech and forms of risk-taking [including drugs and crime] which doesn't connect with the world outside it [culture or the world of the symbolic father]. (quoted in Watts 1997: 3)

To what extent does this description graphically represent one version of what Freud calls narcissism and Lacan calls the Imaginary, a largely socially induced confinement to a psychical dead end of sterile, self-reflecting, infantile phantasy?

In this kind of context, the comment of Helena Kennedy, Chair of the Further Education Funding Council, on how further education is also failing young people, seems tellingly relevant. She says 'There's a real feeling that having aspirations is not cool, that it's "poncy" to go to college.' She traces this 'what's the point' attitude to a deeply entrenched sense of failure (quoted in Watts 1997: 3). From a psychoanalytic perspective, this rejection of further education as un-'masculine' suggests a fear of failing and an underlying despair about the possibility of ever being able to 'measure up' as a man. This may have the whiff of an emotionally or physically absent father whether in a one- or two-parent family.

Klein's work is also suggestive in relation to the absent father but, again, characteristically, she emphasizes the individual rather than cultural dimensions. Her work suggests that if the actual father leaves permanently, or is absent for long periods, the child is likely to idealize him, sometimes to conceal its anger with the father from itself. Since idealization is unrealistic because it obscures the real person with phantasy, this may affect the child's future relationships with partners who may be idealized at first but later denigrated. If the child feels very angry with an abandoning father this may set up frightening phantasies of being attacked by the father in the form of burglars, thieves, rapists and other nightmare attackers. As Julia Segal (1992) suggests, these phantasies may be partly based on real experience of the father and partly on the child's own fears of its own hostile wishes to destroy the mother. These are based on the perception of her as a potential attacker, as a result of projecting its bad feelings onto her. Sometimes when fathers leave, the child feels that this is its fault, that it is the direct result of its own destructive impulses with the result that more reparative, creative phantasies are unable to develop subsequently. However, the absent father continues to play a major conscious and unconscious role in the child's future life.

Although some object-relations theory has tended to marginalize the meaning of the father, Lacan tries to redress this balance with his emphasis on the 'place of the father' or culture. He argues that the dramatic psychical significance of Freud's symbolic father had been watered down and virtually obliterated by an obsession with the mother. But more recent object-relations as well as Freudian theory recognizes the crucial importance of the father for identity and the need to communicate the nature of the father's significance, beyond those working in the clinical sphere: this is in a Britain where four out of ten children in lone-parent families lose contact with the absent parent who is almost always the father (Family Policy Studies Centre 1992, in Watts 1997). Similarly, in the United States, 50 per cent of fathers lose contact with their children after two years (Arendall 1995). In Britain, it has been estimated that 160,000 children annually have parents who divorce and one in four of all children is affected by divorce.

It seems very likely that the disappearance of fathers from their children's lives stems not from lack of feeling but from an emotional inability to cope with the situation both in relation to their ex-partner, their children and new partners who may be seen as competitive rivals for the love of their children. If most men have been culturally required to cut off from their emotions in early childhood, a potent mixture of feelings of grief, sorrow, guilt, anger, resentment and regret provoked by the experience of divorce may be almost intolerable for many men. Denying and obliterating potentially overwhelming feelings by removing themselves from any reminder of these feelings, which often includes cutting off from their children, may tragically be the only emotional option for many men. Walking away may be the best they can do. Men's tendency to re-marry more rapidly than women may reflect the intensity of the denial of what is seen as failure as well as the desire for emotional comfort.

The issue of maintenance is, of course, of huge importance when family split up causes major poverty. Some 70 per cent of lone parents in Britain are on income support and 1.7 million children living on income support are in lone-parent families (Family Policy Studies Centre 1992, quoted in Watts 1997). But refusal to pay adequate maintenance may also often stem from a wish to deny the existence of children and ex-partners who are associated with huge emotional pain and anger. The irresponsibility and denial involved in starting a new family, making it necessary to withhold money from a previous one, may also result from an inability to make contact with potentially overwhelming emotions of loss in some, perhaps many, men.

In conclusion, psychoanalytic perspectives suggest that many men need greater access to their bisexual identity as the means to the emotional creativity and growth which seems to accompany women's acceptance of their cultural 'masculinity' and 'femininity'. But it also suggests that an acknowledgement of the 'feminine' connection with the mother, traditionally denied to men, needs to be firmly placed within the context of the potential for fathering rather than mothering. This makes it less likely to be associated with castration anxiety and fear of potential annihilation than the alternative proposal of simply becoming more 'like the mother'. Interestingly, Freud took the view that women had a greater tendency towards bisexuality than men because the little girl's first love object is the mother. Perhaps this has something to do with it seeming to be easier for women to accept their 'masculinity' than for men to acknowledge their 'femininity'.

Psychoanalytic approaches also strongly suggest that the child, ideally, needs a form of emotional intimacy which is framed within a different order from that of the mother, that is within a male body. Recent research describing the outstripping of boys academically by girls at primary and secondary levels of education in Britain appears to re-inforce women's move into the previously male-dominated territory of knowledge and the cultural power this confers. This, together with widespread unemployment, the predominance of young men between the ages of 18 and 25 in crime, the marked increase in suicide among young men in Britain in the last ten years and the growing cult of 'laddishness' celebrating macho forms of male identity, suggests the urgent need for the general recognition of the importance of fathering as a central lynchpin of a potential male identity. Significantly, the emotional or physical absence of a father is a major reason why adults seek psychotherapy. The film *The Full Monty*, in the midst of the laughter, with great delicacy and subtlety, directs our attention to the effective castration of a group of men compelled to turn themselves into strippers by the emptiness of unemployment and the growing redundancy of their roles as protectors, both socially and psychically.

In the context of the discussion of male envy of women in chapter 6, increasingly emotionally honest and mutually supportive relationships between men and women which recognize the crucial importance of the role of the father as well as the mother, backed by progressive, supportive social change, may offer the best hope for the future.

8

The unconscious roots
of violence

Instead of thinking about why public space has become increasingly
violent and unsafe, the impulse is to exclude, punish and shame those who
have despoiled what was once regarded as safe and reliable.
Susie Orbach, 'Revenge Tragedy', *Guardian*

Destructiveness and the twentieth century

Like each of the individuals who take part in it, history is honeycombed
with contradiction. There have been moments of great vision, creativity,
imagination, generosity, personal sacrifice and social concern for the
well-being of the many rather than the few. Indeed, such moments might
represent some people's definition of 'civilization'. But in parallel with
this positive dimension of human existence there have also been conflicts and acts of dreadful destruction, brutality and sadism by individuals,
groups, governments and alliances of governments. Despite hopes for
cultural progress to match technological progress, the twentieth century
has been no less brutal overall than previous periods of history, but,
rather, brutal on an even greater scale. The increasingly global presence
of the mass media in the second half of this century has left no one in
any doubt of the destructive as well as creative potential of human
beings, both physical and psychological. The horror of the Holocaust,
genocide, ethnic cleansing, torture, small- and large-scale wars in which
there has been the increasing involvement of civilian populations, the
development and deployment of terrifying weapons of mass destruction
and, in the context of the semi-civilized bans on their use, the upsurge
of a myriad of new varieties of anti-personnel weapons, are just some of
the cultural manifestations of human destructiveness we have had to try
to make sense of this century. In fact, scientific and technological

progress has been directed increasingly into the production of even more horrible ways of killing and maiming people. At the level of small groups and individuals, we are bombarded daily with news of violent assaults, murders, rapes, gang warfare, terrorist attacks, racial attacks, domestic violence and general sexual and psychological abuse outside the larger arena of persecution and armed conflict. Such a daily catalogue of information about horrific, often apparently mindless and cruel behaviours, and increasing fears that, whatever we do, none of us is any longer safe in our streets or homes, have provoked frequent discussion in Western countries about the reasons for violence and, in particular, for the perceived escalation of some forms of violence in the last decades of this millennium compared with the inter-war and post-war periods. This is not to overlook a general tendency to feel a nostalgic longing for a return to a golden age of peace and harmony which history suggests never existed in reality.

Some quarters of the British press, in the absence of any alternative paradigm of knowledge to cope with the existence of violence, have fallen back on the well-worn, religious notion of 'pure evil' to describe certain more isolated categories of violence based on particular individuals. These would include the brutal behaviour of such individuals as Hitler and Saddam Hussein as well as the young boys involved in the murder of James Bulger, the West murderers, the perpetrators of the Hungerford and Dunblane massacres, the Belgian child-murderer, Marc Dutroux. Significantly, in contrast, the deportation of political refugees back to their own countries to almost certain torture and death, or the throwing of fire bombs into houses occupied by immigrants or gypsies, do not always attract the same odium perhaps because this treatment is meted out towards people regarded as 'other', the sub-human bearers of the unacceptable parts of the self which psychoanalytic theory suggests some of us unconsciously project into the external world to be rid of them. Many people seem to identify more easily with small children or young women, perhaps because they carry the idealized parts of themselves, the idea of innocence, goodness, beauty and a sense of the future. This means that they feel their deaths as their own or those of their children.

Although we may agree that certain acts are thoroughly evil in their effects, the idea of individuals being the embodiment of 'pure evil' (carried in their genes) or monsters does not get us very far. It fails to appreciate the complexity of the conscious and unconscious ways identity seems to be produced. It seems likely that we are all a product of a complex mix of social, economic, cultural and unconscious factors and there is widespread evidence that those involved in particularly violent and horrific crimes habitually have a history of emotional deprivation and abuse in childhood. In the majority of cases of violence against others and self-destructive behaviour, whose most extreme form is suicide, it is generally recognized that experience of physical or sexual abuse in childhood, often in combination with social deprivation, frequently plays a crucial role. Significantly, in the context of gender, evidence suggests that men (who statistically commit most violent crime) tend to be violent towards others and end up in prison whereas women, perhaps for cultural as well as other reasons, are more likely to turn anger inwards in the form of depression and end up in psychiatric hospitals. Unfortunately, in recent years, in Britain and America, many of those in powerful political positions have chosen to ignore the correlation between poverty and violence which might suggest that the solution to such social illness requires financial resources and higher levels of direct taxation. It seems increasingly that the two-thirds of people in society who are relatively secure and affluent are not willing to have less in order to support those living in poverty or relative poverty and insecurity, even if this does generate violence which ultimately threatens all of us. In some modern cities, this has developed into a fortress mentality, involving fenced, guarded, middle-class ghettos.

Clearly, cultural, historical and economic factors are heavily implicated in outbreaks of violence and brutality. Richard Wilkinson, in *Unhealthy Societies* (1996), strongly suggests that ill health, both physical and psychological, is the direct outcome of the experience of the modern phenomenon of relative poverty. If a society makes people feel that they are outsiders, that they have a justified grievance, such social injury has the same kind of effect as the injury done to the child who is made to feel an outsider in the smaller unit of the family. If sibling rivalry can produce deep feelings of envy and inferiority, what is often referred to as the Cain and Abel effect in the family, it does not seem surprising that, when this occurs in the larger unit of society, its effects threaten to be devastating.

A combination of Freudian and object-relations perspectives offers us a variety of powerful ways of thinking about unconscious feelings and impulses which may underlie destructive and self-destructive behaviour. Although, in drawing on psychoanalytic ideas, the academic world has been mainly concerned with Freudian theory and issues of desire and sexuality, those working in the clinical sphere have moved away from these issues to focus more on the destructive aspects of identity. Let us begin by looking at how Freud analyses the roots of human destructiveness and cruelty and the role of culture in controlling it.

Freud: sadism and masochism

In the early part of his career Freud saw aggression as a sadistic aspect of sexuality which was concerned with the primitive need to gain a sense of identity through mastery and control. He thought this derived from the infantile stage of anal sexuality when the baby gains a sense of pleasure and identity from exercising control and mastery over its bowel movements. Along with oral and phallic forms of the baby's sexuality, this anal form of sexuality constitutes what Freud calls a 'component instinct' which, before the addition of what he describes as adult genital sexuality, provides the baby with its first primitive source of a self, of having a 'real' existence through the experience of pleasure. Freud thought that sadism is concerned with the control and mastery of the external world while its opposite, masochism, results if this aggressive impulse is turned inwards, self-destructively against the self (in, for example, depression, psychosomatic illness or, in extreme cases, self-mutilation or suicide). However, later in his career, when he was preoccupied with finding some explanation for the senseless, unnecessary carnage of the First World War, Freud introduced a new, controversial theory of aggression in his book *Beyond the Pleasure Principle* (1920). Here he argued, for the first time, that there was not one basic sexual drive but two: the life and death drives. However, these two drives, although capable of being isolated from each other, could also be bonded with each other, in varying and different degrees, at different times. He thought the new life drive, consisting of a blend of both the sexual and the self-preservation instincts which he had previously separated from each other, existed together with the death drive. However, the death drive represents a drive towards destruction whose aim is led by what Freud saw as every organism's need to return to its original state of inertia. This idea has always been very controversial among analysts and therapists. Freud went on to argue that, apart from an initial period in our lifetime when they are directed inwards, the destructive drives are directed outwards into the external world in the form of aggressive behaviour. This means that they mostly serve to protect the interests of the life instincts *within* the self in, for example, normal assertive behaviour. Freud thought that aggressiveness also provides us with a high degree of narcissistic enjoyment because it fulfils a primitive, infantile wish for omnipotence and control. But, crucially, he thought that it is the demands of culture, internalized in us in the form of the symbolic father or super-ego, that makes sure that destructiveness is normally, in practice, turned inwards rather than outwards.

In his book *Civilisation and its Discontents* (1930), Freud takes the view that the drive to be destructive formed the greatest barrier to both civilization and the successful prevention of extreme forms of violence and destructiveness. He argues that it is only the presence of guilt stimulated by the super-ego, the father internalized as the representative of culture, which produces what he regards as the veneer of civilization. Just below the cultivated surface, he suggests, lurk aggressive and sexual forces often existing in a fused state. If they are not expressed as normal assertiveness and self-defence, and are also not turned inwards, they will continually threaten to turn civilized men into savage and barbaric murderers. In contrast, Winnicott's object-relations theory rejects Freud's idea of a death drive completely. For most object-relations theory, being more concerned with the development of an individual's sense of reality than with childhood sexuality, barbarity is the specific result of emotional or psychical deprivation or inhibited development.

So, Freud suggests that the inclination to hurt and destroy comes from an original, underlying drive in man which is the most obvious unconscious alternative to the misery of guilt and inhibition, or, in a more extreme form, the self-destruction and self-punishment which often expresses itself in depression or psychosomatic illness. Pessimistically, Freud suggests that violence, in the form of either sadism or masochism, is part of the human condition. In contrast, he was convinced that civilization is a process in the service of Eros or the life drives whose purpose is 'to combine single human individuals, and afterwards, families, then races, peoples and nations into one great unity' (PFL 12: 313). But man's aggressive death drive travelling alongside the life instinct with which it 'shares world-domination' opposes this programme. Rather than combining individuals, it divides them. For Freud, the meaning of civilization is a struggle between Eros and Death. In 1930, nine years before his death, he wrote pessimistically, 'this struggle is what all life essentially consists of, and the evolution of civilisation may therefore be simply described as the struggle for life of the human species' (PFL 12: 314). But, as we have seen, Freud saw the sense of guilt instilled by civilization for its protection as the most important problem in its development. He thought the price we have to pay for its advance is a cumulative loss of happiness or depression brought on by an increasing sense of unconscious guilt as a result of inhibiting our destructive impulses. Our sense of guilt or moral conscience is derived from our father (our earliest authority on such matters as who is allowed to have sexual access to whom) and, at the same time, from our urge for the satisfaction of our drives whose frustration produces the inclination to aggression. In many ways, Freud sees an analogy between the psychical development of the individual and the development of civilization but he argues that, in the individual's development, the main accent is on the urge to be happy (the pleasure principle) whereas the 'cultural urge' (super-ego) is to impose restrictions. But in the development of civilization, by far the most important aim is that of creating a unity between human beings, while the aim of happiness, although still present, is pushed into the background. This, possibly, results in an underlying discontent, or *angst*, if not depression, which then seeks other non-violent ways out of it.

The victim and the victimizer

Freud's work also suggests that if there is a physically or emotionally absent, unreliable or, in particular, abusive father it is difficult for the small boy to resolve his Oedipal crisis by making a productive identification with him. Freud suggests that if a boy grows up unable to internalize an adequate father and, therefore, without an adequate identification with culture, he may remain under the sway of continuing castration anxiety. This means he may be left unconsciously compelled into an oscillation between difficulties with ordinary self-assertion, because of lack of 'masculine' self-confidence which results in depressive, masochistic, self-destructive behaviour, and, conversely, sudden eruptions of destructive, intimidating behaviour towards others which may allow some temporary alleviation of feelings of worthlessness. This can be seen in the case of the bullied and the bully, the self as victim (the small boy) or triumphant executioner (like the phantasized father). In the first case, Freud suggests that what is not used up in the external world in the form of normal self-assertion and self-defence is reincorporated into the self where, as well as sometimes combining with the sexual drive, it also amalgamates with the existing sense of guilt provoked by the punitive presence of an over-harsh super-ego or conscience. Here, where it is in a position to attack the self rather than others, it manifests itself as yet more guilt. So a sense of guilt which is built on larger than usual quantities of incorporated 'spare' aggression can have a range of effects. It may lead to an individual habitually being bullied. Or, Freud suggests, it may make someone severely depressed, tortured by self-reproach, self-hatred and self-punishment and sometimes suicidal or it may result in serious psychosomatic illness. We may see these kinds of outcome, in different degrees, in anyone who has been prevented from expressing sufficient aggression in ordinary self-assertion and self-defence in the family where self-assertiveness has been discouraged or squashed by either or both parents. The predicament of the seriously depressed individual, which Freud discusses in his paper 'Mourning and Melancholy' (1917), also suggests that of the guilty, 'miserable sinner' at the heart of Christian civilization (SE 14: 245).

In the context of relationships, Freud suggests that aggressive instincts, turned inwards in the form of masochism, are likely to result in self-destructive, painful relationships resulting from unconscious compulsions to repeat painful early experiences. These are fuelled by the unconscious wish to resolve unconscious deprivations and conflicts in new relationships which, while feeling new and different initially, turn out to be painfully familiar. He called this pattern of behaviour the 'repetition compulsion'. We can see signs of this kind of behaviour in women who repeatedly end up in relationships with violent men or men who repeatedly find themselves with castrating, undermining women (see Minsky 1996: 81).

We may, like many, be unconvinced about Freud's notion of the existence of a destructive wish to return ourselves or others to an original state of inertia and about the existence of such a drive in everyone rather than only in those who have suffered early experiences of an inadequate, absent or abusive father. However, many of Freud's ideas about culture, morality and destructiveness are still very suggestive in relation to the effects of childhood deprivation. In the context of the dramatic increase in family breakdown, which so often results in physically absent fathers, together with a significant rise in destructive behaviour among young men in the Western world, we may need to take thoughtful account of Freud's focus on the symbolic role of fathers as the symbol of the necessary boundaries imposed by culture. As discussed in chapter 7, Freud's work suggests that fathers need to be encouraged to be emotionally accessible to their children in any kind of family. An emotionally unavailable father may mean the boy is unable to identify fully with male strengths which may then result in the idealization of the cultural characteristics of manhood which in the adult man may take the form of misogyny. And, since a boy may compensate for an absent or damaging father if he can find an alternative cultural source of a father identification within wider culture, societies need to ensure that they provide positive sources of such identifications. Freud's theory suggests that these should include good quality training and meaningful work, both of which confer rather than erode self-esteem. These are likely to militate against the need to identify with destructive gangs or extreme right-wing parties or groups dedicated to finding scapegoats for their aggression, as a symbolic substitute for the father.

Insiders and outsiders

In some urban areas, usually suffering from multiple forms of deprivation, adolescent gangs may offer the only basis for a viable identity based on the strength of mutual identification and solidarity in the absence of adequate possibilities of identification and male solidarity with a father or father substitute often in the context of little social cohesion. In 1921, in *Group Psychology and the Analysis of the Ego* (PFL 12: 98), Freud suggests that the gang leader, as a substitute for the father, is the initial focus for this identity which binds the group together, via an intense emotional tie, into what is experienced as a powerful group identity based on a shared love for the leader which blots out the fragility of the individual identities which go to make it up. Through the process of projective identification, or a sense of an identity held in common, each individual member is able unconsciously to deny his sense of powerlessness in a shared sense of power and 'masculinity'. These erotic bonds, based on what Freud sees as aim-inhibited forms of sexuality (which also connect families, crowds and other groups), link members of the gang in two directions. They explain the hatred for those perceived as outsiders and the chains of love and loyalty which bind the insiders in affection and cooperation. Freud calls this kind of hatred of immediate neighbours (for example, other gangs) the narcissism of minor differences (PFL 12: 131, 305). Some have suggested that the prevalence of authoritarian, emotionally absent fathers may have been a factor in the popularity of German fascist leaders in the 1930s and gangs of 'black-shirts' in an emotionally heightened situation of economic and social decline. In the context of a gang whose members jointly constitute both a symbolic father, and a challenge to the traditional symbolic father, such activities as drug-dealing and territorial skirmishes may become alternative symbols of culture and the 'masculine' world. Intense rivalry between gangs over territory seems to represent the testing of the strength of the joint identity established on the basis of individual identities which are vulnerable and deprived. From this perspective, gang warfare may be a product of both cultural and psychical deprivation.

So Freud's theory suggests that violence, largely associated with men and 'masculinity', may often be a defence against depressive feelings of worthlessness brought about by an over-severe internalized father in the absence of an emotionally accessible actual father who can dispel the small boy's fear of annihilation. Freud's theory about castration anxiety also suggests why male relationships are often so rivalrous. Without an emotionally available father to extinguish the small boy's terrifying phantasies, male identity is forged in the continuing Oedipal phantasy that life is about being a victor or victim, winner or loser, 'an other's gain is my loss', so all outsiders may henceforth be regarded as potential annihilators of identity. As Freud's theory suggests, this may go some way to explaining many individuals' destructive response to 'different' others with whom they are not already bonded as members of a community, for example, on the basis of nationality, ethnicity, religion, ideology, sexual orientation, class, wealth, education, football team. Projection onto different others may then result in persecution and violence at the private or public level. In relation to the subordination of women as the archetypal 'other', this may lead to domestic and public abuse, rape, violence and murder as well as social and legal discrimination. We can see this kind of projective mechanism in relation to those regarded as 'outsiders', often combined with the primitive greed and envy associated with rivalry between siblings, in the persecution of the Jews in the Holocaust, the elimination and oppression of indigenous peoples by colonizers, the persecution of ethnic minorities in previously imperial European nations, ethnic cleansing in Bosnia, tribal rivalries in Africa, between Israelis and Arabs, Loyalists and Republicans in Northern Ireland and between East and West during the Cold War when the threat of violent destruction was symbolized in the symptom of an ever-increasing stock-piling of deadly weapons capable of destroying the world many times over (Mutually Assured Destruction). Clearly, inter-woven with unconscious phantasies of weakness and inferiority and phantasies of omnipotence are powerful conscious factors involving territorial disputes, economic competition and age-old rivalries and hostilities. But the scale of the savagery, cruelty, torture and wish to humiliate and defile sometimes involved in the working out of these conflicts by individuals, groups and governments suggests that uncon-scious motives play an equal if not greater part in this kind of violence than conscious ones. In a very real sense, Freud's ideas suggest that, in many people, a sense of viable identity *depends* on unconscious exploi-tation of difference to sustain it. Unfortunately, the experience of oppres-sion as the rejected 'other', which ideally we might imagine would produce the capacity for empathy and insight, does not seem to prevent the infliction of persecution and violence onto new 'others'. For example, some Israelis, many of whose families have suffered unbearable violence and pain, seem unconsciously compelled to evacuate their experience onto Palestinians, apparently incapable of coping with such experience of abuse in any other way.

At this point I want again to raise the issue of whether the capacity for destructive projection onto the external world exists in everyone, as Freud suggests, or whether it is largely a potential characteristic of some in whom, in Freud's terms, castration phantasy remains unresolved. This means that many may still be locked in a relentless psychical world of rivalry where the only options seem to kill or be killed. The desire for competition and the popularity of games such as football then appear at the unconscious level as ritualized versions of the lingering Oedipal rivalry between the victim and victimizer in many men's internal world. Football offers the possibility of both the agony of symbolic defeat and the ecstasy of symbolic victory and possession of the mother. At the end of a match, fans are either 'gutted' or 'over the moon'. Certainly, object-relations theory, as it has been developed by Winnicott and Bion, suggests that only those of us who have suffered early deprivations as children need to evacuate our sense of violation through bad experiences into the external world so that as adults painful experiences which have never been able to be symbolized or 'thought' are expressed in destructive actions. In some people, these take the form of theft which will symbolically restore integrity to a damaged self as well as violence against others, but in others they take a more self-destructive form. In the context of those individuals who greedily seek positions of power and control in which they become tyrannical and destructive, Freudian and object-relations theory suggests that painful, unconscious feelings of envy and inadequacy may be being buttressed through the acting out of phantasies of omnipotence and denial. This suggests that if a significant number of those in positions of power, in governments, in business organizations, in the military, in the police, in prisons and even, perhaps, in schools and children's homes occupy these positions largely because of a compulsive unconscious need for power and control, then perhaps we should not be surprised if culture sometimes seems dominated by bullying, destructive behaviour. It may be that this results from the influence of relatively few powerful but emotionally damaged individuals. Such people have unknowingly separated themselves from parts of their emotional world – frequently feelings of humiliation, violation and powerlessness – because they are so painful and projected the split-off parts onto others then perceived as malign. Blame replaces the capacity to acknowledge these feelings. Psychoanalytic approaches suggest that some individuals may dominate history because historical circumstances

are contingent with their driving need for power and control stemming from damaging early emotional experience of humiliation and
worthlessness.

Social fragmentation

Freud's book *Civilisation and its Discontents* (1930) suggests that if
culture, in the sense of one large group trying to impose limitations on
such fundamental behaviour as incest and uncontrolled killing, should
lose its quality of unity and bondedness, this would open the floodgates
to violence and destruction. This would result from the breakdown of
large-scale identification among the individuals who go to make it up. As
many people have observed, in Western countries in the past twenty
years there has been an increasing fragmentation of culture. A sense of
bondedness and unity, on the basis of forms of mutual identification,
affection and dependence, has been eroded by increased job mobility,
destruction of old working-class communities, loss of employment and
close work relationships because of large-scale industrial decline, new
technology, insecure contract-based jobs and low-paid, part-time work.
To this, one could add more frequent family break-ups, major cut-backs
in welfare and housing benefits and health provision, and an increase
among many of relative, if not absolute, poverty and exclusion. This
systematic erosion of strongly based identifications founded on common
interests, experiences and values and an increased sense of insecurity,
disconnectedness and isolation is a condition close to what Durkheim,
the founder of sociology, described as *anomie* which he related to an
increased incidence of suicide at the end of the nineteenth century.
Perhaps we are now seeing the same sense of cultural disconnectedness
manifest itself in increasing levels of violence and destructiveness against
the 'other' instead of the self-destructiveness involved in suicide. As
Freud writes in *The Future of an Illusion* (1927), about very unequal
societies:

> In such conditions [of social deprivation], an internalisation of the
> cultural prohibitions among the suppressed people is not to be
> expected. On the contrary they are not prepared to acknowledge
> the prohibitions, they are intent on destroying the culture itself, and
> possibly even on doing away with the postulates on which it is
> based. The hostility of these classes is so obvious that it has caused
> the more or less latent hostility of the social strata that are better
> provided for to be overlooked. It goes without saying that a

civilisation which leaves so large a number of its participants unsatisfied and drives them into revolt neither has nor deserves the prospect of a lasting existence. (PFL 12: 191–2)

Although Freud may have been thinking about the psychosocial roots of revolutions, his comments could also apply to large parts of the current populations of America and Western Europe, some of whose marginalized members seem to have increasingly turned to violence as a response to rising levels of socially provoked anxiety and social damage.

Let us look now at what the two strands of object-relations approaches have to say about the possible unconscious sources of destructive behaviour, beginning with the work of Melanie Klein which in many ways elaborates and re-formulates that of Freud.

Klein: idealization or denigration

Klein's work suggests that, in certain circumstances which provoke feelings of anxiety and helplessness, some people may revert to primitive projection associated with infancy and what she calls the paranoid-schizoid phase (rather than Freud's castration phantasy) as a means of defending themselves against envy and a sense of futility. They may idealize certain people and denigrate others so that phantasy obscures other more realistic ways of responding to events in the external world. Most of us, in certain stressful circumstances, may pick an unjustified fight with someone close to us, or make a cruel remark to expel our own feelings of vulnerability or anxiety. As we have seen, at the cultural level, particularly in the context of feelings of economic or political insecurity or powerlessness, some people may project unacceptable aspects of themselves onto certain groups whom they identify as 'other' who represent 'the stranger within'. Klein's work suggests that some individuals are very prone to destructive projection because of lack of emotional containment as infants. For this reason, they were never able to make an adequate transition from phantasy to reality by entering into the more realistic depressive position in which previous destructive phantasies can be appreciated for what they are, mourned and reparation made. Such individuals may remain trapped in a black-and-white paranoid reality in which destructive projections are expressed as hostile, envious attacks on others in the external world who then need to be controlled because of fears that they will attack. The converse of this is to project valued parts of the self into the external world so that certain people become idealized icons of perfection and goodness. As we have seen, certain individuals may seek powerful positions where they can control and bully others, in the workplace or more widely in totalitarian regimes where they seek to compensate for split-off feelings of worthlessness and precariousness. Such individuals may also be capable of considerable personal charm and charisma as a form of emotional manipulation dedicated to achieving unconscious emotional objectives. But they may also be characterized as particularly competitive, manipulative, secretive, ultra-sensitive to criticism, revengeful, two-faced and unable to experience guilt or admit responsibility for their actions and liable to blame and undermine others.

Other individuals locked in the stark and rigid world characterized by Klein's paranoid-schizoid phase, or in what Freud called a primary state of narcissism still merged with the mother, may 'act out' phantasies of destroying the envied mother more directly in attacks on women. In a cultural context in which many men continue to have unjustified power over women, envying, attacking behaviour on women, particularly in a domestic context, is tacitly reinforced in many cultures. Chasseguet-Smirgel suggests that men's greater tendency to violent phantasies, murder and violent behaviour can be explained by their inability to identify with the procreative capacity of the mother. In this context, sexual attacks and rape may be some men's attempts to re-enter the womb by force (Chasseguet-Smirgel 1986). She argues that because women can identify with the mother's power to reproduce they have more respect for the continuity of life and less appetite for violence. Attacks on children may also represent attacks on unacceptable, vulnerable parts of the self after experiences of emotional deprivation or sexual, physical or psychological abuse as children.

Both Freud's and Klein's theories, by different routes, suggest the presence of destructive inclinations in all of us. They suggest that, if these are not sufficiently resolved, they may be projected onto others in the external world or, self-destructively, projected inwards (introjected) against the self. In Klein's theory, violent destructive behaviour is a defensive form of psychical survival. These theories also suggest, as I have commented elsewhere, that society needs to take care of those who parent (Minsky 1996: 97–100). Social and economic deprivation, as well as the parents' own unconscious history, may make a crucial difference as to whether parents can be adequate for their children's emotional needs or not. If the mother's or parents' behaviour appears to be withholding, rejecting or unloving because of, for example, frustration, anger or depression brought about because of cultural deprivation, the baby may be unable to integrate its initially chaotic inner world. Psychoanalytic theory suggests that this may make destructive or self-destructive behaviour much more likely when the baby becomes an adult.

Contrary to the view that social provision fosters dependency cultures or the 'nanny state', psychoanalytic theory suggests that society needs more rather than fewer containing, maternal institutions concerned with taking care of ordinary human need as well as those paternal institutions which can offer realistic boundaries and the capacity for autonomy. Winnicott's and Bion's emphasis on maternal containment underlines the wisdom of making available such provision, and the relationship between emotional experience and the capacity for thought rather than violent action or 'acting out'. Let's look now at Bion's striking development of some of Klein's ideas.

Bion: the container/contained relationship

The work of Wilfred Bion has been very influential among practising psychotherapists, particularly in the context of his concept of the pre-Oedipal mother–baby relationship as a relationship involving what he describes as the container and the contained. Building on Klein's ideas of projection, projective identification and introjection as ways in which the baby projects parts of its self into the external world and takes parts of the external world into its internal world, Bion sees the mother's role as, above all, a psychical container of the baby's initially chaotic and frightening internal experience which results from its sensory impressions through which it takes in the world. The mother projectively identifies with the baby so that she is able to contain its first instinctual sensations, fears, projections and emotional states – and returns these to the baby in a processed or digested state. In this way she makes them bearable and able to be coped with for the baby who cannot yet do this for itself. Through repeated experience of the mother's containment of its initially confusing and indigestible experience, the baby, whose identity is still fused with the mother, gradually learns to metabolize and contain its own experience. This allows it to begin to make sense and symbolize this experience in the form of phantasies and dream images so that later these 'thing' images can be converted into word symbols. Bion suggests that in the context of a mother who is unable to play her part as the baby's container because of her own unconscious needs, this may mean that the baby, lacking anyone who can make its potentially overwhelming feelings tolerable, has to evacuate them. By expelling them into the external world, it by-passes its potentially annihilating experience as a way of ensuring its continued psychical survival. This evacuation of bad internal objects means that this part of its experience no longer forms part of the baby's psyche because it has been expelled (initially in the form of faeces, wind or later angry, attacking behaviour). Bion distinguishes between the containing and uncontaining mother. Whereas the containing mother allows herself to be psychically used by the baby as, metaphorically, a concave, holding, absorbing surface, the uncontaining mother presents herself to the baby as, at one and the same time, emotionally impenetrable and demanding of attention to her own needs. This kind of mother has been described by Gianni Williams (1996) as like a teapot which can offer the baby only a resistant convex surface which the baby cannot penetrate. At the same time, the mother uses the spout to pour into the baby her own unconscious projections. The baby then has to endure the confused emotions and demands of its mother as well as its own which remain undigested and terrifying. In the adult this kind of early experience of the mother might express itself in various forms of destructive behaviour: violent crime or theft (theft of a self from others), self-destructive behaviour (paradoxically involving evacuation into the body as part of the external world), such as depression, psychosomatic illness, eating disorders such as anorexia or bulimia and drug abuse. Anorexia seems to involve total control of this self-destructive process (domination by the super-ego), whereas bulimia seems to see-saw between total control and being out of control (fluctuations between super-ego and unconscious desire).

Essentially, without the mother's containment of its early raw emotional responses to impressions derived from its senses, what Bion calls its beta elements, the baby cannot emotionally learn to make sense of this chaotic experience for itself and organize it into rudimentary forms of thought and identity. Bion describes these phantasies and dream images, which will eventually allow the child to use language, as the alpha function. In other words, without a containing mother, the baby never acquires the capacity to convert primitive beta elements into alpha elements which are crucial to the capacity for symbolization. If the beta elements can be converted into alpha elements, these are then made storable and available for dream thoughts, unconscious waking thinking, and eventually language and thought (Bion 1967). So beta elements are the undigested facts in existential life that do not evolve into subjective states of mind as alpha elements do. An attack on the child's alpha function in a family where, for example, feelings and internal states are never referred to, may mean that a person never really comes alive and is therefore only partially alive (an example of Bollas's 'normotic' family discussed later in this chapter). A child with a certain kind of narcissistic mother, who constantly projectively identifies onto her child, may be

unable to find an alpha function and be stuck in a primitive communi-
cative exchange characterized by beta 'thinking' and functioning. Bion
argues, from his Kleinian perspective, that the attack on the alpha
functioning comes from the child's hate and envy even while it loves the
uncontaining mother and clings to her.

Shame, blame and the grudge

In the context of Klein's and Bion's theories, we can begin to make some
sense of physical and sexual child abuse in terms of an invasion of the
child's internal world by beta elements which is so overwhelming that
the victim, although internalizing it, cannot contain it. Christopher Dare
(1996) suggests that the idea of the sexual abuse of children, usually by
an adult or older child, is so assaulting that all of us want immediately
to evacuate it and push it away so we don't have to think about it.
Although it has clearly been going on for a long time, as a society we
have been unable to face up to it because we find it quite literally
'unthinkable', that is, impossible to contain in our minds. In describing
the effects of child sexual abuse, Christopher Dare suggests that the child
unconsciously experiences its abuse as monstrous internalized objects
which perpetually confirm or testify to what has happened. This experience produces what analytical psychotherapists sometimes call the destructive circle of shame, blame and retribution or 'the grudge'. The
child's shame turns into blame and then may manifest itself in a life of
living out the grudge in destructive retribution on others. This pattern
might help us to understand all physical child abuse in which the former
victim becomes the victimizer of a new victim who stands in for the
original victimizer and satisfies the desire for retribution. The child has
internalized the monstrous objects of abuser and abused which leads to
shame, a grudge and the idea of a perpetual vendetta. This helps to
illuminate what sometimes seems inexplicable: how those who have
suffered the experience of physical or sexual abuse and violence come
to inflict the same experience on their own children or others. As we
have seen, for Freud this hinges on the phantasy of castration, that is, the
child, and later adult, as either victimizer or victim after having internalized an abusive father. For Klein and Bion, the idea of castration by the
father is replaced by bad internal objects which the child or adult expels
to prevent its identity from being overwhelmed.

We can see the shame, blame, grudge and retribution cycle in play in
some violent, destructive behaviour in young men and in political
situations which seem to be intractable to reason or ordinary human

feeling. We can see it in operation, perhaps, in Northern Ireland where it seems as if the grudge or idea of a vendetta for terrible actions which have been internalized is the result of uncontainable shame and humiliation which can never be given up. The object of the vendetta on either side gets caught up in the notion of 'how can I stop attacking my victimizer for the horrible person he has turned me into?' The more horrible the object becomes, the more it appears to become self-evident that the vendetta can never be stopped in a circle of violence. This situation may be echoed in other areas of political life, for example, between Israeli and Arab, Bosnian Muslim and Serb, Rwandan Tutsi and Hutu, where, buried in among the conscious historical and territorial conflicts, are the unconscious experiences of literally 'unthinkable' abuse which has been internalized so that it has to be continually externalized through a life-long grudge which seeks continual retribution.

Sibling rivalry

Recently, there has been a growing interest among psychotherapists in sibling rivalry and the compulsion to replay these sibling dynamics in mirroring repetitions with new 'others' in later life. Here, in an Oedipal context where the child's feelings of envy and jealousy about the birth of a sibling and perhaps subsequent 'Cinderella' phantasies are not adequately contained by parents who have themselves been able creatively to resolve their envy and jealousy in relation to each other, these feelings may be played out repeatedly through the unconscious mechanism of repetition compulsion. Gerald Wooster (1995), in his paper 'The Resolution of Envy through Jealousy', describes a father who is unable to resolve his own feelings of envy and jealousy about the birth of a new baby with his partner which involves the conversion of the sexual couple into a triangle. Wooster argues that a father in this predicament will be unlikely to be able to reassure and help his small child cope with the birth of a sibling in his or her own version of the potentially painful move from a dyadic to a triangular set of relationships. Freud wrote: 'Up to your nth year you regarded yourself as the sole and unlimited possessor of your mother: then came another baby and brought you grave disillusionment. Your mother left you for some time, and even after her reappearance she was never devoted to you exclusively' (SE 23: 261).

In a situation of sibling rivalry, the powerful emotions often have a quality of intractability revolving, again, around the axes of loss/gain, shame/blame, victim/victor, sadism/masochism, obsessionality (control)/ hysteria (emotionality). We can see these same axes in play in certain kinds of conflict situations within culture where a sibling dynamic seems to be in play. Two individuals or groups may appear to outsiders to be more similar than different, that is, like brothers or sisters, yet be locked in a cycle of fraternal or sisterly destructiveness based on envy and jealousy with no prospect of a peaceful resolution. We may be able to perceive this in a rivalrous work situation or in the arena of international politics. For example, as Mitch Elliot (1996) has suggested, Republican and Loyalist terrorists could be seen to be engaged in what looks like an irresolvable sibling dynamic in the context of parents (Ireland and Britain) who are unable to come together themselves and develop the capacity for emotional and political containment. Similarly, the intractable conflict between Israelis and Palestinians may be seen in the same sibling context where America and the Arab world constitute the parents who lack the capacity to resolve their own envy and jealousy and act as emotional containers.

Let us turn now to the second stream of object-relations theory based on the work of Winnicott.

Winnicott: testing the mother's resilience

Winnicott disagrees with both Freud's and Klein's idea of a dual life and death drive or joint instincts of love and hate and argues, instead, that all human beings are born with a single, uncontaminated life instinct containing love. If our love is accepted we feel creative, alive and full of potential, but if it is rejected we feel potentially psychically annihilated. Only in the deprived baby is creative assertiveness and confidence contained in the life-force turned into destructive, sadistic projections against the 'other' or turned against the self in the form of masochism.

For Winnicott, creativity is bound up with the capacity for ruthlessness. Winnicott argues that the task of the good enough mother is to allow the baby creatively to resolve its gradual separation from her through her ability to contain its ruthless tendencies. For Winnicott, in contrast to Klein, these tendencies are not seen as destructive but related to the baby's impulse for life. They represent the baby's aliveness and capacity for assertiveness and creativity. Winnicott describes the baby's aggression as 'original ruthless virtue' or a 'primitive ruthless love', a form of aggression which he thinks is initially fused in with the baby's primitive impulse to love. For Winnicott, aggression is vitally necessary for the child to achieve its separation from the mother as it begins to experience both its love and dependence as sometimes overwhelming. At first this might take the form of biting the mother's breast. In the baby's play, the mother increasingly has to be able to tolerate the baby's 'ruthlessness' as it seeks to symbolize its growing separation from her, to negotiate the route from its inner world to external reality. If the mother is unable to cope with this ruthless play, the child may never make contact with its creative ability to be its self and, as a consequence, there is a risk that it may destructively turn its aggression inwards leading to psychosomatic illness or depression. So, as the baby matures, the good enough mother, as conceived by Winnicott, has to act as a container for the baby's aliveness even when it takes the form of aggression or non-compliance.

Winnicott also sees the baby's later aggression towards the mother, after its separation from her, what he calls its 'use' of her, as inherently creative. This is the means by which the baby tests the limitations of the environment, after having been part of the mother, rather than expressing a destructive impulse as in Klein. If the baby is not sometimes able to hate, then love will not feel fully real to him or her.

The baby's belief in the durability and reliability of an external world beyond its own phantasies of omnipotence depends on the mother's capacity to survive after these destructive attacks. By surviving, she develops her own autonomy and life with which the baby can identify. This is something different from its earlier fusion with her. The proof of the mother's resilience makes possible a shared reality with her in the external world. In Winnicott's world, what we call reality or culture does not inevitably frustrate the child like the reality of Freud and Klein. It is potentially enriching and reassuring even when it takes the form of disillusionment and the way it sets limits to the baby's omnipotent phantasies of control. Winnicott sees the child's vital transition from phantasy to reality as a means to self-realization and growth rather than a painful confrontation with the loss of the mother as it is for Freud. As Adam Phillips suggests, in contrast to Klein, the baby's own survival is what creates the subject and not, as Klein suggests, his or her reparation to the mother. The mother must be resilient, but in a non-retaliatory way (Phillips 1988).

Adaptation and compliance

For Winnicott, destructive sadism, in contrast to assertive healthy forms of aggression, is the result of maternal deprivation, commonly in the shape of a depressed mother. For this reason, he thinks that Klein, by ascribing hate to the ordinary baby, pathologizes it. The depressed mother is one who, instead of looking after the baby's needs, forces it into adaptation and compliance with her own unmet needs. As a result the baby constructs a false self which represents the denial of an authentic self which has been split off and buried. The mother, by forcing the baby into a compliance with her own conscious and unconscious needs, denies the baby a sense that it is alive and real. By failing to take in the baby's psychosomatic existence for herself and its self, she is unable to help it creatively construct and make sense of itself or the world. As an adult, the child whose real self has gone unnoticed and unappreciated may be lacking in assertiveness and suffer from depression and a sense of futility, confusion and emptiness. In men particularly, anger may express itself in the desire for revenge on women because a woman has been such a powerful but destructive part of his early identity. This desire for revenge might manifest itself through the widespread existence of domestic violence, rape, violent attacks on women and pornography. In pornography, women are often rendered less powerful by turning them into sexualized children who seem to have no purpose other than to provide men with pleasure and an identity, in other words, those things the man's mother was unable to provide for him as a child.

For Winnicott, anti-social acts such as stealing, like Freud's repression, are a symbolic return to a point where the environment failed the child. He or she returns to find the source of his or her deprivation, that is, the psychical gaps in themselves symbolized by the objects they steal. In this way the individual alerts the environment or culture to the deprivation he or she suffered in relation to his or her mother or both parents. So stealing represents a splitting off of bad experience onto objects whose theft represents the possibility of transformation, the repair of what Balint (1984) calls 'the basic fault', and the return of what once rightfully belonged to the child.

Winnicott thought, like Klein, that the baby was born in a state of initial 'unintegration', dominated by its primitive greed for and envy of its mother and the desire to control her totally. After the Second World War, and the horrors of fascism, he speculated about the psychical sources of fascism. He wanted to know how an individual moves from his or her earliest state of primitive greed and helplessness to a sense of relative autonomy in which he or she can relate to other people without too much loss of spontaneity and desire (Winnicott 1986: 210–20). Particularly, within the context of fascism, he asked how the individual achieves this development without resorting to the false solution of a rigid set of self-controlling, life-denying convictions or the idealization of a powerful leader who demands obedience and compliance. If we look at his subsequent work, Winnicott's solution to this question seems, partly, to have been the crucial importance of what happens in the transitional space between the mother and child. Here, the child can resolve issues of intimacy and separation, in a playful emotional climate of make-believe characterized by provisionality and the *absence of absolute values*. If the child makes the transition from phantasy to reality in this creative, imaginative, provisional way it will be unlikely to need a rigid set of beliefs or an idealized external leader who may demand compliance with visions of the future which depend on violence and destruction for their achievement. For Winnicott, fascism is a permanent alternative to the creative transformations of puberty. Here, in adolescence, the working through of conflicts and the creative development of something for ourselves replace the need to comply excessively with the needs of others who constitute the environment. Winnicott compares the indoctrinating leader (and the indoctrinating therapist) to the impinging, pre-emptive, rigid presence of the mother who steals the emergence of a self from her baby. In his paper 'Some Thoughts on the Meaning of the Word "Democracy"' (Winnicott 1964), he suggests that there is a precarious but innate democratic tendency in the developing baby, given the right kind of maternal environment. This seems to be another way of expressing the idea that a 'good' experience in early infancy lays the ground for a wish to repeat the same kind of creative experience in the wider culture, making the need to be violent and destructive much less likely.

So Winnicott suggests that a certain kind of responsive, nurturing mothering produces creative, fulfilled individuals free from destructive elements which need to be projected onto others to avoid damage to the self. However, his concept of the false self suggests that the sources of destructive and self-destructive behaviour initially lie in the depressed mother (rather than Klein's depressed baby), who lacks the unconscious ability to respond to her child's need for her to help it make initial sense of the world and itself.

Violence against women

In relation to violence specifically against women, Winnicott argues that the baby's initial dependence on the mother, inevitably entailing some compliance, underlies both men's and women's attitude to the idea of 'woman' (Winnicott, 1958a: 304–5). He suggests that it is the massive inequality of power between mother and baby, rather than the baby's envy (as suggested by Klein), which leads to the unconscious association of the idea of the mother, and women generally, with the fear of annihilation. Unless the mother is able to transfer her power to her child by sensitively and imaginatively encouraging the baby's sense of its own creativity, the child, whatever gender it is, will associate the mother, 'woman', with the terror of non-being and psychical disintegration. So, both Winnicott and Klein suggest, violence specifically against women, in some men, may involve a mixture of both envy and the fear of annihilation inspired by the mother's power. For Winnicott, those mothers who, for a variety of reasons, cannot be 'good enough' may be experienced as particularly controlling and powerful because their own unmet needs are so suffocating of the baby's self. As I suggested earlier, this may explain some men's resort to pornographic images of women and much younger real female partners as a defence against the internalized mother's power and the sense of powerlessness she provokes. In contrast, many pornographic images, in particular, evoke connotations of little girls who need to be protected or controlled which make some men feel more powerful than they feel.

Christopher Bollas, basing his approach mainly on Winnicott's work, has developed a powerful theory of his own based on the idea of the transformational mother which sheds further light on the origins of creativity and destructiveness. Let's begin by getting a sense of the emotional texture of his theory as a whole.

Bollas: the transformative mother

Christopher Bollas argues that neither classical nor Lacanian psychoanalytic approaches address the character of that part of the psyche that lives in the wordless world behind language. He argues that the baby's first object, the mother, can cast a shadow over the life of the child and later adult without the child having the capacity to process this relation through mental representations or language. The example Bollas gives is the situation in which the mother uses the child to contain her projective identifications. For Bollas, psychoanalysis is partly preoccupied with the emergence into thought of early memories of being and relating, of reliving through language what is known but not yet thought. The early mother is what he describes as a transformational object, and what he sees as the adult's continued search for transformation (through consumer goods, relationships, holidays, 'causes') is in some respects a memory of this early relationship in which maternal care is transferred into the internal self system. Children who are inside a family dynamic which they find impossible to understand cannot successfully organize such experience into phantasies that hold or contain them. This means they store up this 'self-state' determined by a known but ungrasped situation which may subsequently, perhaps, be unknowingly expressed only in moods, but not in thought or language.

Bollas distinguishes, interestingly, between the unconscious ego and the repressed unconscious. For him, the unconscious ego refers to unconscious *form*, whereas the repressed unconscious refers to *content*. He takes issue with both Winnicott and Lacan for associating the true self with the unconscious and the false self with the ego. He argues that this fails to account for what he calls the 'organizing idiom' or way of being of every child, learned from the mother, which he argues is more ego than repressed unconscious. For Bollas, the ego is part of the true self. The baby, with the mother, sets up and develops a highly complex system of organization of its experience, all of which takes place before we exist as a subject for ourself in language. 'The subject arrives rather late in the day' (Bollas 1991: 8). Bollas suggests that by the time of this arrival we are capable of meaningful interpretation of our existence, and the meaningful presence of others, but we have already been constructed by the self or ego's negotiation with the pre-Oedipal maternal environment before our entry into language. Phantasy is not the same as the true self but represents the first representation of what Bollas calls the 'unthought known' in the baby's mind. It forms an idiom of the baby's being and is the first means of representation in the gradual and complex development of an internal world. He suggests that the phantasy of the Oedipus complex involves the child in the formation of mental representations that engage the child in unconscious *thought* and in this respect psychical activity in the Oedipal phase differs fundamentally from that in the pre-Oedipal world of the unthought known.

So Bollas's idea of the self is formed by what it intuitively knows but cannot yet think, by its own complex system of 'grammar' which is partly inherited and partly acquired. In our early life, we 'know' these 'grammatical' rules about the business of 'being' but only some of them have so far been thought. But Bollas suggests that a significant part of our adult existence is determined by this unthought known. Bollas also argues that there is no one unified self because it is made up of many different internalized relationships. For him, the idea of the self should refer to the positions or perspectives from which and through which we sense, feel, observe and reflect on distinct and separate experiences of being and over time we develop a general sense of this relation, of what we take ourselves to be like.

Bollas places great emphasis on the transformative role of the mother, describing it as an aesthetic experience which responds in a particular way to the baby's desire and needs. She both sustains the baby's life and transmits, through her own special idiom of being, an aesthetic of being that becomes an aspect of the baby's identity. This is the way she acts as what Winnicott calls the 'facilitating environment' through her way of holding the infant, responding to its gestures, selecting objects, and perceiving its internal needs. The language of her inter-subjective relationship with the baby is gesture, gaze and utterance, and all this negotiated experience coalesces around the rituals of the psychosomatic needs of the mother's care: feeding, changing, soothing, playing and sleeping. So the mother, as the other half of the infant's self, transforms the baby's internal and external environment and, in this process, offers the experience of being prior to systems of language. Bollas stresses that there is no delusion operating in the child's early identification with the mother as Lacan suggests. With the transformation of being through this symbiotic knowing, the mother *does* actually transform the baby's world. The acquisition of language is perhaps the most significant transformation but learning to handle and differentiate between objects and to remember objects which are not present are transformative experiences which crucially change the nature of the child's internal world. Given this level of identification with the mother, it is not surprising that a failure by the mother to provide this kind of nurturing environment through prolonged absence or 'bad handling' (for example, narcissistic projection onto the baby) can cause the collapse of the baby's self or ego and precipitate huge psychical pain.

So, Bollas (1991: 33) argues that the baby takes in the form as well as the content of the mother's communication – how she transforms inner and outer realities. The aesthetic of this experience is 'the particular way the mother transforms emptiness, agony and rage into fullness and content'. The baby gets both milk and aesthetic handling from the mother. In doing this, the mother protects the child from the premature development of thought. She gives a sense of continuous being through her reverie or rapport with the baby at a time when thought is irrelevant to survival. The words of language are later a new transformational object which substitutes for the mother and 'leads from deep enigmatic privacy to culture and the human village' (Bollas 1991: 34). Language is the discovery of the word as a representation of the self and it allows further development of the individual's personal aesthetic or idiom. 'So the first human aesthetic passes into the formal aesthetics of language which represents a continuity from the mother's cooing, mirror-uttering, singing and so on' (Bollas 1991: 35). As part of this transition we carry the framework of the maternal aesthetic, our primary 'theme' of being with her that will affect all future ways of being with her and in other close relationships. Contrary to Lacan's idea, the historical subject comes on the scene after the basic rules have been established. 'Whether accepting and facilitating or refusing and rigid or a mixture of both, the mother's handling will influence our way of handling the self' (Bollas 1991: 36). We learn a grammar of our being from the mother. If there is a failure at the point of the child's entry into language, 'words will be meaningless expressions of the child's internal world which may feel useless and dangerous.' Bollas suggests that this may lead to the dissociation of language from feeling so that 'moods are registered exclusively in a person's way of being' (Bollas 1991: 36). Ideally, the ego stores the rules for handling the self and objects and, when the structure coheres, the baby will begin to express its early knowing through phantasy, thought and relating to an object. This known but unthought, Bollas insists, is the substance of the core of one's being and will be the basis of all subsequent infantile and child phantasy life.

So, for Bollas, the transformational mother allows the child to form a sense of harmony with the outside world. But, Bollas argues, the child whose mother is not emotionally present, who is not emotionally containing, has to construct her out of nothing, for example, out of moods of isolation, despair, helplessness, frustration and rage. In doing this, it forms a substitute object which contains these feelings but out of what Bion calls 'loving hate'. The child dreads abandonment which causes intense hatred but it also treasures the mother as all it has.

Theft of the self and the violent acting out of inner states

Bollas draws on Bion's concepts of the alpha and beta elements outlined earlier to argue that seriously disturbed mothers or parents may unknowingly attack the baby through projective identification so that they deposit a large, unwanted and destructive part of themselves in the baby, leaving it in possession of their confusion as well as its own and potentially overwhelmed with destructive feelings. This may mean, Bollas argues, that the child becomes perpetually delinquent, registering its identity not in language and relationships but through 'acting out' in actions which testify to its rebellion against what has happened to it. The child unconsciously perceives the parent(s) as an attack on life itself and feels that its parents are trying to strangle its life out of existence. It develops a disposition to 'empty' itself which, Bollas suggests, might reflect a death drive which has been created in the child by the 'death work' of a certain kind of family life. In the context of self-destructive behaviour, Bollas describes the situation where the parent and child organize a shutting out of 'thinking'. Bollas describes as 'normotic' the person who comes from a family where internal or feeling states are not referred to, where parents are unable to be alive to the child's inner reality so that he or she fails to symbolize in language his or her subjective states of mind. Language is used only for control. Here the violence is experienced by the child in the enforced shutting out of feeling and life. Nothing emotional is ever put on the table to be shared and discussed.

So Bollas argues that a person who has continually had important elements and functions of his or her psyche extracted during childhood will experience a certain kind of loss. He or she will feel that a primary injustice has occurred and they may seek vengeance based on a bitter, agitated despair that forms a kind of unconscious mourning. They may become dominated by the idea of an eye for an eye, a tooth for a tooth. Here we return to the idea of the grudge. Drawing on Winnicott, Bollas suggests that a man who becomes a burglar may be violating a home to steal internal objects of a family and that the act may mirror what happened to him as a child when there were thefts of parts of the child's mind that the child can know only through a sense of primal loss and a sense of prevailing harm having been done to him. It has occurred in a wordless, violent manner which, in the same way, he may then inflict onto others in the external world in theft or violent acts. Similarly, psychopathic lying may be seen as an omnipotent manipulation of the object-world which mirrors the way a family effectively lied to a child about what was happening to it. For example, a child who may be being abused physically or psychologically may be told repeatedly 'You're a very lucky little girl to have such loving parents and such a happy childhood and everything you want compared with what we had.'

In many ways, Bollas elaborates the ideas of Winnicott and Bion while adding his own emphases. His idea of the mother as someone who brings about transformation in the child's psychical life is particularly rich and suggestive. Again, his ideas, like the others discussed in this chapter, bring home the importance of social provision which promotes emotional containment and growth in adults who become parents rather than feelings of helplessness, anxiety and resentment.

Violent crime and the need for mourning

In this chapter we have explored some psychoanalytic ideas which may help us to understand some of the unconscious as well as cultural and historical roots of violence. These ideas suggest that there are deep-structure unconscious factors enmeshed in most forms of destructiveness of which we need to take serious account. However, an analysis of different forms of destructiveness may sometimes make us feel uncomfortable because it may stir up anxiety and pain derived from our own personal histories. As Christopher Dare (1996) suggests, we may find such subjects as child sexual abuse and other forms of abuse, torture and persecution 'unthinkable' because they evoke in us the pre-verbal memory of a time when we found many experiences unbearable and impossible to contain. But we need at least to try to 'think' the unbearable in order to help us find ways of reducing the quantity of unbearable things anyone has to face in a life. Literature is often one of the best ways of allowing us to find the words or 'think' the unbearable.

Psychoanalytic understandings have a direct bearing on the way society deals with violent individuals since they strongly suggest that much violent behaviour results from some form of physical, sexual or psychological abuse in early life. It suggests that not only does society need to be protected from very destructive, violent individuals but also that the principle of retribution only adds further to the cycle of violence in which many violent individuals are already caught up. This seems very important in the context of debates about the value of increased government emphasis on prison and retribution, particularly in Britain and America. Arthur Hyatt Williams (1996), influenced by Klein's and Bion's work, and by the experience of working with violent offenders in British prisons, argues that, if punishment leads not to atonement but to a further grievance, it leads to a negative therapeutic reaction which escalates the committing of violent crimes. He argues that if prisons treat prisoners well, it facilitates their capacity to make contact with unbearable feelings and mourn, which can achieve positive change. He also argues that the brutalization of prisoners tends to be copied by the victims. This happens during war when the victim identifies with the enemy and commits the same atrocities. The passive recipient of violence becomes an active perpetrator. As Freud (1911) suggests in 'Formulations on the Two Principles of Mental Functioning' (PFL 11: 29) and, as we have seen, Bion develops, brutalization usually involves an evacuation of violence to relieve the self of the unthinkable. What is psychically indigestible is expelled in increasingly worse forms of the original abuse. Individuals treat new victims with the same violence to which they have been subjected. Reparative action in the form of good treatment and, perhaps, psychoanalytic therapy may turn the corner from brutalization to the restoration of healthy, creative behaviour. Hyatt Williams stresses the importance, after a brutal crime, of opportunities for repeated mourning and regretting of the crime on a daily basis so that painful feelings and memories associated with it may be felt and digested so that they will not be evacuated in further violent behaviour. Mourning consists of the ability to contain painful feelings of badness and guilt and allows phantasy to be used as a substitute for 'acting out' in a violent action. Hyatt Williams distinguishes between manic reparation and real mourning that is repeated day after day. In prolonged mourning the internalized object which has been hurt can be repaired and restored. This takes the form of the prisoner becoming able to identify with the victim. Hyatt Williams argues that prisons have to humanize the prisoner rather than de-humanizing him or her by demonization.

In thinking about forms of group violence, Hyatt Williams argues that events involving mobbing and bullying often begin with as few as two aggrieved members. He agrees with Bion that the particular group dynamic and the herd instinct are of central importance. In contrast to Freud, he does not see attachment to a leader as always evidence of disturbed behaviour. He stresses that in dealing with gangs or mobs, it is necessary to deal with the mob leader by detaching him and attaching him to a different group. He suggests that followers may have only a very mild inclination to sadistic, destructive behaviour, which is mainly a result of the violence the leader had to suffer passively before. This only becomes activated into sexual excitement if encouraged by a seriously aggrieved leader. Hyatt Williams argues that it is very difficult to change a mob without removing the central core of the mobbers but that retaliation against this causes acceleration because it is perceived as scapegoating. This intensifies the situation and introduces a heroic element. Such situations, argues Hyatt Williams, need psychological insight and empathy rather than sadistic retribution. In his experience of violent offenders, there had always been a bad example in the form of a sadistic parent or an act which has resulted in the internalization of an authority figure who is sadistic. This had produced the shame, blame, grudge cycle leading to brutalization and retribution. In some individuals, Hyatt Williams suggests, again drawing on Bion, revenge is experienced as indigestible to the self which may lead to a self-destructive act such as suicide or psychosomatic illness. (This does not rule out the possibility that some suicides committed in prisons and detention centres, more recently particularly by young people on remand, are those of young, vulnerable individuals who suffer at the hands of the violent.) Hyatt Williams suggests that in turning anger outwards the individual is saying that he or she can't love other people, whereas in turning anger inwards the individual is communicating that he or she can love other people but are being potentially overwhelmed by uncontainable feelings.

One important question raised earlier in this chapter is whether being male or female has any connection with whether anger is turned outwards or inwards? As I commented earlier, it is certainly the case that it is mostly men who go to prison and women who end up in mental hospitals. There are clearly cultural inhibitions on women and girls expressing anger, though recently there has been a significant increase in the number of girls involved in violent crime, but we cannot rule out the possibility that there may be biological factors involved. However, suicide rates among 15–24-year-olds generally in Britain have increased dramatically in the past fifteen years and an Oxford study predicts that some 20,000 young people will be referred to hospital in any one year as a result of deliberate self-injury (Hawton and Fagg 1992).

Cultural responses

Psychoanalytic approaches generally suggest that, rather than the punishment and retribution recently favoured by most 'tough on crime' approaches to violent crime, the provision of the opportunities for psychotherapy and creative relationships is likely to be among the most effective ways of tackling some of the causes of crime and helping those driven to violent, abusive behaviour. Although it is expensive, this kind of approach reflects the psychoanalytic view, supported by most psychotherapists working in the clinical field, that harsh punishment only compounds bullying, sadistic behaviour. Without being utopian, the wider national and international levels of violence, the ending of poverty, and the cultural engendering of experiences which generate hopefulness and a sense of worth rather than futurelessness and worthlessness, seem to be a priority. Democratic as well as totalitarian governments sometimes adopt social and economic policies which promote institutionalized forms of violence. These include such things as poverty, homelessness, unemployment, de-humanizing, meaningless work, isolation and a wide division between 'haves' and 'have nots', rather than opportunities for emotional integration and creative forms of boundary and independence. This reproduces cycles of deprivation, frustration and despair for many people. In some people these states of mind may frequently activate early unconscious experiences of helplessness, confusion, pain and rage. When this is reinforced within the psychical as well as social context of the family, psychoanalytic theory suggests that severe psychical damage, both destructive and self-destructive, is likely to result.

Although escalating costs of health care suggest that psychotherapy will not form a standard part of health provision in the foreseeable future, it already offers help to some individuals, especially adolescents, who are caught up in a cycle of violent behaviour. Psychoanalytic approaches suggest that individuals who have been damaged by violence may be unable later, as parents, to avoid handing on to their children the injury done to them, often in a cycle of unconscious damage which is passed from one generation to the next. In a climate of increased public awareness of the psychical as well as cultural roots of destructive behaviour, such a service may one day be a vote-winner in a climate where there is a loss of confidence in more punitive, vengeful approaches to violent behaviour.

Violence and representation

Finally, in this chapter, let us look briefly at what may be the underlying unconscious sources of the enjoyment of images of extreme violence in the cinema and on video. Since we live in a violent world in which, in Europe and America particularly, violence seems to be on the increase, we would expect this to be reflected in cinematic and video representation. But, despite the existence of violence within culture, most individuals' lives do not bring them into regular contact with the kind of sadistic violence and graphic detail we now regularly encounter in many contemporary films and videos unless we make stringent efforts to avoid it. For me, this raises two questions: why do so many individuals want to watch very violent images, which the commercial success of these films suggest is the case, and are cinematic and video representations likely to provoke violent crime in any of those who watch them? A Kleinian response to the first question would be that many of us gain satisfaction from explicitly violent images because they reflect the chaotic, violent primitive impulses which she argues, controversially, underlie the conscious identity of us all. Through the process of identification with visual symbols of violence, Klein suggests that many of us gain symbolic access to unconscious, primitive phantasies which derive from the paranoid-schizoid position. The representation of violence therefore has the effect of catharsis similar to that inspired by Greek tragedy and Shakespeare's tragedies through allowing us to take part in the repeated symbolization of powerful feelings rather than converting them into destructive action. Bettelheim (1991) argues that fairy-tales also make possible the symbolization of primitive inner states of the child's mind. Both these forms of representation have something in common with the therapeutic session in which the patient becomes able to symbolize or 'think' internal states of feeling or conflict, something previously known but not yet thought.

However, importantly, this eventually leads to long-term emotional change rather than temporary emotional release. So Kleinian psychoanalytic theory suggests that many people go to violent films which, through the process of identification, allows them to express violent phantasies which culture forbids them destructively to 'act out'. In most violent films it is always clear who are the good and bad guys so we identify with good as well as bad within a moral context of right and wrong. However, in the best 'cops and robber' films there is no clear line drawn between good and evil. There are bad cops and good villains, so good and evil are a part of each other and not completely split off from one another. We could argue that this representation of the existence of good and bad in the same people represents a more psychically complex and realistic approach to identity characteristic of Klein's depressive position than the stark, binary division of good and bad more characteristic of paranoid-schizoid thinking. However, films such as *Pulp Fiction* (1994), directed by Tarantino, may pose problems. It has been widely suggested that *Pulp Fiction* engages us in a psychopathic experience through identification without the need to experience the consequences. Some regard this as pornographic in the sense that there is no good object with which to identify. But watching violent films even from an exclusively psychopathic point of view for most people *is* a quite different experience from that of the psychopathic individual who 'acts out' their murderous phantasies in the 'real' world because they cannot distinguish between their inner world of phantasy and the external world. Such individuals remain psychically dominated by delusions of the paranoid-schizoid position without access to the 'reality' of the depressive position. As we have seen, Bion's work further suggests that these individuals have been so damaged by their early experiences that they use violent action as a means of evacuating their 'bad' experience. This 'acting out' is a form of 'self' preservation in the absence of being able to consciously 'think' the experience through the symbols of language. Under normal circumstances, most of us are able to distinguish adequately between our inner world and the outer world of external reality, between internal phantasy and action (or 'acting out') in the world outside.

So, psychoanalytic theory suggests that the consumption of violent images in films and videos does not directly provoke the 'acting out' of violent crime except in those who are already preoccupied with and disposed to violence because of their early experiences. The young boys in the Bulger case may have been watching a violent video before they murdered the toddler James Bulger, but there was a family history of deprivation and violence. It is unclear whether the video played any part in their action. Psychotherapists specializing in the treatment of very violent borderline and psychopathic patients see a violent father as one of the most important indicators of violent criminality.

A more Freudian perspective suggests that the popularity of very violent cinematic and video images reflects the need to symbolize unconscious primitive anal sadistic phantasies about control and unresolved castration phantasies of being locked in Oedipal combat with the father. We gain satisfaction through being able to identify with the protagonists. If football and other team games are ritualized forms of violence or war, this interpretation seems suggestive. As we have seen, Klein's theory also suggests the need to symbolize primitive destructive feelings but for Klein these murderous feelings are provoked by envy of the mother rather than by fear of the father. We express destructive emotions based on oral phantasies about attacking and being attacked by the breast (devouring, biting, tearing apart) and anal phantasies (controlling, sadistic) symbolically through the identifications we make in violent cinematic and video images of devouring monsters and monstrous acts which give us a form for our primitive phantasies. Bion's, Winnicott's and Bollas's object-relations theories strongly suggest that it is mainly those of us who have been emotionally deprived as babies, in whom destructive and sadistic unconscious experiences remain unprocessed, who positively enjoy violent images. But since so many individuals seem to be drawn to visual images of an increasingly horrific nature it is difficult to avoid the conclusion that many people have suffered considerable emotional deprivation in early childhood. In the past, gladiatorial combat, animal baiting and public executions, which continue to take place in some parts of the world, seem to have fulfilled the same kind of function. Some analytical therapists would argue that those of us who dislike violent film and video images are denying our own violent feelings, perhaps because our early experiences have led us to be more masochistic than sadistic. Others suggest that some individuals have no interest in violent images because early destructive feelings have been integrated into consciousness rather than remaining unconscious or split off.

If we turn to the issue of the technical production of increasingly graphic images of violence in film and video, the question arises whether the current focus on the techniques used to achieve these images stems only from the need to symbolize primitive, violent feelings. Or do these images simply reflect the evolution of a cult of ultra-realistic fictional murder and mayhem which is connected with the fashionable, postmodern concern with the constructedness of what we call 'reality' and the need to break new boundaries of cultural 'transgression'? From a psychoanalytic standpoint, the portrayal of extremely realistic violence may be related to an unconscious need to control our fear of violence and death. A film such as *Pulp Fiction* presents violence in a context not of exploring mindless brutality but from within a framework of emotional shallowness, spectacle, style, irony and the idea that in the post-modern world, no 'reality' exists anyway. There are only illusions that we encounter in different forms of representation. Psychoanalytic insights suggest that part of the successful transition from phantasy to what we call 'reality' is about coming to terms with our phantasies of omnipotence and the idea that we are immortal. They suggest that one of the most important things about growing up is the recognition of the undoubted 'reality' that we cannot be in control of everything and that one day we shall all die. The 'message' in recent films such as *Pulp Fiction* is that violence and death are amusing and funny, even stylish and 'cool' when they are represented in a technically accomplished way. Psychoanalytic approaches generally suggest that this may be a defensive splitting off from what death and violence and destruction mean to us unconsciously, particularly in the context of mounting fears about violence in the street encroaching into our homes. The point about violent death is that we cannot control it. It is final and uncompromisingly the end of everything we know. It represents a monumental potential loss of control which our narcissism resists. With the modern decline of religious belief most people these days cannot rescue themselves with the expectation of an afterlife. Increasingly we have to square up to the idea of our death as something final and nowadays, as in many periods in the past, we may fear that it may be a violent one. As anyone who has experienced any violence knows, violence is usually painful, emotional, shocking, ugly both visually and psychologically. In fact, it is everything *Pulp Fiction* appears to be denying. Are the smart, sterilized, even objectively beautiful and witty images of films like *Pulp Fiction* being unconsciously used to help us master what horrifies us about the 'real life' images of death and destruction which crowd in on us via our television screens?

9

Consuming 'goods'

One of the fascinating aspects of the word 'consumption' in the setting of psychoanalytic theory is that it seems to refer back directly to the baby's earliest experience of consuming the mother so that it can survive not only physically but also psychically. Along with the nourishment contained in the mother's milk, the baby also takes in a pleasurable primitive sense of identity, of having what Winnicott calls a 'real' existence. In this psychoanalytic context, pleasurable cultural experiences of many kinds, though in different degrees, may be seen as symbolizing our earliest experience of the 'good breast'. Symbolically, we may 'consume' or incorporate other people, ideas or material objects into ourselves as a means of psychical survival.

The increasing availability and consumption of consumer 'goods' has been a defining characteristic of post-war culture in Western countries. Intrinsic to this process has been both the massive development of science and technology and the marketing of these 'goods' in terms of meanings with which individuals, by means of mass advertising, have been invited to identify. As many writers have observed, the second half of the twentieth century has seen the steady development of the marketing of desire in the form of symbolic 'goods' which represent longed-for aspects of ourselves that we unconsciously imagine we can acquire from the external world. Advertisers have tried to persuade us that we can buy whatever we want to be. They have also been able to define the particular commercial forms our unconscious wishes might take so that cars or beer, Coca Cola or a pair of Nike trainers may come to represent, for example, sexual wishes, power, status, security, comfort or a sense of belonging. The success of this marketing enterprise and the mass consumption of an increasing quantity and diversity of goods as they become available, as well as the concepts of fashion and style which persuade us that we constantly need to re-invent the meanings of ourselves in specified ways, can be understood only in terms of a combination of historical, cultural and psychical factors.

In the latter half of the twentieth century there has been unprecedented technological and economic development and the intensifica-
tion and globalization of the capital and power required to make
financial profit out of these developments. In Western countries, and
increasingly further afield in developing nations such as those in the
Pacific rim, this has resulted in jobs, higher wages and an increased
surplus available for spending on consumer 'goods' among many people
despite low wages and unemployment among significant minorities in
many places. In the past twenty years the gap has widened significantly
between the 'haves' and 'have nots', both globally and within individual
countries. But the success of the modern phenomena of consumerism
and shopping as major sources of pleasure and identity for many people
cannot be explained only by technological and economic development.
A psychoanalytic perspective suggests that millions of individuals'
pleasure in consumption and their willingness to invest so much of
themselves in consumer commodities, often working long hours in
unrewarding work in order to do so, are directly related to the erosion
of other sources of identity which used to be more readily available
within culture. For many, the painful experience of living under communism in Eastern Europe seems to have been intensified by the absence
of consumer goods as a pleasurable means of easing the burden of so
many assaults on identity and meaning.

Fragmentation, dislocation and an increasing sense of disconnection
from others have been seen as characterizing contemporary culture by
both modernist and post-modernist writers. Central to this fragmentation
have been at least three major social changes. One of them has been the
gradual, post-war decline and breakdown of old, stable communities
which, without idealizing them, frequently provided large numbers of
individuals with many of the positive experiences in their lives (even
though they were also sometimes experienced as suffocating and inhibiting). Such communities provided many people with a secure basis for
the development of a sense of identity through nurturing feelings of
belonging, of being known and recognized, of being an insider rather
than an outsider, and through a sense of shared meanings, solidarity and
mutual support in times of hardship and ill health. Such communities,
often based on extended kinship, with their network of identifications
and social affiliations, have declined for many complex reasons but
particularly because of the increase in job mobility, developments in
communication and, in many cases, mass-housing schemes which have
dispersed people onto and isolated them in vast estates on the edge of
cities away from the more intimate, if old-fashioned, inner-city neigh-
bourhoods. Together with these kinds of attack on urban and rural

communities, and on the sense of identity and continuity they helped to provide, there has been further fragmentation in an unprecedented increase in family break-up in the last three decades of the twentieth century. In Great Britain one in three families now split up.

All other things being equal (in the sense that there has been no significant physical, sexual or emotional abuse, and even sometimes when there has), family break-up causes emotional trauma. It means that individual identities may also break up as a result of unbearable feelings of grief and loss. Psychoanalytic perspectives suggest that the child's identity is made up of the internalizations of both parents, however imperfect one or both may be. When a family breaks up this identity is suddenly split down the middle. This may mean that there are two competing halves associated with mother and father respectively pulling in two different directions, with all the associated feelings of loss, disorientation, guilt, anger, anxiety and helplessness. Psychoanalytic approaches suggest that, apart from feelings of loss of part of their identity when a parent leaves, children often tend to feel that the break-up is their fault, that it is because of their 'badness', whether it is in terms of guilty desire or angry feelings. But divorce and break-up of the microcommunity of the modern, relatively isolated nuclear family is usually experienced by parents as well as children as a major assault on identity.

Another source of significant cultural change in Western Europe and America has been a political assault on what has been seen as welfare dependency. In the past fifteen years, for ideological as well as economic reasons, there has been a sustained attack on the post-war concept of the socialized community supported by taxation and national insurance which, via the state, accepts the responsibility for caring for people during times of economic hardship, unemployment or ill health. Many people had grown accustomed to this post-war idea of social nurture and responsibility based on the sense of social cohesion generated in the war-time years. Recent high unemployment, job insecurity, increasing tendencies to employ people on short-term contracts, justified by the need for a flexible response to the exigencies of the global market, and the rapid removal of much of the social fabric of welfare and health provision, have been other recognizable factors in widespread feelings of anxiety, insecurity, disconnection, lack of self-esteem and helplessness.

In the kind of cultural context outlined above, psychoanalytic knowledge suggests that consumption of consumer 'goods' may play a central role in encouraging, if not creating, escapist or narcissistic forms of identity. For some of the two-thirds of the British population who are economically in a position to take an active part in it this may help, temporarily, to plug the psychical gap left by early unresolved experiences of loss and separation and also by the loss of other nurturing sources of identity within culture based on fulfilling, sustaining networks of relationships in the family, community or society more generally. Kleinian theory, in particular, suggests that certain experiences and deprivations brought about by cultural experience provoke high levels of anxiety which, in some more vulnerable people, cause primitive defence mechanisms to resurface as a way of defending a sense of meaningful identity. Freudian theory suggests that shopping and the purchase of consumer 'goods', which are symbolically laden with longed-for aspects of ourselves, may, in the short term at least, be one reliable form of gratification in the context of rapid social change and fragmentation. Even for those in work, long working hours, bureaucratic and hierarchical line-management work structures, high levels of general stress including, for women in particular, that involved in combining work and family commitments and the easy availability of credit facilities may all contribute to the attraction of consumer 'goods'. Shopping offers a form of active power which many may feel they lack in other areas of their life and, for some, may act as a defence against feelings of culturally or psychically induced emptiness and meaninglessness. Indeed, it could be argued from this perspective, following Lasch (1980), that contemporary culture encourages us to substitute infantile forms of gratification for emotional integration. From a Freudian perspective, consumer 'goods' may evoke childhood phantasies of achieving a state of bliss and completion with the mother, whereas from a more Winnicottian perspective, they may evoke comfort, closeness and security also associated with early, pre-Oedipal experience. The car may often symbolize phallic power and sexuality but also the comfort, security and containment associated with the womb. Such unconscious symbolic meanings may well be a factor in the reluctance to exchange the car for public transport, even if the latter were to become cheap and frequent. Of course, conscious factors, such as convenience, economy and environmental considerations, are interwoven with unconscious meanings but psychoanalytic theory suggests that, for many, the unconscious meanings are likely to be the most salient.

Let us look now, in more detail, at some of the unconscious processes which may be involved in cultural consumption of a variety of kinds, including the consumption of romantic fiction, films, videos, TV programmes and celebrities. This involves looking, particularly, at the psychoanalytic meaning of the consumption or 'taking in' which is embedded in concepts such as incorporation, identification, narcissism, the ego-ideal, projection and introjection and projective identification.

Oral 'incorporation'

For Freud, the consumption of the mother's milk is the baby's first way of relating to itself and the outside world – it almost literally eats or incorporates the mother. As we have seen, in the highly pleasurable 'taking in' of the mother's milk, the baby not only gains nourishment but also its first sense of having a real existence or identity, at that time still merged with the breast. Through this process of the baby's identification with or incorporation of the mother, the breast represents both its physical and psychical survival. In his *Three Essays on the Theory of Sexuality*, Freud (1905) describes this process of incorporation of both milk and a primitive sense of identity as the oral phase of sexuality, followed by and overlapping with the anal, phallic and genital phases (PFL 7: 31). Freud suggests that as adults we all carry vestiges of this kind of oral behaviour in the need, sometimes, to incorporate or consume substitute forms of the symbolic 'good breast'. In states of anxiety or boredom we may seek the comfort associated with the breast by smoking, drinking, taking drugs, eating chocolate and comfort-eating generally. Oral behaviour also includes activities such as kissing, having conversations in which we consume a lot of space and time, soaking up television or the sun, or going on a shopping spree. Afterwards we may feel temporarily better, or more substantial, like the baby after a good feed because we now have something in our inner world which acts as a substitute for the meaning of the 'good breast'. These activities evoke memories of our earliest experience of the breast as a source of pleasure, comfort and identity.

However, Freud argues that if a baby experiences difficulty or trauma during the oral stage of its infancy, its future development as an adult may be particularly unconsciously preoccupied with the idea of incorporation as a means of gaining access to a sense of identity. There may be a feeling that nothing and no one is ever enough to fill an overwhelming psychical hunger. In close relationships, such an individual may be experienced as very emotionally demanding. In extreme forms, and particularly in situations which provoke anxiety and feelings of helplessness, adult oral behaviour may involve, for example, excessive drinking and greedy eating, which may involve eating disorders such as bulimia, and drug addiction. The pleasure of incorporation or 'taking in' may be achieved through the mouth, nose, ears or eyes, skin, intravenously or through 'greedy' shopping and the appropriation of large quantities of consumer objects (an extreme example would be Imelda Marcos's consumption of over 3,000 pairs of shoes). All these forms of 'consuming' behaviour may enable an individual to achieve a fragile, but temporary, sense of identity which, in early infancy, was the only basis for identity available to the baby. Some extreme forms of adult oral behaviour, involving, for example, alcohol or drug abuse, are often regarded by therapists as an attempt at self-medication, as a temporary way of boosting confidence and obtaining a sense of psychical substance and identity in order to obliterate a yawning sense of emptiness and isolation. Therapeutic groups such as Alcoholics Anonymous often seem to be effective because they offer the possibility of forming meaningful relationships with whole people rather than a part-object (the breast). These are based on shared experience and objectives and mutual support which offer the potential for other less destructive, less dependent, emotionally richer forms of identity to begin to emerge.

Narcissism and the ego-ideal

Freud's theory of narcissism and the idea of the ego-ideal and Lacan's concepts of the Imaginary and ideal ego have been widely used in the analysis of culture and particularly in the analysis of consumerism. These concepts seem to suggest why desires or needs and their temporary satisfaction can be so easily constructed in consumer societies. Let's look first at Freud's theory of narcissism.

Freud first used the term 'narcissism' in 1910 when he was trying to explain why homosexual men choose a lover who is the same rather than different from themselves. He came to the conclusion that they take themselves as their sexual object, narcissistically, and therefore seek a partner who resembles themself. This means that they can then love their lover as their mother loved them. Later, in his paper 'On Narcissism' written in 1914, he suggests that narcissism is a transitional stage between what he calls the baby's auto-eroticism or desire for pleasure from its own body and its desire for an external object, seen as a whole rather than part-object (initially the mother and later other objects) but with whom its identity is still merged (PFL 11: 65–97). In the narcissistic phase the baby projects its own body onto the mother whom it then loves as itself. In this way the baby forms a phantasied but satisfying, coherent image of its self reflected back to it by the mother's behaviour. Previously, in *The Three Essays on the Theory of Sexuality*, Freud had seen this identity as being made up entirely of pleasurable sensations. So the baby is given what Lacan calls an Imaginary sense of a free-standing 'self' or ego (Lacan's 'mirror stage') even though it still shares an identity with the mother. So the baby, and later narcissistic adult, projects its 'self' onto an object in the external world and then internalizes this external relationship with the object as its self while mistakenly imagining itself to be separate and independent from this external object or idea. This may happen in heterosexual as well as homosexual relationships when individuals often choose someone very like themselves.

Freud distinguished between two types of love: narcissistic love ·characterized by the desire to be loved (to be given idealized reflections of the self) and anaclitic love characterized by the desire to love. Freud thought some narcissistic types of relationship conformed to the kind of love characteristic of heterosexual relationships, and falling in love with the ideal of a perfect partner. (He also thought it was involved in some women's wish to be worshipped and adored.) In romantic love we often fall in love with our self projected onto the other. We speak of finding our 'other half', our self in another. This might explain a sensation characteristic of the initial stages of falling in love, what I call 'kissing into infinity'. During the kiss we project our self onto the other – all our phantasies and desires – and then, in the process of psychical incorporation, we feel a sense of oneness and what Freud described as the 'oceanic feeling' which may turn our legs to jelly with the sheer weight of what we have momentarily invested in the other person, sometimes on the basis of very flimsy evidence! Freud's theory of narcissism suggests we're actually kissing our phantasized self merged in the other. Traditionally, popular ballads about romantic love refer to the sensation of head-spinning dizziness, of 'walking on air', of having someone 'under our skin', references to a powerful feeling of unreality and identification. But as we get to know the person better and gain a more realistic view of them, we usually lose these sensations because we have to deal with a 'real' person who cannot, realistically, carry all our phantasies. As mentioned in chapter 5, the movements associated with the computer-generated, non-stop drum-beat of the dance music played at raves, whether or not combined with drugs, seem to induce the same kind of 'head-spinning' trance-like sensation of bondedness with others, of oneness with the universe. This again may be a psychical return to the 'oceanic feeling' reminiscent of our once merged, bonded existence with the mother. As well as the feeling of being in love, this seems also to be associated with deeply held religious feelings and experiences. In the context of relationships with consumer 'goods', we may fall in love in a similar way with the idea of a holiday, a car, a pair of boots or even a glistening new white fridge. Freud's theory of identification suggests that the new fridge reflects back to us a transformed, pristine, immaculate self ready to embark on a new life. The first scratch or stain, the first piece of plastic trim which falls off, the first hint of perished rubber and our phantasies of it and ourselves begin to dissolve as the reality of real fridges in everyday use sets in. Both we and the fridge have to sink back into the imperfect mundanity of the real world and we have to abandon our self-idealization. This phenomenon may help us to explain the lure of the spotlessly new in many other contexts which seems so intrinsic to marketing, fashion and the need to keep up to date. These are used to justify the need for continuous consumption of commodities for the purpose of refuelling our identities as well as satisfying the needs of a capitalist economy.

As we saw earlier, Freud thought the love of parents for their children was another form of loving ourselves in the other so that children are experienced by their parents as a psychological as well as a physical extension of themselves. He also thought love for a much younger partner was another form of narcissistic love which involves the idea of loving the 'self' we used to be or would have liked to have been, that is, a feeling of renewal. Freud argued that, although we normally eventually transfer our narcissistic love from the narrow confines of a relationship in which our identity is fused with someone else (at first the mother) to a love-object we experience as separate, we always retain some potential for love based on narcissism. The problem with relationships based on narcissism is that part of our unconscious identity is projected onto someone or something else in the external world which, in making us very psychically dependent on them, makes us very vulnerable if that person rejects us or dies. It seems clear that narcissism or love of the same can express itself in both heterosexual and gay relationships since 'masculinity' and 'femininity' or difference may exist in an infinite number of mixes, in male or female bodies.

Freud's notion of the ego-ideal is central to narcissism in both its normal and pathological forms. In his paper 'On Narcissism' he suggests that the love which was originally fixed on our self in its merged state with the mother is, after the separation and loss of the mother at the end of the Oedipal crisis, turned inwards onto a mother whom we have now internalized as an inner object. Freud argues that when we abandon or lose an object, we don't just leave it behind us. Instead, we internalize the idea of the loved object so that it lives on inside us and contributes to who we are. In this sense we are made up of abandoned love-objects. Having internalized the lost mother so that she becomes part of who we are, we then turn the full beam of our love inwards, which, since she is now a part of us, means onto our self. The ego-ideal, then, represents an unconscious strategy for returning to the earlier state of merged dependence on the mother through the installation of her as an idealized object, part of our self, in our internal world. It seems to refer specifically to the internalization of the bonded 'oneness' between the mother and baby and our attempt to hold on to this idea of completion with the mother for ever. In contrast, the super-ego (also an internalized object) is linked to three people, the father who represents culture and the reality beyond the mother and baby couple (Frosh 1991: 82). The ego-ideal in the adult, therefore, is best understood as representing the pursuit of narcissistic nirvana with a substitute for the mother, the pre-Oedipal pursuit of oneness, a pre-social time where the self and the mother are still merged, where incest has not been recognized, where there is no father, no difference and no structure (Frosh 1991: 82). It therefore represents an attempt at recovering the baby's sense of omnipotence and the reinstatement of illusion or phantasy. In contrast, the super-ego or symbolic father represents restriction, boundary, constraint, the recognition of symbolic castration, that is culture and adult forms of pleasure and sexuality. As Frosh (1991: 83) puts it, 'In a nutshell, the ego-ideal represents escapist imagination, the super-ego reality.'

Freud's powerful idea of the ego-ideal has been clarified and helpfully elaborated by Janine Chasseguet-Smirgel:

> The violent end to which the primary state of fusion is brought by [the baby's] helplessness obliges the infant to recognise the 'not me'. This seems to be the crucial moment when the narcissistic omnipotence that he is forced to give up is projected on the object, the infant's first Ego-Ideal, a narcissistic omnipotence from which he is henceforth divided by a gulf that he will spend the rest of his life trying to bridge. (Chasseguet-Smirgel 1985: 6–7)

This first overwhelming loss, the gap between what we are and what we want to be, as Lasch and others have suggested, then underlies all other cultural forms of alienation, for example, historical myths of a golden age, of the first expulsion from paradise or primary fall from grace which is central to many religions. However, as Frosh argues, as well as inspiring nostalgia for an idealized past, a need for oceanic experience, the desire for states of trance, it also inspires a search for re-unification which can underlie the motive for art as well as 'regressive longing' (Frosh 1991: 84). But Frosh distinguishes between the narcissism involved in creativity and regressive narcissism which involves our seeking an idealized self in, for example, a new car or a new partner. Frosh sums up the crux of the argument:

> creativity, like mental health in general, is concerned with facing reality, with acting upon it, transforming it, expressing, repairing, re-generating it, and the emotions it produces. Narcissism,

embedded structurally in the attempt of the ego to merge with the ego-ideal, is the denial of difference in favour of an imagined land in which there is no separation and loss, no unmet desire, and indeed no work. The ego-ideal, even though it fulfils a reality principle function, by establishing the existence of plans and hopes (i.e. post-ponements of pleasure) holds out a seductive promise of return to the longed for early state when ego and non-ego were merged; it is, therefore, more a carrier of regressive rather than creative urges. (Frosh 1991: 84)

One of the central emotional 'truths' at the heart of psychoanalytic knowledge is that, in order to remain creatively rather than regressively in touch with our inner world, we have, at the same time, to be able to recognize loss, frustration, uncertainty and contradiction. Chasseguet-Smirgel argues, importantly, that it is not the ego-ideal itself that is regressive, but the striving for the ego-ideal without the mediation of reality, without the acceptance of separation, symbolic castration, the recognition of loss and difference, in fact everything that results from a relatively successful resolution of Freud's Oedipal crisis, Lacan's transition to the Symbolic, Klein's depressive position or Winnicott's transitional space.

So Chasseguet-Smirgel argues, following Freud, that the pursuit of pleasures or ideals, whether in the form of consumer 'goods', political causes, religions, heroes and cultural icons or belief systems in the form of 'grand narratives', may be, but is not always, a regressive desire for an escape from the need to face reality. But she suggests that a rigid adherence to anything – nationalism, communism, fascism, the market, psychoanalytic theory or any other belief which argues that it alone represents the 'truth' – is a failure to face up to the reality of difference and is based on the desire for merged perfection with the mother. But this does not mean, as some post-modernists such as Lacan want to argue, that we have to give up all values and sense of moral purpose. There are causes we may want to defend but, when we embrace these values, psychoanalysis generally suggests that we need to do it within a context of being able to separate escapist phantasy from reality. We have to live with the reality that life is full of uncertainty, ambivalence, conflict and contradiction which we can never omnipotently control but it is this realization which allows us access to emotional growth and creativity.

Psychoanalysis generally, then, suggests that if we consistently unconsciously confuse the meaning of ourselves with objects outside ourselves in the external world, we remain potentially very fragile. By refusing the difference between our self and the meanings the object has outside as a 'not me' object, we cannot relate to the world beyond the projections we make onto it. Although we may gain short-term pleasure, it is always at the expense of an underlying sense of meaninglessness. From within an object-relations perspective, Winnicott argues that extreme forms of narcissism result from early maternal deprivation. This may result in varying degrees of what he calls a false self which is alienated from a self which remains undeveloped and in hiding. This false self remains in a state of undifferentiated fusion with the mother who is then confused with objects in the external world which we mistake for ourselves.

Lacan, building on Freud's ideas, defines narcissistic identifications as the realm of the Imaginary. Here we are beset by a hall of mirrors which represents a dead-end consisting of images which we misrecognize as a coherent identity. For Lacan, this blinds us to our essential de-centredness, filling the gap in our being where desire, loss and longing are permanently installed. The difference between Freud's and Lacan's conception of identity is that Lacan takes the self or ego to be entirely under the illusory sway of the Imaginary, distinguishing it clearly from a precarious subjectivity which we can obtain only in language. In contrast, Freud sees the ego or consciousness as an identity which may be constructed more or less narcissistically but which may equally well become relatively emotionally integrated. As we have seen, for Lacan, identities in both the Imaginary and the Symbolic are unstable in different ways, whereas, for Freud, consciousness can remain relatively undisturbed by unconscious eruptions. Kenneth Wright, writing from a Winnicottian perspective, distinguishes between the gap or absence left by the loss of our mothers which we fill by the process of symbolization and the gap with which some of us are left because we failed to have 'good enough', 'non-impinging' mothering (Wright 1991). This means that we never had the fundamental bedrock ingredients for a primary sense of self or what Winnicott calls the feeling of being 'real' rather than of just existing. This reassuring feeling continues to occupy the psychical centre of the child whose mother could be 'good enough' even though it has had to relinquish her.

In the context of the particular form of the 'taking in' or identification with public figures and celebrities known mainly through the media, let us consider for a moment the massive public response to the death of Diana, Princess of Wales in 1997 and what may be its significance in unconscious terms. Contrary to the view of some commentators at the time, that Diana was being narcissistically consumed as an idealized, de-humanized icon of perfection and saintliness, for the most part the public reaction seemed eminently realistic and 'healthy' rather than hysterical. The stunned mourning of her death seemed to centre on the perception of her as an imperfect mixture of qualities with which many could identify rather than as the embodiment of total goodness and truth. As Klein's theory emphasizes, phantasy in the form of idealization (and denigration) always prevents us from perceiving what is real and distinctive about individual human beings and the contradictions, ambiguity and ambivalence which exist in all of us. The public response to Diana's death suggested that she symbolized a complicated mixture of beauty and vulnerability, narcissism, insecurity, impulsiveness, humanity, humour and an intuitive capacity for spontaneous emotional generosity in relating to others, albeit in a glamorous, privileged setting. A wide diversity of people seemed to identify with her emotionally painful experiences and her struggle to make something positive out of them and herself so she could help other 'outsiders' who are damaged, despised or rejected. In the context of the increasing experience of social fragmentation and isolation mentioned earlier in this chapter, many people also seemed to find comfort in a transient sense of community and collectivity with others while they testified with their flowers and messages to their sense of shared identification with her and sorrow that she had suddenly been taken out of the symbolic structure of their lives. Through ordinary as well as narcissistic identification, her loss contained the loss of something of themselves as the loss of most things we value or love inevitably does.

The public's response to Diana's death may represent a major cultural turning point in the sense that the public allied itself uncompromisingly with the spontaneity and intuition traditionally associated with the 'feminine' but, importantly, blended with the activity and assertiveness associated, perhaps, with the bisexuality inherent in the meaning of the name of Diana, the Hunter Goddess. In other words, Diana perhaps represented a blurring of rigid gender boundaries. In Kleinian terms, Diana's death revealed a public alliance with the emerging realism and creativity associated with the depressive position and the beginning of emotional integration. The public mood challenged the rigidity of what Klein describes as the paranoid-schizoid position or Winnicott's false self encapsulated in what they perceived as the control and unreality of patriarchal 'masculinity' and authority. This was symbolized, in the public perception, in the monarchy. In his powerful funeral tribute, Diana's brother, Earl Spencer, referred directly to Diana's intuition. 'Your greatest gift was your intuition . . . your instinctive feel for what was really important in all our lives.' This echoes the language of Winnicott. Diana's death seems to have reinforced a huge and growing national longing for emotional growth, integrity, creativity and imagination in public life and an end to what people perceived as the sterility of control, rigidity and denial. This may have begun with the landslide Labour victory four months before. The public may also have intuitively recognized the unconscious womb-envy implied in the ambivalence or hostility of much of the media and the palace. Diana seemed to represent the mother and the intuitive, emotional world associated with the mother but she was also beautiful and becoming increasingly articulate and potent. This could do her no good in many quarters. As a result of her death, the public (men as well as women), many surprised by the depth of their feelings, seems spontaneously to have been struck with a collective deluge of emotional insight provoked by powerful feelings of loss. Contact with these feelings seemed to provoke a public transformation of consciousness through the emergence of a valuable kind of intuitively derived 'truth'. It is difficult to see this insight as the product only of language.

Finally, in this section, let us look at the meanings of a new car as an example of a narcissistic muddling of ourselves with material objects in the external world. Most of us are concerned about the design for practical and aesthetic reasons. We think about the engine and the size and shape of the body of the car in terms of economy, reliability, comfort, security and the overall appearance. Many people are also concerned with the image and, in particular, whether the car looks 'sexy' or 'muscular'. These terms would imply real or imagined levels of power, agility and performance. It is often important that the capacity for high performance connoted by fuel injection or turbocharging, for example, is symbolized literally in the car's presentation in the form of 'badging'. In BBC2's intriguing and often moving television documentary series about motoring, *From A–B* (BBC2, 1994), a company sales rep tells how he and his wife sat at home one evening and wept after the discovery that his company had allocated him a smaller car than he had expected and without the coveted 'i' after the car type number, indicating petrol injection. The man identified his car with himself and he felt his entire 'masculine' being had been humiliatingly called into question by the incident. In telling the story he showed all the signs of feeling himself to be a castrated and broken man. The loss of the 'i' represented the loss of himself. His experience is not so surprising if we recall the number of times we have seen advertisements for large, powerfully built cars caught almost *in flagrante* with beautiful, desirable women. Of course, many modern advertisements, most recently for jeans, beers and perfumes, sell identities, sexual and otherwise, in much more subtle ways but the mechanism through which we are seduced to invest ourselves in these meanings remains the same.

Idealized and denigrated consumer goods

Klein's theory also suggests that consumption is about the projection of our idealized selves onto consumer goods as well as other individuals, ideas and causes. We subsequently re-introject these idealized objects as ourselves (projective identification). In the context of what many see as a culture dominated by infantile longing, such ideas are very illuminating. Both Klein's concept of projective identification reminiscent of the rigidity and over-simplification of the paranoid-schizoid phase and Freud's victim/victimizer remnants of symbolic castration allow us to detect the presence of idealization and denigration in relation to consumer goods as well as people. We idealize those goods with which we identify and denigrate 'others'. Through a process of denigration we may turn consumer objects, like people, into rejected 'others' on the basis of their perceived difference from ourselves. This seems very like Foucault's 'dividing practices' as they apply to consumer commodities. We create certain consumer objects, as well as people, groups, ideas and causes as symbolic others, that is like inanimate lepers, criminals, deviants or 'defectives'. Fashion plays a major role in allowing us constantly to bolster our sense of who we are by indicating how we can renew ourselves by continually creating new arrangements of objects as psychical vehicles for idealization or denigration. We may redefine our selves and create new others on the basis of objects being 'in fashion' or identified with a group with which we want to be associated. Fashion thus allows us to continually re-create our selves whether in relation to cars, clothes, lager or anything which has been commodified. We sometimes express this matter of taste in the quite passionate terms of love and hate. We may say we 'wouldn't be seen dead' in some item of clothing or a particular car or describe something we don't 'fancy' as 'rubbish'. Perhaps the idealization of the self made possible by the acceptance of some goods and the denigration of others is most obvious in adolescents who, in the throes of trying to gain a viable sense of identity, often make passionate identifications with certain kinds of clothes, music, motorbikes or football teams which involve equally impassioned rejections of others, often to the point of getting involved in fights. Adults may be doing something similar when they identify with one particular way of thinking or theory to the exclusion of all others, thus closing off vast tracts of insight and possibility. It seems likely that a primitive need to maintain a sense of identity on the basis of idealizing some things and denigrating others may form the basis of the desire to compete rather than cooperate in many areas of life.

So both Klein and Freud seem to suggest, within different conceptual frameworks, that projection as a primary means of establishing a fragile form of identity may pervade many of our relationships with consumer objects as well as individuals and groups perceived as 'other'. (This might help us to explain why modern consumer-based culture has been so stunningly successful.) To what extent does the political ideal of consumer 'choice' depend on this 'productive' sado-masochistic dynamic based on competition? Let us look now at a more Winnicottian view of the unconscious meanings of consumption.

The transformational role of consumer objects

Christopher Bollas, like Kenneth Wright, builds on Winnicott's central idea of the transitional object. He emphasizes the transformational role of the mother for the baby's psychical development. Elaborating on Winnicott's idea of the transitional object (a small piece of torn-off blanket or rag which the baby carries around with it), he suggests that the baby's creation of what he calls a 'transformational object' is the baby's displacement of the transformational process with the mother onto this object and later innumerable objects in the outside world as the baby evolves from the experience of a process to what Bollas calls 'the articulation of experience'. It finds symbolic equations which stand in for and compensate for the loss of the mother. Bollas argues that the search for transformational objects continues in adult life. For some, religion offers the chance for a metamorphosis of the self echoing the earliest experience of a bond with the mother within a mythic structure. For many others, in secular life, hope is invested in new objects: a new car, consumer goods, job, move to another country, holiday, change of relationship. Bollas says all these can be seen as a request for transformation and signify the experience of transformation first experienced in the process of the baby's development with the mother. Advertising actually promises that a product will alter the subject's external environment and therefore change their internal mood. This is in contrast with Freud's and Lacan's theories which suggest that these objects signify the narcissistic or Imaginary search for total, unending bliss and completion with the mother and therefore evoke false, unjustified hopes for a unity of being which can never be possible. Bollas takes a different view. He argues that these signifiers evoke the promise of transformation because they chime with pre-verbal memories of a self or ego. They evoke our unconscious response not by offering us the illusion of wholeness and completeness but by putting us back in touch with very early experiences with the mother which have never been symbolized in thought or language. But Bollas also points to aesthetic moments when an individual feels a deep subjective rapport with an object: a painting, poem, symphony, landscape or love-song. They too usually chime with a pre-verbal ego memory. However, Bollas argues that some people may seek negative aesthetic experiences which refer back to early negative ego experiences and manifest the particular negative structure of their personal unconscious or what Bollas calls 'unthought known'. This is very similar to Freud's repetition compulsion in which individuals repeat traumatic situations because, through them, they remember how they came into being existentially, not cognitively.

But Bollas asks, drawing on Winnicott, what happens to people who fail to be disillusioned by, for example, consumer goods or other perceived transformational objects not living up to expectations. He argues that various disturbances emerge from such failure such as the compulsion to gamble, the criminal who seeks the perfect crime to repair unconsciously defects in his or her identity and, externally, bring wealth and happiness. In addition, Bollas gives the example of the search for the perfect partner. All constitute a deficiency in our experience of having an identity or, as Michael Balint (1984) put it, they offer the chance to repair the 'basic fault'. As an example of a failed maternal relationship, Bollas cites the mother who makes her child into a mythic object for her and itself (for example, the 'special' child whose extraordinary gifts will transform the fortunes and standing of the family) rather than looking after its needs as a child rather than her own. As the 'golden larva', the child experiences no psychical space of its own. Its inner space exists for and belongs to the mother. 'As an adult the child's existential despair is flung into a mythic narrative in an order where the real is used to populate the fantastic' (Bollas 1991: 20).

So Bollas argues that the search for transformation is perhaps one of the most widespread, archaic ways of relating which is not desire or craving or longing as Lacan would have us believe. It arises from the idea that the object will deliver change and have the capacity to resuscitate memory of early change and transformation but this is existential, pre-verbal memory, not cognitive memory. Bollas cites extremist political movements as examples not so much of a wish to consume or re-merge with the mother but of the belief that they will effect a total transforma-tion which will deliver everyone from a whole spectrum of 'basic faults' – social and moral. The certainty of the revolutionary, he argues, which is striking to the observer, is not based on desire but on the longing for change and delivery from a perceived deficiency in the self. For Bollas, transformation is not the search for gratification in the Imaginary, as

Lacan suggests, but emerges out of some people's frustration about ever being able to achieve emotional insight and growth through other means. Similarly, Bollas reminds us, 'aesthetic moments are not always beautiful and wonderful but sometimes ugly and terrifying but none the less moving because they tap an existential memory' and put us in touch with ourself (Bollas 1991: 27).

Narcissism and creativity

So psychoanalytic theory argues that narcissism, which to some extent exists in all of us, risks bypassing the most creative dimensions of who we are because, in denying difference between ourself and objects outside us, it is also a denial of the difference between subject and object, phantasy and reality. In contrast, artistic creativity, in some ways like Winnicott's transitional object, whether in the form of a painting, a poem or a garden, involves being able to negotiate and play with the experience of inner and outer 'reality', subject (me) and object (not me), phantasy (good or bad around the mother) and reality (culture) in order to create something new out of this mixture. Drawing on both Freud and Winnicott, Joyce McDougall (1992a) suggests that the creative part of who we are usually entails the successful integration of the 'masculine' and 'feminine' parts of ourselves inherent in bisexuality together with the capacity to symbolize the successful integration of our oral, anal and phallic forms of infantile sexuality and identity when it is unimpeded by the inhibitions and 'sterility' produced by early traumas. Such traumas can result in the pleasurable 'taking in' of the contents of the mother's breast being replaced by a fear of being devoured by the mother who the baby experiences as an attacker. Trauma can also result in the pleasurable anal 'giving out' of faeces, that is the baby's precious internal contents, delivered to the mother in the spirit of a generous 'gift' (its first creative product) being subsumed by humiliating feelings of worthlessness and self-disgust if the gift is rejected in the course of oversevere toilet training. In the phallic stage, the trauma might involve the pleasure of masturbation in relation to the desire for the mother being replaced with feelings of guilt, denial, punishment or even fear of death. All these traumatic outcomes can lead to the psychical blocking off of the potential for fulfilling sexual relationships and the ability to play which is inherent in creativity. This means the fore-stalling of the capacity to love and work creatively as a separate, relatively independent individual capable of creating symbolically his or her own worlds.

Kenneth Wright (1991) describes artistic creativity as the means of finding a form for our experience by forcing the chosen medium in the external world to bend to our interior vision of what we want so the final product can resonate a self back to us like the responsive, containing mother we actually experienced or wished we had had. In allowing us to combine our inner, subjective world with an outer, objective one, in the crucial mixture of subject and object we once were in the transitional space with our mother, creativity, following the way first prepared for it by the baby's transitional object, enables us to separate from our shared relationship with the mother rather than perpetuating it.

Marion Milner (who also uses the pseudonym Joanna Field), in her books *A Life of One's Own* (1986) and *On Not Being Able to Paint* (1971), employs Winnicott's concept of transitional phenomena to explore the nature of genuine happiness, creativity and art. In *On Not Being Able to Paint*, she suggests that painting, and by implication all artistic experience, takes place in an intermediate space where 'body and mind meet in expressive action' in the kind of state of absorption which we normally associate with day-dreaming. She describes painting as finding a bit of the outside world, whether in chalk, paint or paper, which is willing to fit in temporally with our dreams or inner world, where a moment of illusion is made possible in which inner and outer reality seem to coincide and merge. Like Winnicott, Milner sees this creative intermediary space as involving a process of reciprocity between phantasy and the external world, as an attempt to express the wholeness of certain attitudes which logic and science, on their own, can never do. Art brings subject and object together in a special kind of unity. It is a way of trying to create ourselves, make sense of our loves and hates and, at the same time, the world outside. Our view of ourselves inter-penetrates with the view of the external world because of our capacity to project. This is why a grey day sometimes makes us feel bleak or sad. She suggests that creative expression in art sometimes makes the internal chaos we all feel easier to face because we can combine it with the external world – paint, paper, stone – and give it a life in the world. For Milner, embodying the experience of illusion in artistic activity provides the vital basis for 'realising, making real, for feeling as well as knowing the external world', for what she describes as 'contemplative action', a state of combining both being and doing (Milner 1971: 140). Art can allow the individual to think without being drowned in feeling. Always concerned with the nature of creativity generally, she differentiates between two kinds of creativity within culture: creativity in art is about making symbols for feeling, and creativity in science is about making symbols for knowing. Insisting that these must be complementary even though our culture encourages us to value one rather than the other, Milner argues for an education which integrates feeling and reflective thinking, never one based on reason and logic alone.

So, for Milner, like Winnicott, art provides the opportunity for us to give up the apparent certainty of logic and reason for an experience which, like play, is a state where dream and the external world are fused. She likens it to an active stillness of waiting and watching that includes inner and outer in a unity which, crucially, also recognizes that these dimensions are separate (Milner 1971: 93). She, like Winnicott, sees the artist as engaged in what everyone is doing all the time. The freedom to do this in art is derived from having entered into an active relationship with the 'other', external reality. She describes this as 'spreading out the Imaginative body in wide awareness' (Milner 1971: 107). Like Winnicott, imagination and creativity must always be integrally linked to the ex- perience of the self as embodied, the sensation that we exist inside our own body and not outside it.

It seems likely that when we respond deeply to art it is because the artist's experience for which she or he has found a form, echoes our own and we also feel held or contained or responded to by the artistic product. It may act as a resonating, responsive mother for us as well as the artist.

Culture and the need for containment and boundary

As suggested earlier, much has been written by critics of contemporary culture about fragmentation, dislocation, disconnection, a preoccupation with surface and shallowness. For some this has been a cause for celebration but, for others, mourning. But psychoanalytic theory, taken as a whole, suggests that both individuals and culture need and can achieve a sense of relative cohesion and stability. Ideally, a relatively stable identity emerges within the mother–baby relationship during infancy and early childhood. Freud emphasizes the importance of the child's identification with culture via the symbolic father as the third term whose constraining meaning the child must recognize, whereas Winnicott highlights the significance of reliable, empathic mothering and the creative role of the transitional object and transitional space. For Klein, a relatively integrated identity rests on the baby's experience of guilt and reparation in the depressive position as it learns to take responsibility for its own bad feelings rather than blaming others in the external world. Psychoanalytic theory as a whole also suggests that we can gain a sense of relatively integrated identity without a return to

grand, omnipotent, all-encompassing narratives or the denial of difference. Such an identity depends on a variety of levels of experience
which include intuitive and empathic, artistic ways of being and knowing
as well as experience which is mediated by the narratives through which
we name and 'create' much of our experience.

Psychoanalytic theory generally suggests that culture can supplement
our early childhood experience and provide opportunities for emotional
growth. It suggests that nurturing, containing cultural institutions such as
adequate health care, social services and welfare benefit systems can
continue the child's experience of maternal care in the adult context or
compensate for the lack of such early experience. Similarly, it suggests
that we need institutions which represent the authority of the symbolic
father but only in the sense that they confront us with the need for some
law, boundary and constraint on our phantasies of total freedom. Lacan
would argue that this is the role of all language and representation. A
major problem, then, is that the particular distorted form which 'masculinity' has often taken throughout history has traditionally been based on
unjustified power and the need, therefore, to control. One of the effects
of this defensive conception of 'masculinity' in the modern world has
been to under-value human need in the project to improve efficiency
and profits. This means that this 'masculine' defence has therefore often
failed to make the need for culturally 'feminine', containing institutions
a priority. Psychoanalytic approaches also suggest that we need a greater
proliferation of a new type of 'masculine' institution, more concerned
with human need and aspiration (including unpredictable periods of
enforced passivity and dependency if we become suddenly sick, disabled, homeless or old) than economic expediency. They also suggest
that this may be the only way of undermining the powerful attraction of
an environmentally damaging 'consumer culture' and the potential lure
of powerful leaders who promise deliverance from the 'real' by identifying an enemy within and encouraging the phantasies necessary for
scapegoating and violence.

Let us look now at how psychoanalytic ideas can shed light on some
of the unconscious processes inherent in some specifically economic
aspects of cultural experience.

Relative deprivations

In spite of the widespread availability of consumer commodities, significant minorities of those living in consumer societies in the developed as
well as developing world have very limited access to consumer goods.

As Galbraith argues in *The Culture of Contentment*, the 'economically and socially fortunate' have taken over as the contented, largely self-approving majority and rule under what he sees as the 'rich cloak of democracy, a democracy in which the less fortunate do not participate' (Galbraith 1993: 15). Nowadays, we describe much of this lack of access to consumer goods and social 'goods' of any kind, which the majority take for granted, as 'relative' poverty because many of the people involved, caught up in what Galbraith describes as a 'hopeless enthral-ment' (Galbraith 1993: 39), are not actually starving in Britain at least (though they may be inadequately nourished). The situation in Britain and America, at least, appears unlikely to change in the near future as it seems very difficult to persuade the affluent two-thirds who are comfort-able and doing well to make some sacrifices, for example in significant increases in direct taxation, in order to give the other third greater equality. Increasingly, as Galbraith (1993: 41) argues, 'In what is the accepted, and, indeed, only acceptable view, the underclass is deemed the source of its own succor and well-being; in the extreme view, it requires the spur of its own poverty and it will be damaged by any social assistance and support.'

In his book *Unhealthy Societies*, Richard Wilkinson (1996) argues that inequalities of health are the result of social inequality. Relative poverty, as well as dire poverty, leads to ill health. Low status, insecurity, unemployment, high levels of stress at the lower end of the social structure are social diseases which cause illnesses in relatively deprived as well as deprived areas. In a consumer society, if some people are denied access to 'goods' available to most people because of low pay, unemployment, job insecurity, like the child who is emotionally neg-lected or abused in the family, they are turned into outsiders with poor self-esteem and few means of participating in the culturally ac-cepted means of bolstering identity. Denial of access to consumer goods which the rest of us can take for granted, in a society based on consumption, represents a form of cultural emotional abuse which may well be externalized in violence against the self or others. Delinquent behaviour by young men who have never been employed and who have little prospect of employment is generally recognized to be linked to a sense of deep frustration about being excluded from the pleasures and status conferred by consumer commodities which lie permanently out of reach.

The idea of relative deprivation must inevitably involve the gap between the rich developed countries and the poor less-developed countries. Many regard the starkness of this geographical divide between the 'haves' in the northern hemisphere and 'have nots' in the south, as an economic and environmental time-bomb lying in wait for us in the first decades of the coming millennium. Despite awareness of this explosive scenario, exacerbated by tribal conflict, famine, war-devastated territory, the rise of fundamentalism, and the decimation of populations and economies by AIDS, the governments of rich countries, together with the World Bank and the IMF, seem unwilling to instigate radical action to alleviate this situation. This might initially involve the cancelling of crippling loans, efforts to combat extreme poverty and compensatory economic treatment. From a psychoanalytic perspective, a failure to grasp the potentially dangerous reality of the developing situation, not least in terms of self-preservation from potential violence against Western countries, as well as within developing countries, seems to represent a narcissistic short-sightedness characterized by greed, denial and projection. There seems to be a refusal, on the part of substantial sections of the electorates of the developed world, to give up the developing world as a site for the unconscious projection of the unacceptable 'stranger within', even in these post-colonial, post Cold-War times. Here, Kristeva's idea of the 'abject' is useful.

Kristeva (1982) associates what she describes as the 'abjected mother' with the baby's attempt to develop boundaries between the pre-Oedipal mother and itself during the Oedipal crisis. The mother both attracts and repels, threatens us with distinctions and the separation that the child knows it must make and, as a consequence, she gets tarred with ideas of defilement, pollution and contamination. The mother as a container of the baby's identity, and from whose body the baby has emerged, must be psychically turned into something horrific and contaminating in order to be controlled and confined, that is to be put aside despite the longing to remain with her. Kristeva argues that this sense of horror and disgust is then, in the form of adult misogyny, associated not just with the mother from whom the child has barely managed to separate, but with all women as the despised other. In one sense, in the adult man, this fear and disgust stems from his own concealed sense of continuing, unconscious dependence. Kristeva suggests that the man is revolted by the idea of having emerged from the visceral horrors of the woman's birth canal. The woman may be caught up in collusive self-disgust by her awareness of being the same as the one she needs to revile in order to separate. Since the psychical mechanism of projection begins with the baby's merged identity with the mother, all those who come to represent a projected, externalized part of the self may be tarred with the same brush of abjection.

In the context of the idea of the abject, the developing world, with which ex-colonial Western nations have shared such a close relationship in the past, may continue to represent a state of being which inspires the kind of rejection, fear and aggression which, Kristeva argues, we come to associate with the abject mother. This is perhaps the reason why the developing world has received so little support from the rich nations by whom they were previously economically exploited. But, although colonialism was about the patriarchal imposition of European law and customs ('cleanliness and godliness'), in order to facilitate economic exploitation of the 'other', it also entailed certain kinds of intimacy and close, shared knowledge of the colonizer's most private life. Servants, associated with the abject and 'dirty', parodoxically brought up the colonizer's children and attended to the most personal needs of their parents. Despite the ascriptions of racial superiority and inferiority, colonizers and colonized seem often to have been caught up in a love/hate relationship with the other on whom, in countless ways, they were dependent. At the unconscious level, this evokes the texture of the mother–child as well as 'masculine'–'feminine' relationship. Significantly, sex between colonizer and colonized was often regarded with the same kind of horror as incest. In unconscious rather than conscious terms, de-colonization may be seen as not only the giving up of the greedy appropriation of the symbolic milk supplied by the colonized but, also, the acceptance of separation, autonomy and learning to stand on one's own feet on the part of the ex-colonialists, although this is not how the withdrawal from colonial rule was commonly perceived. On the contrary, it was rationalized more in terms of giving the ex-colony (perceived as child rather than mother) the opportunity to stand on its own feet. So, from a psychoanalytic stance, de-colonization may also be seen as a movement from a greedy infantile phantasy of omnipotence to the reality of separation and independence. From within this kind of perspective, tied aid to developing countries by ex-colonial nations looks like a more covert form of continuing narcissistic greed and further hidden appropriation of the mother. In an increasingly unstable world where globalization, the concentration of capital by a diminishing number of global companies and the speed and scale of access to information threaten to denude individual nation states of their former power to control events, the electorates, governments and financial elites of economically developed nations may still unconsciously need underdevelopment in ex-colonial countries to maintain a declining sense of identity and direction. In many ways it looks as if under-development, for some nations, may maintain the myth of infantile dependence of the ex-colonized rather than the ex-colonizer and the idea of Western nations as more in control of their own identity and destiny than they really are, in spite of the serious dangers this entails.

As I have suggested, the unconscious relationship between colonizer and colonized and ex-colonizer and ex-colonized seems to mirror patriarchal gender relations and mother–child relations. At the level of the unconscious, the former may be viewed as synonymous with the latter in many ways in that patriarchal 'femininity' is often a form of infantilization. For example, it seems no accident that women are often referred to as 'babe' or 'chick' and male servants were habitually called 'boy' by their masters and mistresses. In the colonial situation, the powerful, literate colonizer in charge of the symbolic in the form of the paternalistic rhetoric of colonial government and the law projects his own vulnerability onto the lacking 'feminine' other, the 'dark continent' of the colonized who, like the 'woman', is culturally associated with the 'abject' and inferiority, unfathomability, mystery and desire as well as being associated with the child. In other words, the colonizer is unconsciously dependent on those he controls. In the colonial situation, the 'feminized', infantilized, abject, colonized 'other', for a time, supports the colonizer's projections and his unjustified and exploitative power and meaning. These projections onto the indigenous inhabitants become naturalized as 'what the natives are like' just as patriarchal projections onto women become naturalized as women's 'nature'. But even after the end of colonial power, through tied aid and the encouragement of the growth of cash crops, ex-colonies are still under the economic control of the excolonizers, just as many women are still economically controlled. For example, in Britain, despite legal changes, on average, women still earn two-thirds of the male wage and, at the upper levels of management, have to contend with such things as the 'glass ceiling'.

Increasingly, huge and powerful global commercial organizations based on rootless capital, spurring even higher levels of consumption, wield power over people and the planet, so far largely without interference from democratic processes and nation states. If we apply a psychoanalytic perspective to the relationship between global business conglomerates and the environment, many of those who control giant multi-national companies may appear like omnipotent babies, greedily consuming the earth's resources, ruthlessly fighting off all opposition, constantly embroiled in internecine, Cain and Abel-like rivalry with others whom they seek, cannibalistically, to devour in increasingly massive take-overs. This perspective might offer insight into the lack of responsibility and concern about the fate of not only human beings but also the earth's physical inability to tolerate unbridled economic growth. At one level, this view of global business as driven by predominantly infantile needs is over-simplistic and reductionist but if there is any grain of 'truth' in it, it does not bode well for the future. Without changes in the attitudes of the directors and major share-holders in these global organizations (parodoxically often in the form of investment companies containing pension funds which have to be protected), and in those of governments in, for example, the Group of Seven most powerful nations, it is difficult to envisage how things will change without policies of sustainable development. The American electorate continues to be wedded to extravagant, gas-guzzling cars and cheap energy in spite of knowledge about the greenhouse effect, acid rain, and global warming. Without human and environmental catastrophies on a scale which goes beyond the horrors of such incidents as Chernobyl, Seveso and Bhopal, oil spillages such as the Exxon Valdez tanker disaster and other major forms of chemical pollution of land, sea and air and human beings, it is difficult to imagine how cultures dependent on greedy electorates and global business interests, which now operate largely outside the orbit of national governments, can alter modes of consumption and bring about change. Correspondingly, smaller-scale institutions in Western European states have developed increasingly instrumental, bureaucratized organizations which exhibit many of the characteristics of larger, uncaring, irresponsible business enterprises and their activities are similarly articulated in a euphemistic language of 'mission'-based rationality. Encouraged by governments of all political colours eager to embrace the free market, uphold the values of business and divest themselves of the burden of as many public services as possible, they also increasingly prioritize economic efficiency above concern for the well-being of human beings or the planet.

In the context of contemporary changes in the lives of men and women discussed in chapter 6, let us speculate for a moment on the possibilities for positive change in the foreseeable future.

Cultural change

If, as suggested in chapters 6 and 7, more men and women become more able to own the different aspects of their identities without projecting what is unacceptable onto each (perceived as the) 'other', relationships between men and women may possibly become more creative and mutually fulfilling in the future. This may mean relationships become less prone to break down, at least during the childhood and adolescence of children when children are most vulnerable. This might then reduce one form of unconscious damage. If women become increasingly active and fulfilled in both their work and their relationships they may be less likely to suffer from depression and therefore more likely to be able to be the containing, 'good enough' mothers that psychoanalytic theory suggests children need in the early stages of childhood. In the next decades, many more men (and 'masculine' women) may become able to abandon defensive, controlling, oppressive forms of 'masculinity'. This may then affect institutional arrangements so that more men may feel able to share child care and be more physically and emotionally available, adequate fathers. These changes, in combination with other positive cultural changes, could lead to greater levels of emotional integration rather than continuation of the defensive need to control. This might then lessen the appeal of regressive forms of narcissistic pleasure and satisfaction and eventually set limits to economic growth, at least in some Western countries.

Stated baldly like this, such developments seem rather utopian although they may be the only way to prevent what a growing number of environmental experts now regard as inevitable environmental catastrophe in the middle of the next century. These experts suggest that without major changes in patterns of consumption it is unlikely that we or our planet can survive. To the extent that the planet symbolizes a nurturing 'mother earth' on whom, ultimately, we all depend, contemporary technology-driven consumer cultures could be said to be sucking the mother dry. Psychoanalytic approaches suggest that this situation is not only the result of the desire for a higher standard of living by ever-growing numbers of the earth's inhabitants. They suggest that it is also the result of contemporary levels of consumption in developed nations being so powerfully tied up with our need to satisfy infantile forms of identity in the widespread absence of other possibilities. This is in the context of the gradual erosion of other sources of identity in an increasingly fragmented culture which may have led to what many psychotherapists see as the modern disease: a sense of isolation, emptiness and lack of meaning in many people. Shopping, and a relatively high level of material consumption or standard of living, in the short-term at least, may offer many people some kind of psychical compensation for a sense of 'hollowness' and lack of depth to living. For many, living may increasingly feel like virtual living. Shopping and other forms of consumption, compared with this, may feel 'real'.

In the next and final chapter, I shall discuss the focus of many academics on Lacan's psychoanalytic theory. Among other things, this theory has led to the view that, since language lacks a direct connection with the external world, there are no grounds for values because all points of view are equally valuable or, put another way, unstable. Apart from being a position which is contradicted by other psychoanalytic perspectives which cannot be written off as grand, imperialistic narratives, this is unhelpful in the context of needing to solve huge human, economic and environmental problems. In other words, a deodorizing theory of signifiers, divorced from unmediated bodily experience, disguises both the theoretical smell and the 'real' smell coming from the world's rivers and oceans, more literally, the world's drains.

10

Fragrant theory and the sweet scent of signifiers

Psychoanalysis in the academic world

In this concluding chapter let us look at what has happened to psycho-analysis in the academic rather than clinical world, particularly in relation to the psychoanalytic theory taught in arts and humanities departments rather than those which are oriented towards the practice of psycho-therapy. Although, in recent years, there has been an intense interest in academic circles in the body and its cultural construction, the idea that our bodies and our early psychosomatic experience might have any direct, rather than culturally mediated, effect on our identity and culture has usually been greeted with scepticism or even derision. In this culturalist climate such an idea has been regarded as essentialist, that is based on a belief that there is some direct relationship between our biological bodies and our 'masculine' or 'feminine' identity, and therefore unthinkable. In many university departments, psychoanalysis has come to mean mainly Freudian theory and, more specifically, Lacan's seductive development of it. Those who ally themselves with this linguistic version of psychoanalysis are, like Lacan, often unwilling to contemplate the possibility that bodies and biology may have any direct role to play in the production of who we are. For example, women's biological capacity to have, feed and, perhaps because of their bodily connection, emotionally nurture very young babies in a specially attentive way (what Winnicott (1975: 302) calls primary maternal preoccupation) is not considered likely to play any part in the formation of some aspects of 'femininity' because this idea subverts the notion that gender completely crosses the boundaries of the body so that men can be as 'feminine' as many women and vice versa. Even the significance of the fact that 'masculine' women can have babies but 'feminine' men cannot often seems to be played down in the interests of our maintaining a sense that we, or rather culture, is entirely in control of who we are. For Lacan, language as a metaphor for bodily experience excludes any direct, unmediated effects which relate to our bodies.

In some ways, the emphasis on culture and a deep suspicion of experience is understandable. Historically, essentialist theories and the idea of experience-based knowledge as the basis for certainty and absolute 'truth' have been and, in some quarters, continue to be used ideologically and oppressively to perpetuate existing power arrangements, cause suffering and prevent political change. At the mass level in the tabloid press, crass biologism and genetic determinism are widely used to explain a wide variety of social and psychical forms of injury. But some academics seem to have entrenched themselves firmly in a position where personal, embodied experience as the source of intuitive wisdom and a certain kind of 'truth' about how to live has been invalidated. The focus of post-modernist theory generally, including that of Lacan, has been on the cultural representation of experience. In Lacan's theory we speak our selves into existence through the narratives we create, driven by the movement of our repressed desire for the mother (Lacan 1977a: 259). But, although in Lacan's theory we are connected to the personal, family world by our Oedipal desire, our early pre-Oedipal experiences of emotional intimacy with our mother or both our parents, out of which object-relations theory argues that we are crucially partly constituted, seem to be left out of the account. All experience outside the realm of language and representation is considered delusory.

The sweet scent of control

Lacan's influential development of Freud's theory has been welcomed by many of those in universities because in his theory, the social/cultural world of language and culture has become fused with the personal, sexual world of the unconscious and the child's perception of actual bodies and sexual difference. In Lacan's theory, the penis has been transformed into the cultural sign of the phallus which Lacan conceives of as the blue-print for all the other cultural meanings also based on the idea of difference. By welding together Freud's theory of the unconscious and Saussure's linguistic theory of semiotics, Lacan makes human identity into nothing but the self which the world of language eventually enables us to speak. In fact, Lacan regards all forms of identity which lie outside language and signification as false, and reserves the idea of 'subjectivity' only for our identity in language, the best we can achieve. So, in Lacan's theory, not only has psychoanalytic theory been made irresistible to some because it is so theoretically coherent and clever, but it has also been made particularly appealing because of the sweet, because distancing, scent of structural linguistics and the possibility of achieving total control of who we are, which has also seemed enticing to many academics. In contrast, Freud's and object-relations theory, which offer much less opportunity for control, looks, metaphorically, positively simple-minded and 'smelly'. They both confront us with a psychosomatic view of gendered identities which is partly dependent on biology (Freud never rules out the possibility of some 'constitutional' factors) and, in the case of object-relations theory, focus our attention on the milky, murky, confused, chaotic and, at times, anxiety-ridden world of the pre-Oedipal baby and the need for the mother's physical and emotional containment. Freud's theory threatens us with the pain of our exclusion from our mother and father's sexuality, the price of our becoming fully human and, at its best, object-relations theory threatens some of us with the uncertain horrors of such things as spontaneity, intuitiveness and ways of knowing associated with our earliest experience of pre-verbal relating and a form of intuitive wisdom running alongside rationality and desire. To some, object-relations theory, in particular, looks potentially like a biological and psychical quagmire which, alarmingly, in emphasizing so many dimensions of who we are which lie outside culture and language, lies beyond our control.

The body and intuitive ways of knowing

A reluctance to recognize the possible role of biological as well as cultural influences on identity and the 'truth' of certain intuitive, empathic ways of being and knowing rules out most of the insights produced by object-relations theorists like Klein and Winnicott and followers such as Bion, Bollas, Wright and McDougall as well as much of Freud's work. Crucially, these writers, unlike Lacan, see identity as a psychosomatic unity. If we don't feel 'real' in our bodies as well as our minds something is the matter. Unlike Lacan's, object-relations approaches do not write off early experiences of becoming and relating, what Christopher Bollas calls the baby's personal 'grammar' or idiom of being, as only narcissistic delusion (Bollas 1991: 36). Object-relations approaches highlight and value the pre-Oedipal experience of relating to the mother or both parents, and a special, personal way of being with the baby which is our first experience of the world. They emphasize the importance of the intuitive, spontaneous dimensions of being, knowing and relating which are, ideally, part of the baby's earliest experience of 'good enough', containing mothering. They also suggest that it is possible to achieve what they see as a significant degree of psychical integration without succumbing to the idea that we can achieve absolute wholeness, stability or perfection. (Most psychoanalytic theories recognize that the best we can achieve is a state of living with precariousness creatively.) But, rather, they suggest that a *relative* degree of integration of both pre-Oedipal and Oedipal experience into our consciousness is both possible and desirable. The capacity emotionally to digest and process raw experience and use phantasy, initially as a primitive form of thinking, is considered valuable and vital to successful development.

The seductiveness of Lacan's theory

If we think about how Lacan's theoretically enticing theory works its magic over some of us, we can see that, like Freud, he focuses on unconscious desire, sexuality, the Oedipal crisis, the symbolic father and identity. But he inventively transposes these concepts developed by Freud from the personal, sexual realm of the family to the social realm of language and culture. In this way Lacan makes the long sought connection between sociology and psychoanalysis, culture and the unconscious. Lacan's theory, like Freud's, also emphasizes the unclosable gap between what we are and what we desire, the lack and 'want to be', that underpins us all and makes us human. He then links this to our drive towards language and knowledge where desire fuels our continuous search for 'truth' and the ultimate theory, the unity and completion that we longed for with our mothers. But at what cost? In the moment we are seduced by Lacan's theoretical coherence and cleverness, at the same time that we succumb to the powerful embrace of his scented, sexualized and gendered signifiers, in that moment we lose touch with all our experiential sense of the meaning of ourselves, our bodies and culture. We lose our sense of the value of what we make emotionally of personal, lived experience and the wisdom or 'truth' it often produces beyond the realm of rationality and beyond even the satisfaction of the 'feminine' form of desire that Lacan describes as *jouissance*. This French word suggests a form of sexual bliss which, for Lacan, is unrelated to phallic forms of sexuality (Lacan 1975: 70–1). For Lacan, sexuality has nothing to do with 'real' bodies. He sees heterosexuality and human love generally as the means of satisfying need (or what he calls Demand) rather than Desire which can only be satisfied in language (Lacan 1977a: 281–91). Sexuality for him is only to be found in language in the *jouissance* produced by the play of Desire. This entails the freedom involved in symbolizing unconscious desire in 'full' rather than 'empty' speech, in free associating within the endless loops of meaning within language as we speak and write in poetry which defies the constraints of rational language.

In Lacan's idea of the play of repressed sexual desire in language there is little sense of anything like Winnicott's psychosomatic 'continuous sense of being alive'. Lacan's idea of the pleasures of *jouissance* seems very different from the intuitive, embodied playfulness characteristic of Winnicott's concept of the transitional space in which the capacity for artistic creativity and for creative cultural enjoyment take place. At first sight, both Lacan's pleasurable celebration of repressed desire in language and Winnicott's intuitive negotiation of the relationship between phantasy and reality through play and artistic expression and enjoyment seem to be referring to similar states of being. The difference is, perhaps, that Lacan's playful pleasure takes place in a world where actual bodies and bodily sexuality have been split off and made much less important than words and language. In fact, for Lacan, heterosexuality has become a sad, misguided farce. The complicated meanings and pleasures of human sexual/emotional relationships have been devalued and replaced by artistic or literary pleasures within the relative safety of texts. Even though Winnicott's theory focuses much more on 'being' and relating than desire, when we play in Winnicott's transitional space it does not entail the denigration and giving up of our embodied emotional and sexual relationships. We can love and relate intuitively and meaningfully to others and be involved in artistic forms of 'truth'. The same is true of Klein's theory; in our creative use of cultural symbols in the depressive position, where we also negotiate the gap between our phantasies and reality, our desire for oneness with the mother and our necessary separation, our sexuality in human relationships and our capacity to love are not invalidated. Art and knowledge do not need to exclude love and intimacy.

For Lacan, becoming a subject within the inter-subjectivity which language, driven by unconscious Desire, makes possible is the best form of identity and knowing available to us. But, to be fair, Lacan argues that even this is bogus because the status of the powerful meaning of the phallus is always subverted by the unconscious knowledge of symbolic castration (the father retains the mother, not the little boy). For Lacan, all earlier identities are illusory because they are still entirely fused with the mother rather than being involved in the metaphorical pursuit of this fusion in the search for 'truth' in knowledge. Object-relations theory, however, suggests that pre-verbal identities cannot be written of as delusions because they contain within them the vital ingredients for reaching a full-blown human identity in language, or not, if the mother's containment has not been 'good enough'.

Most psychoanalytic theories would agree that we can't regard any theory as over-archingly 'true' because words are always arbitrary substitutes for our early losses, without any direct relationship to the reality they describe. Building on this idea, Lacan argues that since all meanings and knowledge are based on a phallus which has been symbolically castrated, this must always undermine their cultural power and make them bogus. At some level, it seems, we cannot avoid the idea that, in one sense, language and knowledge must always be illusory. It is therefore surprising that Lacan's post-modern theory is often taught rather as if it were the psychoanalytic equivalent of Einstein's theory of relativity, outstripping but also, at some important level, incorporating, not invalidating, Newton's mechanical ideas. Lacan's theory in no way encompasses the insights of Freud and other psychoanalytic theories; we could argue that it either distorts them in the case of Freud's theory or, in the case of object-relations theory, leaves them out altogether.

An eclectic approach

If we really want to see what light psychoanalysis can shed on the cultural issues which confront us, as I have argued in this book, it seems necessary that we should try to use psychoanalytic ideas eclectically and make creative links between them, for example between some of Lacan's ideas about language and desire and the object-relations view that our very entry into language and cultural identity depends on the quality of our earliest psychosomatic experiences within what Christopher Bollas calls our first transformative relationship with the mother. It is here that we can find the basis for what Peter Lomas calls wisdom, or an intuitive sense of morality, meaning morality in the sense of having a feeling based on experience, about the best way to live (Lomas 1994: 10). As Winnicott, Bion and Bollas suggest, ideally, our early experience with our mothers is about the mother's capacity to contain the baby's earliest potentially overwhelming feelings of helplessness, anxiety, conflict and instinctual sensations. This means that the baby is then able to emotionally contain and intuitively organize these for itself and take this primitive organizing capacity, the psychical ingredients necessary for development, into the symbolic which offers new opportunities for unravelling experience. As such, our dynamic 'absorption' of pre-verbal experiences cannot be simply written off as delusions, what Lacan calls Imaginary, self-reflecting misrecognitions. They may be narcissistic in the sense that the baby's being is still fused with the mother but at the same time they contain a crucial potential for something else that has grown out of the texture of the intuitive, empathic maternal relationship.

The feminist writer, Julia Kristeva, has developed her own theory out of some of Lacan's ideas about language but she is critical of his exclusion of the pre-Oedipal mother's role in the construction of meaning and culture. But, although she emphasizes the importance of the pre-Oedipal mother, she describes the baby's early experience mainly in terms of a pre-Oedipal patterning process made up of the play of oral and anal drives which eventually emerge in language as what she calls the 'semiotic', a symbolizing force which both contributes to the rhythms and music of language but also continually challenges and disrupts its meanings and any identities based on it. However, although she is mainly interested in the early organizing effects of infantile drives rather than emotional containment, she also warns that we should not forget that the child's *love* for the mother pre-exists its *desire*.

In his idea of the 'mirror stage' Lacan gives us the image of the mother holding the baby up to the mirror so that the baby suddenly takes itself to be coherent and whole, to be something that looks convincingly like a 'self' even though it still feels physically and psychically uncoordinated. But, Lacan argues, the baby misrecognizes itself because it is looking only at a reflection, an illusion of itself (Lacan 1977a: 1–7). This contradicts Winnicott's idea that the mother's crucial role is to mirror or reflect an identity back to the baby which it internalizes as, ideally, a good object or self (Winnicott 1971a: 111–18). It is the taking in or incorporation of the emotional quality of the mother's reflections or responses to the baby – the containment in her mind as well as her arms, gaze, utterances – which gives the baby an authentic sense of itself as lovable, valuable, a pleasure to itself and others, or not. This is an experience which object-relations theory argues is real, not delusion. It cannot be adequately summed up in the idea of narcissism. The mother or both parents give the baby a form of non-representational knowledge, an existential knowledge of 'being' which involves its capacity to relate to itself and others emotionally and spontaneously which it will take into language and all its future relationships. This is what Bollas calls the *form* rather than the *content* of the unconscious which is a part of what he sees as our ego or identity which exists right from the start (Bollas 1991: 7–10). Here, it seems, the unconscious represents both emotional intimacy with *and* desire for the mother.

So, unlike Lacan, object-relations theory suggests that pre-Oedipal experiences potentially constitute some of the essential stuff of what we are; in fact, they make a significant and dramatic difference to whether we are 'ordinarily' precarious because of the repression of our unconscious Oedipal loss of the mother or much more seriously precarious because we cannot contain and 'think' our earliest experiences. We lack the emotional, empathic repertoire that we need for a creative, relatively independent and integrated life which can draw on intuitive as well as theoretical insight.

Anxiety and the rejection of biology and experience

If practising psychotherapists and analysts can use object-relations approaches eclectically and successfully, in combination with Freud's ideas, I wonder why it is difficult for some academics to use the same kind of eclectic approach in the knowledge that no theory is perfect – we are never going to get a perfect theory because we ourselves can never be perfect. This is surely at the core of post-modern views on theory. What then might be emotionally at stake in some academic circles, in the rejection of biological factors, bodily sexuality and personal, psychosomatic experience, in the sense of personal intuitive wisdom as a source of a certain kind of 'truth'? Why do some academics even balk at the possibility of the existence of a tangled web of biological, cultural and unconscious elements which produce at least three ways of knowing? These are intuitive awareness of how to 'be' oneself and relate to others, knowing through the ability to use reason and the capacity to represent the world poetically through the play of unconscious desire.

I wonder if the answer may be that the crucial difference between psychotherapists and many academics who use psychoanalytic theory is that most psychotherapists have had psychoanalytic therapy as part of their training whereas many academics have not. This means that therapists are more likely to be psychically relatively comfortable with themselves, more able to work eclectically, to put theories in their place intuitively and more able to rely on their empathic experience of ordinary, spontaneous relating and living. They are therefore potentially more likely to feel able sometimes to take some thoughtful risks without provoking too much anxiety in themselves as a result of doing so. For many academics, the concepts of identity and experience might be more emotionally troubling than subjectivity and language because they may refer more directly to what Bollas calls the 'unthought known' of early, unremembered experience. Certainly, eclectic psychoanalytic clinical practice considers the empathic, intuitive texture of the relationship between therapist and patient to be at least as important in the successful outcome as theoretical rigour and clever interpretation.

I wonder, therefore, if, in some academic circles, a retreat from the dimension of personal experience as a valuable source of wisdom or value to cultural representation and the denial of the basis for any kind of 'truth', and a retreat from the biological body and embodied forms of love and sexuality, may be based on a high degree of anxiety and denial. This may involve the fear of the return of painful feelings associated with Oedipal and very early pre-Oedipal experience and the need for theories which allow us to feel that we, and not uncontrollable forces such as biology, embodied Oedipal desires or early psychosomatic experiences, are in control of our destiny and mortality. I want to suggest that the distaste for the idea that there may be some biological factors in the construction of identity, for the concept of identity rather than subjectivity, for the idea of desiring bodies as well as desiring words, and for the notion of personal, intuitive ways of knowing which are not adequately expressed in the idea of the free play of desire, springs from anxiety and lingering omnipotent phantasies of control. If we acknowledge the possibility that our biology and our complicated personal, bodily as well as culturally mediated experience are both extremely likely to have some bearing on who we turn out to be, we cannot, at the same time, escape a confrontation with three major aspects of reality. These are the painful reality of sexual difference, whether we turn the meaning of the penis into an empty, arbitrary signifier or not, the certainty that we shall die, that we are not omnipotent, and the disturbing resonances often provoked by pre-Oedipal known but unthought and therefore consciously unknown experience.

Freud as well as Lacan, in a different way, tells us that intellectual activity can be a cultural substitution for the mother, a defensive form of mastery and control of painful Oedipal emotions, and object-relations approaches also suggest that rationality and theory may often be a flight from early painful experience to a false self, a retreat from what Winnicott calls a break in our continuous sense of 'going on being'. If the need for knowledge as a form of control rather than creativity inevitably involves unresolved phantasies of omnipotence associated with difficulty in making the transition from phantasy to reality, these omnipotent denials must surely further threaten the integrity and therefore value of any theoretical knowledge we may produce. However inherently precarious all theories might be because of their roots in unconscious loss, some degree of emotional integrity and contact with the feeling level of existence is surely a necessary component to knowledge which can comfortably engage with a range of crucial but different elements of reality. These are: *biology*, which reminds us that we are going to die and that sexual difference exists, *identity* (rather than subjectivity), which reminds us of feelings in relation to the fact that our parents' sexual relationship excluded us and that we may have lacked a 'good enough' mother with whom we could learn intuitive, empathic ways of being and knowing and, linked with this, early pre-Oedipal, *unthought but known experience*. Such reminders of certain aspects of reality may be so disturbing, together with anxieties provoked by rapid change and living in contemporary global culture and the ordinary demands of living, that they have forced some of us into a retreat into the reassuring arms of the particular theoretical perspectives and affiliations which can best protect us from this pain. From this point of view, the theoretical unity and coherence of Lacan's post-modernist theory, once we've overcome the difficulty of his writing, look rather defensive and omnipotent. His theory seems to have split off much of what is unacceptable, like experience and suffering and real bodies that make us more than 'routinely' precarious, onto modernism and humanistic theory.

Freud and Lacan

If we take a distinctively Freudian approach to Lacan's ideas, then in Lacan's theory Freud's idea of human sexuality and love, and what we make of it, have been radically disconnected from desire and relegated to what Lacan sees as the much more mundane level of the satisfaction of need. If we look behind the scenes, in the spaces between Lacan's words, this demotion of the status of what Freud described as the central 'primal scene', that is the sexual scene between our parents, enables the psychical impact of this idea and the painful recognition of it we all have to make to become fully human, to be defused. Lacan achieves this by substituting the potentially devastating reality of our parents' excluding sexuality with a linguistic 'reality' in which poetic language from which none is excluded, the linguistic rather than bodily celebration of our 'want to be', becomes not just the superior but the *only* form of human sexuality. In what looks like an attack on the meaning of the primal scene, in Lacan's theory words and thinking replace rather than stand in for bodily sexuality and love and *jouissance* eclipses orgasm. Art and poetry replace life and embodied feeling. And, in one sense, by placing all desire and the 'feminine' within language, we can possess the mother for ourselves whenever we feel like poetically throwing over the constraints of rationality redefined as the place of the father in Lacan's theory. The symbolization of unconscious desire seems to have been confused with what feels like a kind of 'acting out' within language so that the free play or integration of 'masculine' (conscious) and 'feminine' (unconscious) signifiers, that is the bisexuality which always seems to be associated with creativity, becomes the *only* form of authentic sexuality. In Lacan's theory there is a strong sense of the narcissistic one-ness of the mother's identity incorporating that of the child rather than the two-ness of the mother and child who have managed to separate. Even though Lacan makes the idea of the child's symbolic castration, the failure to split up the parents, *conceptually* so central, his theory seems *unconsciously* to represent at one level a refusal of the primal scene of the sexual relationship between the mother and father. What can be seen as a transgressive 'theft' of the 'masculine' and 'feminine' creativity in the primal scene which is present in so many forms of creativity, for Lacan, seems to entail the sterility and denial of the pleasures of actual human sexual relationships. The striking conversion of the actual penis as the bodily sign of sexual difference into the cultural sign of the phallus, with all that follows from this, even though this symbolizes loss as well as power and mastery, also has the unconscious flavour of a narcissistic or manic refusal of the reality of sexual difference and the symbolic castration this must mean to the child. From this Freudian perspective, Lacan's conceptual focus on the idea of the lack and symbolic castration looks as if it might be a powerful, unconscious reaction formation which conceals the attack on both these 'realities' which seems to lie at the heart of Lacan's theory.

So it can be argued that Lacan's theory depends on specular and intellectual images and representations as if no intuitive forms of relating are going on. In his theory, at one level psychoanalysis, like all forms of knowledge, becomes another false knowledge based on a false self which, even here, tries to disown the actual body which seems to be experienced as a persecutor. Thinking has become a substitute for feeling and sexuality which, in the clinical context, is a form of splitting or dissociation normally associated with a way of dealing with an unreliable mother. In this sense, in Lacan's theory, thinking always has the tinge of masturbatory activity used to deaden and blot out painful feeling associated with loss and deprivation and a sense of futility and despair. In the linking of the phallus with language there may be a fetishistic element so that the mother (only clearly revealed in poetic language or free association) becomes the mother with a penis which partially denies sexual difference (see chapter 5 on fetishism). If this is the case, to what extent can we connect this with the Lacanian cultural preoccupation with voyeurism, particularly in film studies?

Lacan's post-modernist ideas, and developments of them (in the work of Cixous, Kristeva, Irigaray and Derrida), are fascinating and illuminating in many ways in that they make us challenge assumptions and suggest new ways of looking at aspects of identity, representation and culture. But theories can often be very interesting and illuminating on the way to being wrong or inadequate in important ways. If we look beyond language conceived of as only signifiers driven by desire, then we can see that ordinary language is permeated with metaphors drawn from psychosomatic experience of embodied relationships. These continually span the space between the word and biology, but also between language and pre-verbal relational, intuitive experience. The concrete of ordinary, material living and psychosomatic relating, as well as of desire and early drives, has been turned into a wealth of expressions such as, for example, someone getting under our skin, elbowing us out, cold shouldering us, getting up our nose, making our ears burn, not putting a foot wrong, putting their foot in it, not being able to see beyond the end of their nose, getting it off their chest, having their fingers in every pie, chancing their arm, putting their shoulder to the wheel, having their back to the wall, having to knuckle under, putting their nose to the grindstone, making us sick. We see people as nosey, tongue in cheek, a pain in the neck, headstrong, skin deep, brass-necked, lippy, iron-fisted, tight-fisted or tight-arsed, all fingers and thumbs. All language and metaphor has its roots in both conscious and unconscious 'truth' and the experience of embodied living and relating as well as desire.

Despite its emphasis on the precariousness and lack of unity of all identity and knowledge, the seduction of Lacan's theory is that once we manage to gain some grasp of it, it is paradoxically remarkably stable and coherent. But is this, as I have suggested, only because of what it excludes? It seems to deny or subtract a huge part of our experience from consideration, both bodily sexuality and the pre-Oedipal emotional intimacy associated with the mother. But all this is concealed in the apparent but illusory totality of Lacan's all-encompassing world of language and signification, what he makes into the linguistic place of the father. There are no loose ends in Lacan's theory, perhaps because, as unpalatable Oedipal and pre-Oedipal psychosomatic experience, they seem to have been projected elsewhere onto the 'other' of object-relations theory. Only by doing this can Lacan's theory cut such a dashing figure in the theoretical arena.

The need to engage with complexity

In the context of what has formed the subject of this concluding chapter, it seems a matter for concern that students in some university arts and humanities departments may be largely unaware of certain areas of psychoanalytic theory because many of those teaching and writing about psychoanalysis for the purposes of analysing culture find Lacanian theory more psychically comfortable than specifically Freudian or object-relations approaches. This is not a very happy situation for many students who may not encounter psychoanalytic ideas again at close quarters. It cuts them off from the richness, diversity and complexity of psychoanalytic ideas and gives a distorted view of their potential, used eclectically, for the purposes of analysing ourselves and cultural phenomena. This is, of course, always in combination with historical, social and cultural approaches. It may also put them off the idea of psychoanalytic therapy should they ever consider having it and encourages them to invalidate their own personal, intuitive knowledge or wisdom derived from their experience. Perhaps most importantly, by theoretically oversimplifying, which may sound an odd thing to say about Lacan's conceptually difficult work, it cuts them off from the appreciation of the complexity of the factors which produce ourselves and human culture. Although Lacan is conceptually very coherent, complex and clever, by denying the validity, value and meaning of bodily sexuality and early psychosomatic experience and identity usually associated with the relationship with the mother, his work can be seen as lacking an important dimension of emotional and therefore theoretical integrity. Like the narcissistic patient, it lacks the aspect of complexity which hangs on a respect for personal embodied experience and intuitive, empathic ways of knowing as well as on rationality and the play of desire in language. We need to be able to cope with complexity and difference in theories as well as in other areas of life rather than denying them by creating them as 'others', in order to engage with the massive problems which confront us.

An exclusively culturalist view is often accompanied by the idea that theories must incorporate the possibility of change. Of course it is more comfortable to work with the political possibility that we can change oppressive meanings and systems but it is also dangerous if this blinds us to those things we may not be able to change and therefore prevents us from finding the most creative ways of preventing them being exploited oppressively. If we are tempted to use knowledge as a form of mastery and denial of painful emotion we may be prone to this way of thinking. It is highly likely that identity is not exclusively culturally, unconsciously or biologically determined but a complex and shifting product. In the context of the widespread popularity of Lacan's theory, it is as if, for some people, the body and the unconscious need to be metaphorically shampooed and deodorized through the medium of modern linguistics before they can be theoretically handled without fear of contamination or emotional pain. In this metaphorical climate of fragrance and smells which I find difficult to resist, it is perhaps significant that smell is one of the most primitive senses. One of the main ways very young babies can differentiate between their mother and others is through their sense of smell. It is also interesting that sometimes patients in psychotherapy may begin to give off body odours when they become very anxious. We may not be able to speak our primitive anxieties but we can 'make a stink'. Signifiers, in offering us distance from potentially disturbing Oedipal and pre-Oedipal feelings, seem to offer the possibility of a cultural deodorant, keeping us 'sweet', 'good' objects for ourselves.

Faced with an infinitely complex world, it seems unwise to throw away anything that can be of use to us in addressing this complexity. We need to be able to allow ourselves eclectic access to a range of psychoanalytic insights, not only those which, it could be argued, have been made conceptually fragrant to distance us from some of their meanings and make them acceptable to those of us who work in academic institutions: those who may, for our own unconscious reasons, prefer signifiers and abstract notions of desire to desiring bodies and a notion of knowledge, 'truth' and morality derived from embodied personal experience.

Bibliography

Abraham, K. (1922) 'Manifestations of the female castration complex', *International Journal of Psychoanalysis*, 3: 1–29.

Adorno, T. (1978) 'Freudian theory and the pattern of fascist propaganda', in A. Arato and E. Gebhardt (eds), *The Essential Frankfurt School Reader*, pp. 118–37, Oxford, Blackwell.

Adorno, T. (1994) *The Authoritarian Personality*, London, Norton.

Andermatt Coneley, V. (1984) *Hélène Cixous: Writing the Feminine*, Lincoln, University of Nebraska Press.

Andermatt Coneley, V. (1992) *Hélène Cixous*, Brighton, Harvester Wheatsheaf.

Appignanesi, L. and Forrester, J. (1992) *Freud's Women*, London, Weidenfeld.

Arcana, J. (1979) *Our Mothers' Daughters*, London, The Woman's Press.

Arendall, T. (1995) *Fathers after Divorce*, London, Sage.

Balint, M. (1984) *The Basic Fault*, London, Tavistock and Routledge.

Barrett, M. and McIntosh, M. (1982) *The Anti-social Family*, London, Verso.

Baudrillard, J. (1983) *Fatal Strategies*, London, Pluto Press.

Baudrillard, J. (1996) *The System of Objects*, London, Verso.

Bell, D. (1993) 'Primitive mind of state', paper presented at the Conference on Psychoanalysis in the Public Sphere, London, University of East London.

Benjamin, J. (1990) *The Bonds of Love*, London, Virago.

Benvenuto, B. and Kennedy, R. (1986) *Jacques Lacan: an Introduction*, London, Free Association Books.

Berke, J. (1989) *The Tyranny of Malice*, London, Simon Schuster.

Bersani, L. (1990) *The Freudian Body*, New York, Columbia University Press.

Bettelheim, B. (1954) *Symbolic Wounds: Puberty Rights and the Envious Male*, New York, Macmillan.

Bettelheim, B. (1967) *The Empty Fortress*, New York, The Free Press.

Bettelheim, B. (1990) *Recollections and Reflections*, London, Thames and Hudson.

Bettelheim, B. (1991) *The Uses of Enchantment*, London, Penguin.

Bion, W. (1991) [1962] *Learning from Experience*, London, Karnac.

Bion, W. (1993) [1967] *Second Thoughts: Selected Papers on Psycho-Analysis*, London, Karnac.

Bocock, R. (1993) *Consumption*, London, Routledge.

Bollas, C. (1989) *Forces of Destiny: Psychoanalysis and the Human Idiom*, London, Free Association Books.

Bollas, C. (1991) *The Shadow of the Object: Psychoanalysis of the Unthought Known*, 2nd edn, London, Free Association Books.

Bollas, C. (1992) *Being a Character: Psychoanalysis and Self-Experience*, London, Routledge.

Bollas, C. (1995) *Cracking Up: Unconscious Work in Self-Experience*, London, Routledge.

Bott Spillius, E. (1988) *Melanie Klein Today*, 2 vols, London, Routledge.

Bowie, M. (1991) *Lacan*, London, Fontana.

Bowie, M. (1993) *Psychoanalysis and the Future of Theory*, Oxford, Blackwell.

Bowlby, J. (1963–80) *Attachment and Loss*, 3 vols, London, Hogarth Press; New York, Basic Books: 1 *Attachment* (1963); 2 *Separation, Anxiety and Anger* (1973); 3 *Sadness and Depression* (1980).

Breen, D. (1989) *Talking with Mothers*, London, Free Association Books.

Breen, D. (1993) *The Gender Conundrum*, London, Routledge.

Brennan, T. (ed.) (1989) *Between Feminism and Psychoanalysis*, London, Routledge.

Brennan, T. (1991) *History after Lacan*, London, Routledge.

Brennan, T. (1992) *The Interpretation of the Flesh: Freud and Femininity*, London, Routledge.

Britton, R. (1989) 'The missing link', in R. Britton, M. Feldman and E. O'Shaughnessy (eds), *The Oedipus Complex Today*, London, Karnac.

Brown, J. A. C. (1960) *Freud and the Post-Freudians*, London, Penguin.

Butler, J. (1990) *Gender Trouble*, New York and London, Routledge.

Butler, J. (1993) *Bodies that Matter*, London, Routledge.

Castioradis, C. (1987) *The Imaginary Institution of Society*, Cambridge, Polity Press.

Chasseguet-Smirgel, J. (1981) *Female Sexuality*, London, Virago.

Chasseguet-Smirgel, J. (1984) *Creativity and Perversion*, New York, Free Association Books.

Chasseguet-Smirgel, J. (1985) *The Ego-Ideal: a Psychoanalytic Essay on the Malady of the Ideal*, London, Free Association Books.

Chasseguet-Smirgel, J. (1986) *Sexuality and the Mind: the Role of the Father and the Mother in the Psyche*, New York, New York University Press.

Chodorow, N. (1978) *The Reproduction of Mothering: Psychoanalysis and the Sociology of Gender*, Berkeley, University of California Press.

Chodorow, N. (1989) *Feminism and Psychoanalysis*, Cambridge, Polity Press.

Chodorow, N. (1994) *Femininities, Masculinities, Sexualities*, London, Free Association Books.

Cixous, H. (1976) 'The laugh of the Medusa', trans. K. Cohen and P. Cohen, *Signs*, 1 (4): 875–91.

Cohn, N. (1993) *Cosmos, Chaos and the World to Come*, New Haven, Conn., Yale University Press.

Coleman, J. (1997) *Key Data on Adolescence*, Brighton, Trust for the Study of Adolescence.

Coltart, N. (1993) *Slouching Towards Bethlehem ... and Further Psychoanalytic Explorations*, London, Free Association Books.

Coltart, N. (1996) *The Baby and the Bathwater*, London, Free Association Books.

Connel, R. W. (1995) *Masculinities*, Cambridge, Polity Press.

Coward, R. (1984) *Female Desire*, London, Paladin.

Craib, I. (1989) *Psychoanalysis and Social Theory*, London, Harvester Wheatsheaf.

Craib, I. (1994) *The Importance of Disappointment*, London, Routledge.

Creed, B. (1993) *The Monstrous Feminine*, London, Routledge.
Crowley, H. and Himmelweit, S. (1992) *Knowing Women*, Milton Keynes, Open University Press and Cambridge, Polity Press.
Dare, C. (1996) 'Shame, blame and retribution: individual and family dynamics around the experience of child abuse', paper presented at a Conference on Psychoanalysis and the Young Adult, Cambridge Psychoanalytic Forum, Cambridge, June.
Deutsch, H. (1925) 'The psychology of women in relation to the functions of reproduction', *International Journal of Psychoanalysis*, 6: 405–18.
Deutsch, H. (1932a) 'On female homosexuality', *Psychoanalytic Quarterly*, 1: 484–510.
Deutsch, H. (1932b) 'The significance of masochism in the mental life of women', *International Journal of Psychoanalysis*, 11: 48–60.
Deutsch, H. (1933a) 'Female sexuality', *International Journal of Psychoanalysis*, 19: 34–56.
Deutsch, H. (1933b) 'Motherhood and sexuality', *Psychoanalytic Quarterly*, 2: 476–88.
Deutsch, H. (1944–47) *The Psychology of Women*, vol. 1, New York, Grune and Stratton; vol. 2, London, Research Books.
Dinnage, R. (1988) *One to One*, Harmondsworth, Penguin.
Dinnerstein, D. (1978) *The Rocking of the Cradle*, London, Souvenir Press.
Doane, J. (1992) *From Klein to Kristeva*, Michigan, University of Michigan Press.
Eichenbaum, L. and Orbach, S. (1982) *Outside in, Inside out*, Harmondsworth, Penguin.
Eichenbaum, L. and Orbach, S. (1985) *Understanding Women*, Harmondsworth, Penguin.
Elliot, A. (1996) *Subject to Ourselves: Social Theory, Psychoanalysis and Postmodernity*, Cambridge, Polity Press.
Elliot, A. and Frosh, S. (1995) *Psychoanalysis in Contexts*, London, Routledge.
Elliot, M. (1996) 'Cain and Abel: a study in the social dynamics of conflicted group identities', Department of Psychoanalytic Studies, University of Essex, November.
Fairburn, W. R. D. (1994) *Psychoanalytic Studies of the Personality*, London, Routledge.
Fairburn, W. R. D. (1995) *From Instinct to Self: Selected Papers of W. R. D. Fairburn*, New York, Aronson.
Featherstone, M. (1991) *Consumer Culture and Postmodernism*, London, Sage.
Feder Kittay, E. (1984) 'Womb-envy: an explanatory concept', in E. Trebilcott (ed.), *Mothering: Essays in Feminist Theory*, New York, Rowman and Allanheld.
Field, J. (Milner, M.) (1986) *A Life of One's Own*, London, Virago.
Flax, J. (1990) *Thinking Fragments*, Berkeley, University of California Press.
Fletcher, J. (ed.) (1990) *Abjection, Melancholia and Love*, London, Routledge.
Follett, M. P. (1930) *Creative Experience*, New York, Longmans, Green and Co.
Forrester, J. (1985) *Language and the Origins of Psychoanalysis*, London, Macmillan.
Forrester, J. (1991) *The Seductions of Psychoanalysis*, Cambridge, Cambridge University Press.
Foucault, M. (1981) *The History of Sexuality*, 2 vols, trans. R. Hurley, Harmondsworth, Penguin.

Freud, A. (ed.) (1986) *Sigmund Freud: the Essentials of Psychoanalysis*, Harmondsworth, Penguin.

Freud, S. (with Breuer, J.) (1895) *Studies on Hysteria*, SE 2, PFL 3.

Freud, S. (1900) *The Interpretation of Dreams*, SE 4–5, PFL 4.

Freud, S. (1905) *The Three Essays on the Theory of Sexuality*, SE 7: 123–245, PFL 7.

Freud, S. (1908a) 'Character and anal eroticism', SE 9: 167–75, PFL 7.

Freud, S. (1908b) 'On the sexual theories of children', SE 9: 205–26, PFL 7.

Freud, S. (1910) 'A special type of choice of object made by men', SE 11: 163–75, PFL 7.

Freud, S. (1911) 'Formulations on the two principles of mental functioning', SE 12, 213–26, PFL 11, 29–44.

Freud, S. (1912) 'On the universal tendency to debasement in the sphere of love', SE 11: 177–90, PFL 7.

Freud, S. (1914) 'On narcissism: an introduction', SE 14: 67–102, PFL 11.

Freud, S. (1917a) 'Mourning and melancholy', SE 14: 237–58, PFL 11.

Freud, S. (1917b) 'The taboo of virginity', SE 11: 193–208, PFL 7.

Freud, S. (1920a) *Beyond the Pleasure Principle*, SE 18, PFL 11.

Freud, S. (1920b) 'The psychogenesis of a case of homosexuality in a woman', SE 18: 145–74, PFL 9.

Freud, S. (1921) *Group Psychology and the Analysis of the Ego*, SE 18: 69, PFL 12: 91.

Freud, S. (1922) 'Some neurotic mechanisms in jealousy, paranoia and homosexuality', SE 18: 221–32, PFL 10.

Freud, S. (1923) *The Ego and the Id*, SE 19, PFL 11.

Freud, S. (1924) 'The dissolution of the Oedipal complex', SE 19: 173–9, PFL 7.

Freud, S. (1925a) *An Autobiographical Study*, SE 20.

Freud, S. (1925b) 'Negation', SE 19.

Freud, S. (1925c) 'Some psychical consequences of the anatomical distinction between the sexes', SE 19: 243–58, PFL 7.

Freud, S. (1926a) *Inhibitions, Symptoms and Anxiety*, SE 20: 70, PFL 10: 227.

Freud, S. (1926b) *The Question of Lay Analysis*, SE 20, PFL 15.

Freud, S. (1927a) 'Fetishism', SE 21: 147–57, PFL 7.

Freud, S. (1927b) *The Future of an Illusion*, SE 21, PFL 12: 183.

Freud, S. (1930) *Civilisation and its Discontents*, SE 21, PFL 12.

Freud, S. (1931a) 'Female sexuality', SE 21: 223–43, PFL 7.

Freud, S. (1931b) 'Libidinal types', SE 21: 215–20, PFL 7.

Freud, S. (1933a) 'Femininity', Lecture 33, *New Introductory Lectures on Psychoanalysis*, SE 22: 112–35.

Freud, S. (1933b) *New Introductory Lectures on Psychoanalysis*, SE 22, PFL 2.

Freud, S. (1937) 'Constructions in analysis', SE 23: 257.

Freud, S. (1938) *An Outline of Psychoanalysis*, SE 23, PFL 15.

Fromm, E. (1990) *The Anatomy of Human Destructiveness*, London, Penguin.

Frosh, S. (1991) *Identity Crisis: Modernity, Psychoanalysis and the Self*, London, Macmillan.

Frosh, S. (1994) *Sexual Difference*, London, Macmillan.

Fuss, D. (1989) *Essentially Speaking: Feminism, Nature and Difference*, New York, Routledge.

Galbraith, K. (1993) *The Culture of Contentment*, Harmondsworth, Penguin.

Gallop, J. (1982) *Feminism and Psychoanalysis: the Daughter's Seduction*, London, Macmillan.

Gallop, J. (1985) *Reading Lacan*, Ithaca and London, Cornell University Press.

Gallop, J. (1990) *Thinking Through the Body*, London, Routledge.

Gay, P. (1988) *Freud: a Life for our Time*, London, Macmillan.

Gay, P. (1990) *Reading Freud*, New Haven, Conn., Yale University Press.

Gay, P. (1995) *The Freud Reader*, London, Vintage.

Gemosko, G. (1994) *Baudrillard and Signs*, London, Routledge.

Gibson, C. (1995) 'On becoming a father', paper presented to the Conference on Re-Finding the Father, Institute of Psychoanalysis, London.

Gilligan, C. (1982) *In a Different Voice*, Cambridge, Mass., Harvard University Press.

Gilman, H., Porter, R., Rousseau, G. and Showalter, E. (1993) Hysteria beyond Freud, Berkeley, University of California Press.

Gilman Sander, L. (1993) *Freud, Race and Gender*, Princeton, NJ, Princeton University Press.

Girard, R. (1979) *Violence and the Sacred*, trans. P. Gregory, London, The Johns Hopkins University Press.

Goldman, D. (1993) *In Search of the Real: the Origins and Originality of D. W. Winnicott*, New York, Aronson.

Grolnick, S. (1978) *Between Reality and Phantasy*, New York, Aronson.

Grolnick, S. (1990) *The Work and Play of Winnicott*, New York, Aronson.

Grosskurth, P. (1985) *Melanie Klein*, London, Maresfield Library.

Grosz, E. (1989) *Sexual Subversions: Three French Feminists*, Sydney, Allen and Unwin.

Grosz, E. (1990) *Jacques Lacan: a Feminist Introduction*, London, Routledge.

Grunberger, B. (1989) *New Essays on Narcissism*, trans. D. Macey, London, Free Association Books.

Guntrip, H. (1971) *Psychoanalytic Theory, Therapy and the Self*, New York, Basic Books.

Guntrip, H. (1975) 'My experience of analysis with Fairburn and Winnicott (how complete a result does psychoanalytic therapy achieve?)', *International Review of Psychoanalysis*, 2: 145–56.

Hainhault, M. L. and Roy, J. Y. (1993) *Unconscious for Sale: Advertising, Psychoanalysis and the Public*, Minneapolis, University of Minnesota Press.

Harroway, D. (1991) *Simians, Cyborgs and Women*, London, Free Association Books.

Harroway, D. (1992) *Primate Visions*, London, Verso.

Hawton, K. and Fagg, J. (1992) 'Deliberate self-injury or self-poisoning in adolescents', *British Journal of Psychiatry*, 161: 816–23.

Heald, S. (1994) *Anthropology and Psychoanalysis*, London, Routledge.

Herman, N. (1987) *Why Psychotherapy?*, London, Free Association Books.

Herman, N. (1988) *My Kleinian Home*, London, Free Association Books.

Hinshelwood, R. D. (1989) *A Dictionary of Kleinian Thought*, London, Free Association Books.

Hobsbawm, E. (1997) *On History*, London, Weidenfeld and Nicolson.

Hoggett, P. (1993) *Partisans in an Uncertain World: the Psychoanalysis of Engagement*, London, Free Association Books.

Hoggett, P. (1998) 'Hatred of dependency', paper presented at the conference 'Psychoanalysis in the Public Sphere', London, January.

Homes, J. and Bateman, A. (1995) *Introduction to Psychoanalysis*, London, Routledge.

Hornby, N. (1992) *Fever Pitch*, London, Gollancz.

Horney, K. (1924) 'On the genesis of the castration complex in woman', *International Journal of Psychoanalysis*, 5: 50–65.

Horney, K. (1926) 'Flight from womanhood', *International Journal of Psychoanalysis*, 7: 324–39.

Horney, K. (1932) 'The dread of woman', *International Journal of Psychoanalysis*, 13: 348–60.

Horney, K. (1933) 'The denial of the vagina', *International Journal of Psychoanalysis*, 14: 57–70.

Horney, K. (1967) *Feminine Psychology*, London, Routledge and Kegan Paul.

Horney, K. (1994) *The Neurotic Personality of our Time*, London, Routledge.

Hudson, L. (1993) *The Way Men Think*, New Haven, Conn., Yale University Press.

Hyatt Williams, A. (1996) 'Brutalisation or civilisation', paper presented at a Conference on Psychoanalysis and the Young Adult, Cambridge Psychoanalytic Forum, Cambridge, June.

Hyatt Williams, A. (1997) 'Cruelty', Bion Reading Group, Cambridge, April.

Irigaray, L. (1981) 'This sex which is not one' and 'When the goods get together', both trans. C. Reeder, in E. Marks and I. de Courtivron (eds), *New French Feminisms*, Brighton, Harvester Press.

Irigaray, L. (1985) *Speculum of the Other Woman*, trans. G. C. Gill, Ithaca, Cornell University Press.

Irigaray, L. (1987) *Sexes et parentés*, Paris, Minuit.

Irigaray, L. (1993a) *The Irigaray Reader*, ed. Margaret Whitford, Oxford, Blackwell.

Irigaray, L. (1993b) *An Ethics of Sexual Difference*, trans. C. Burke and G. Gill, London, Athlone Press.

Iverson, M. (ed.) (1994) *Psychoanalysis in Art History*, Oxford, Blackwell.

Jacobs, M. (1992) *Sigmund Freud*, London, Sage.

Jacobs, M. (1995) *Winnicott*, London, Sage.

Jacoby, R. (1975) *Social Amnesia*, Hassocks, Harvester Press.

Jacoby, R. (1987) *The Last Intellectuals*, New York, Basic Books.

Jameson, F. (1991) *Post-Modernism or the Cultural Logic of Late Capitalism*, London, Verso.

Jardine, A. (1985) *Gynesis: Configurations of Woman and Modernity*, Ithaca and London, Cornell University Press.

Jones, E. (1922) 'Notes on Dr Abrahams's article on the female castration complex', *International Journal of Psychoanalysis*, 3: 327–8.

Jones, E. (1927) 'The early development of female sexuality', *International Journal of Psychoanalysis*, 8: 457–72.

Jones, E. (1933) 'The phallic phase', *International Journal of Psychoanalysis*, 14: 1–33.

Jones, E. (1935) 'Early female sexuality', *International Journal of Psychoanalysis*, 16: 263–73.

Jones, E. (1948) *Collected Papers on Psychoanalysis*, London, Baillière, Tindall and Cox.

Jones, E. (1964) *The Life and Work of Sigmund Freud*, Harmondsworth, Penguin.

Jukes, A. (1993) *Why Men Hate Women*, London, Free Association Books.

Kahr, B. (1993) *Winnicott*, London, Sage.

Kakar, S. (1989) 'The maternal-feminine in Indian psychoanalysis', *International Review of Psychoanalysis*, 16 (3): 355–62.

Kaplan, A. (1990) *Psychoanalysis and Cinema*, London, Routledge.

Keller, E. (1985) *Reflections on Gender and Science*, London and New Haven, Conn., Yale University Press.

Kennedy, R. (1993) *Freedom to Relate*, London, Free Association Books.

Khan, M. M. R. (1974) *The Privacy of the Self*, London, Hogarth Press and The Institute of Psychoanalysis.

Khan, M. M. R. (1975) 'Introduction' to D. Winnicott, *Collected Papers: Through Paediatrics to Psychoanalysis*, London, Tavistock.

Khan, M. M. R. (1981) *The Case for a Personal Psychotherapy*, Oxford, Oxford University Press.

Khan, M. M. R. (1983) *Hidden Selves*, London, Hogarth Press and The Institute of Psychoanalysis.

Klein, M. (1930) 'The importance of symbol formation in the development of the ego', *International Journal of Psychoanalysis*, 11 (1): 724–39.

Klein, M. (1931) *The Psychoanalysis of Children*, London, Hogarth Press.

Klein, M. (1956) 'Envy and gratitude', in J. Mitchell, *Melanie Klein*, Harmondsworth, Penguin, 1986.

Klein, M. (1957) *Envy and Gratitude*, London, Tavistock.

Klein, M. (1961) *Narrative of a Child Analysis*, London, Hogarth Press.

Klein, M. and Riviere, J. (1937) 'Love, guilt and reparation' in *Love, Hate and Reparation*, London, Hogarth Press.

Kneller, G. (1965) *The Art and Science of Creativity*, New York, Holt, Reinhart and Winston.

Kohon, G. (1986) *The British School of Psychoanalysis: the Independent Tradition*, London, Free Association Books.

Kovel, J. (1988) *White Racism*, London, Free Association Books.

Kristeva, J. (1980) *Desire in Language*, trans. L. S. Roudiez, Oxford, Blackwell.

Kristeva, J. (1981) 'Woman's time', trans. A. Jardine and H. Blake in *Signs*, 7 (1): 13–15.

Kristeva, J. (1982) *Powers of Horror*, trans. L. S. Roudiez, New York, Columbia University Press.

Kristeva, J. (1984) *Revolution in Poetic Language*, New York, Columbia University Press.

Kristeva, J. (1991) *Strangers to Ourselves*, trans. L. S. Roudiez, New York, Columbia University Press.

Kristeva, J. (1992) *The Kristeva Reader*, trans T. Moi, Oxford, Blackwell.

Kurtz, S. (1992) *All the Mothers are One: Hindu India and the Cultural Reshaping of Psychoanalysis*, New York, Columbia University Press.

Lacan, J. (1975) *Encore: Le Seminaire XX, 1972–3*, Paris, Seuil.

Lacan, J. (1977a) *Ecrits: a Selection*, trans. A. Sheridan, London, Tavistock.

Lacan J. (1977b) *The Four Fundamental Concepts of Psychoanalysis*, ed. J. Alain Miller, trans. A. Sheridan, London, Hogarth Press and The Institute of Psychoanalysis.

Laing, R. D. (1960) *The Divided Self*, Harmondsworth, Penguin.

Langer, M. and Hollander, N. (1992) *Motherhood and Sexuality*, New York, Guildford Publications.

Laplanche, J. (1976) *Life and Death in Psychoanalysis*, Baltimore, Md, and London, The Johns Hopkins University Press.

Laplanche, J. and Pontalis, J. B. (1985) *The Language of Psychoanalysis*, London, Hogarth Press.

Lasch, C. (1980) *The Culture of Narcissism*, London, Sphere Books.

Lasch, C. (1984) *The Minimal Self*, London, Picador.

Lechte, J. (1990) *Julia Kristeva*, London, Routledge.

Lemaire, A. (1977) *Jacques Lacan*, trans. D. Macey, London, Routledge.

Lemoine-Luccione, E. (1987) *The Dividing of Women or Woman's Lot*, London, Free Association Books.

Lindner, R. (1986) *The Fifty Minute Hour: a Collection of True Psychoanalytic Tales*, London, Free Association Books.

Lomas, P. (1966) 'Ritualistic elements in the management of childbirth', *British Journal of Medical Psychology*, 39: 207.

Lomas, P. (1973) *True and False Experience*, London, Allen Lane.

Lomas, P. (1987) *The Limits of Interpretation: What's Wrong with Psychoanalysis*, London, Penguin.

Lomas, P. (1992) *The Psychotherapy of Everyday Life*, London, Penguin.

Lomas, P. (1994) *Cultivating Intuition: an Introduction to Psychotherapy*, Harmondsworth, Penguin.

Lunt, P. and Livingstone, S. (1992) *Mass Consumption and Personal Identity*, Buckingham, Open University Press.

Lyotard, J. F. (1984) *The Postmodern Condition*, Manchester, Manchester University Press.

MacCannell, J. (1986) *Figuring Lacan: Criticism and the Cultural Unconscious*, Beckenham, Croom Helm.

McDougall, J. (1989) *Theatres of the Body: Illusion and Truth on the Psychoanalytic Stage*, London, Free Association Books.

McDougall, J. (1992a) Public Lecture 'Trauma and creativity' for the Squiggle Foundation, London.

McDougall, J. (1992b) *Theatres of the Body: a Psychoanalytic Approach to Psychosomatic Illness*, London, Free Association Books.

Maguire, M. (1995) *Men, Women, Passion and Power*, London, Routledge.

Maltsberger, J. (1996) *Essential Papers on Suicide*, London, Taylor and Francis.

Marcia, I. (1996) *Remembering the Phallic Mother: Psychoanalysis, Modernism and the Fetish*, Ithaca, NY, Cornell University Press.

Marks, E. and de Courtivron, I. (eds) (1981) *New French Feminisms: an Anthology*, Brighton, Harvester Press.

Meltzer, D. (1978) *The Kleinian Development: Part 2, Richard Week-by-Week*, Perthshire, Clunie Press.

Mens-Verhulst, J. (1993) *Daughtering and Mothering*, London, Routledge.

Miller, A. (1987) *The Drama of Being a Child*, London, Virago.

Miller, A. (1990) *The Untouched Key*, London, Virago.

Miller, A. (1991) *Banished Knowledge*, London, Virago.

Miller, A. (1992) *Breaking Down the Wall of Silence*, London, Virago.

Miller, J. (1983) *Towards a New Psychology of Women*, Harmondsworth, Penguin.

Milner, M. (Field, J.) (1971) *On Not Being Able to Paint*, London, Virago.

Milner, M. (Field, J.) (1986) *A Life of One's Own*, London, Virago.

Milner, M. (Field, J.) (1987) *The Suppressed Madness of Sane Men*, London, Routledge.

Minsky, R. (1990) 'The trouble is it's ahistorical – the problem of the unconscious', *Feminist Review*, 36: 4–14.

Minsky, R. (1992) 'Lacan', in H. Crowley and S. Himmelweit (eds), *Knowing Women*, pp. 188–205, Buckingham, Open University Press and Cambridge, Polity Press.

Minsky, R. (1994) 'Reaching beyond denial – sight and in-sight – a way forward?' *Free Associations*, 34.

Minsky, R. (1996) *Psychoanalysis and Gender*, London, Routledge.

Minsky R. (1998) 'Fragrant theory: the sweet scent of signifiers' in *Free Associations*, forthcoming.

Minsky, R. (1998) 'Control or containment: coping with change' in *Free Associations*, forthcoming.

Mitchell, J. (1975) *Psychoanalysis and Feminism*, Harmondsworth, Penguin.

Mitchell, J. (1986) *The Selected Melanie Klein*, Harmondsworth, Penguin.

Mitchell, J. and Rose, J. (eds) (1982) *Jacques Lacan and the Ecole Freudienne: Feminine Sexuality*, London, Macmillan.

Moi, T. (1985) *Sexual Textual Politics*, London, Methuen.

Moi, T. (ed.) (1986) *The Kristeva Reader*, Oxford, Blackwell.

Moi, T. (ed.) (1987) *French Feminist Thought*, Oxford, Blackwell.

Money-Kyrle, R. (1978a) *Collected Papers*, Perthshire, Clunie Press.

Money-Kyrle, R. (1978b) *Man's Picture of his World*, London, Duckworth.

Moore, S. (1988) 'Getting a bit of the other – the pimps of post-modernism', in R. Chapman and J. Rutherford (eds), *Male Order: Unwrapping Masculinity*, pp. 165–92, London, Lawrence and Wishart.

Mulvey, L. (1996) *Fetishism and Curiosity*, Bloomington, Ind., Indiana University Press.

Mulvey, M. (1991) *Visual and Other Pleasures*, London, Macmillan.

Oliver, K. (1993) *Reading Kristeva*, Bloomington, Ind., Indiana University Press.

Olivier, C. (1991) *Jocasta's Children: the Imprint of the Mother*, London, Routledge.

Orbach, S. (1994a) *Between Women*, London, Arrow Books.

Orbach, S. (1994b) *What Do Women Want?*, London, Fontana.

Orbach, S. (1994c) *What's Really Going on Here?*, London, Virago.

Orbach, S. (1997) 'Revenge tragedy', *Guardian*, 16 August.

Pajaczkowska, C. (1981) 'Introduction to Kristeva', *m/f*, 5 (6).

Phillips, A. (1988) *Winnicott*, London, Fontana.

Phillips, A. (1994) *On Flirtation*, London, Faber.

Pines, D. (1993) *A Woman's Unconscious Use of her Body*, London, Virago.

Power, A. and Tunstall, R. (1997) *Dangerous Disturbance: Riots and Violent Disturbances in Thirteen Areas of Britain, 1991–1992*, York Publishing Services in association with the Joseph Rowntree Foundation.

Randall, P. (1996) *Adult Bullying: Perpetrators and Victims*, London, Routledge.

Rayner, E. (1990) *The Independent Mind in British Psychoanalysis*, London, Free Association Books.

Rayner, E. (1995) *Unconscious Logic: an Introduction to Matto Blanco's Bi-logic and its Uses*, London, Routledge.

Rich, A. (1976) *Of Woman Born: Motherhood as Experience and Institution*, New York, Bantam Books.

Richards, B. (ed.) (1984) *Capitalism and Infancy: Essays on Psychoanalysis and Politics*, London, Free Association Books.

Richards, B. (1989a) *Images of Freud: Cultural Responses to Psychoanalysis*, London, Free Association Books.

Richards, B. (1989b) *Crises of the Self*, London, Free Association Books.

Richards, B. (1994) *Disciplines of Delight: the Psychoanalysis of Popular Culture*, London, Free Association Books.

Roazen, P. (1971) *Freud and his Followers*, New York, Da Capo Press.

Robinson, P. (1993) *Freud and his Critics*, Berkeley, University of California Press.

Roland, A. (1997) *Cultural Pluralism and Psychoanalysis*, London, Routledge.

Rose, J. (1986) *Sexuality in the Field of Vision*, London, Verso.

Rose, J. (1993) *Why War? Psychoanalysis, Politics and the Return to Melanie Klein*, Oxford, Blackwell.

Ross, J. M. (1994) *What Men Want: Mothers, Fathers and Manhood*, Cambridge, Mass., Harvard University Press.

Roudinesco, E. (1990) *Psychoanalysis in France 1925–1985*, London, Free Association Books.

Roudinesco, E. (1997) *Jacques Lacan*, Cambridge, Polity Press.

Rustin, M. (1982) 'A socialist consideration of Kleinian psychoanalysis', *New Left Review*, 131: 71–96.

Rustin, M. (1991) *The Good Society and the Inner World*, London, Verso.

Rycroft, C. (1985) *Psychoanalysis and Beyond*, London, Chatto and Windus.

Rycroft, C. (1995) *A Critical Dictionary of Psychoanalysis*, Harmondsworth, Penguin.

Rycroft, C., Gover, G., Storr, A., Wren-Lewis, J. and Lomas, P. (1968) *Psychoanalysis Observed*, London, Penguin.

Sachs, W. (1992) *Global Ecology*, London, Zed Books.

Samuels, A. (ed.) (1985) *The Father: Contemporary Jungian Perspectives*, London, Free Association Books.

Samuels, A. (1993) *The Political Psyche*, London, Routledge.

Sayers, J. (1986) *Sexual Contradictions*, London, Tavistock.

Sayers, J. (1991) *Mothering Psychoanalysis: Hélène Deutsch, Karen Horney, Anna Freud and Melanie Klein*, London, Hamish Hamilton.

Schneiderman, S. (1983) *Jacques Lacan: the Death of an Intellectual Hero*, Cambridge, Mass., Harvard University Press.

Segal, H. (1986) *Delusion and Artistic Creativity and other Psychoanalytic Essays*, London, Free Association Books.

Segal, H. (1989) *Klein*, London, Fontana.

Segal, J. (1985) *Phantasy in Everyday Life*, London, Pelican.

Segal, J. (1992) *Klein*, London, Sage.

Segal, L. (1990) *Slow Motion: Changing Masculinities*, London, Virago.

Segal, L. (1992a) *Is the Future Female?*, London, Virago.

Segal, L. (1992b) *Sex Exposed*, London, Virago.

Segal, L. (1992c) *Straight Sex*, London, Virago.

Seidler, V. (ed.) (1991) *Re-creating Sexual Politics*, London, Routledge.

Seidler, V. J. (ed.) (1992) *Men, Sex and Relationships*, London, Routledge.

Shamdasani S. and Munchow, M. (1994) *Speculations after Freud: Psychoanalysis, Philosophy and Culture*, London, Routledge.

Shiach, M. (1991) *Hélène Cixous: a Politics of Writing*, London, Routledge.

Silverman, K. (1988) *The Acoustic Mirror*, Bloomington, Ind., Indiana University Press.

Skelton, R. (1993) 'Lacan for the faint-hearted', *British Journal of Psychotherapy*, 10 (2).

Skelton, R. (1995) 'Is the unconscious structured like a language?', *International Forum of Psychoanalysis*, 4: 168–78.

Spivak, G. (1988) *In Other Worlds: Essays in Cultural Politics*, London, Routledge.

Sprengnether, M. (1990) *The Spectral Mother: Freud, Feminism and Psychoanalysis*, Ithaca, NY, Cornell University Press.

Stoller, R. J. (1975) *Perversion: the Erotic Form of Hatred*, London, Maresfield.

Stoller, R. J. (1991a) *Pain and Passion*, New Haven, Conn., Yale University Press.

Stoller, R. J. (1991b) *Porn*, New Haven, Conn., Yale University Press.

Stoller, R. J. (1992) *Presentations of Gender*, New Haven, Conn., Yale University Press.

Stoller, R. J. (1994) *Sex and Gender*, London, Karnac.

Storr, A. (1979) The Art of Psychotherapy, London, Butterworth–Heinemann.

Storr, A. (1990) *Freud*, Oxford, Oxford University Press.

Storr, A. (1991) *The Dynamics of Creation*, London, Penguin.

Storr, A. (1992a) *Human Aggression*, London, Penguin.

Storr, A. (1992b) *Human Destructiveness*, London, Routledge.

Storr, A. (1993) *Music and the Mind*, London, Flamingo.

Strong, R. (1987) *Gloriana: the Portraits of Queen Elizabeth I*, London, Thames and Hudson.

Suttie, I. (1988) *The Origins of Love and Hate*, London, Free Association Books.

Tomlinson, A. (1990) *Consumption, Identity and Style*, London, Comedia.

Tong, R. (1993) *Feminist Thought: a Comprehensive Introduction*, London, Routledge.

Trosman, H. (1996) *Contemporary Psychoanalysis and Masterwork of Art and Film*, New York, New York University Press.

Turkle, S. (1992) *Psychoanalytic Politics: Jacques Lacan and Freud's French Revolution*, London, Burnett Books.

Ward Jouve, N. (1997) *Female Genesis*, Cambridge, Polity Press.

Watts, J. (1997) 'A future in the balance', *Guardian*, 25 June.

Weatherill, R. (1994) *Violence and Privacy: Psychoanalysis and Cultural Collapse*, London, Free Association Books.

Welldon, E. V. (1988) *Mother, Madonna, Whore*, London, Free Association Books.

Wernick, A. (1991) *Promotional Culture*, London, Sage.

Whitford, M. (1989) 'Re-reading Irigaray', in T. Brennan (ed.), *Between Feminism and Psychoanalysis*, London, Routledge.

Whitford, M. (1991) *Luce Irigaray: Philosophy in the Feminine*, London, Routledge.

Whitford, M. (ed.) (1991) *The Irigaray Reader*, Oxford, Blackwell.

Whitford, M. (ed.) (1994) *Knowing the Difference*, London, Routledge.

Wilkinson, R. (1996) *Unhealthy Societies*, London, Routledge.

Williams, G. (1996) 'Foreign bodies: failure of the container-contained relationship in eating disorders', paper presented at a Conference on Psychoanalysis and the Young Adult, Cambridge Psychoanalytic Forum, Cambridge, June.

Williamson, J. (1979) *Decoding Advertisements: Ideology and Meaning in Advertising*, London, Marion Boyars.

Winnicott, D. (1950) 'Some thoughts on the meaning of the word "democracy"', in *Home is Where We Start From* (1986), London, Pelican.

Winnicott, D. (1957) *The Child and the Family: First Relationships*, London, Tavistock.

Winnicott, D. (1958a) *Collected Papers: Through Paediatrics to Psychoanalysis*, London, Tavistock/New York, Basic Books.

Winnicott, D. (1958b) 'Hate in the counter-transference', in *Collected Papers: Through Paediatrics to Psychoanalysis*, London, Tavistock/New York, Basic Books.

Winnicott, D. (1958c) 'The manic defence', in *Collected Papers: Through Paediatrics to Psychoanalysis*, London, Tavistock/New York, Basic Books.

Winnicott, D. (1964) *The Family and Individual Development*, London, Tavistock.

Winnicott, D. (1965a) 'The development of the capacity for concern', in *The Maturational Processes and the Facilitating Environment*, London, Hogarth Press and the Institute of Psychoanalysis.

Winnicott, D. (1965b) *The Maturational Processes and the Facilitating Environment: Studies in the Theories of Emotional Development*, London, Hogarth Press and The Institute of Psychoanalysis.

Winnicott, D. (1971a) 'Mirror-role of mother and family in child development', in *Playing and Reality*, London, Routledge.

Winnicott, D. (1971b) *Playing and Reality*, London, Routledge.

Winnicott, D. (1971c) 'The use of an object and relating through identifications', in *Playing and Reality*, London, Routledge.

Winnicott, D. (1975) *Collected Papers: Through Paediatrics to Psychoanalysis*, London, Tavistock/New York, Basic Books.

Winnicott, D. (1977) *The Piggle: an Account of Psychoanalytic Treatment of a Little Girl*, London, Penguin.

Winnicott, D. (1986) *Home is Where We Start From: Essays by a Psychoanalyst*, London, Pelican.

Winnicott, D. (1988) *Human Nature*, London, Free Association Books.

Wisdom, J. (1992) *Freud, Women and Society*, New Brunswick, Transaction Publishers.

Wolfenstein, E. (1993) *Psychoanalytic Marxism*, London, Free Association Books.

Wollheim, R. (1971) *Freud*, London, Fontana.

Wooster, G. (1995) 'The resolution of envy through jealousy', Sib-Links Workshop, London, unpublished paper.

Wright, E. (ed.) (1992) *Feminism and Psychoanalysis: a Critical Dictionary*, Oxford, Blackwell.

Wright, K. (1991) *Vision and Separation*, London, Free Association Books.

Young-Bruehl, E. (1990) *Freud on Women*, London, Hogarth Press.

Index